A JEALOUS GOD

A JEALOUS GOD

Science's Crusade against Religion

PAMELA R. WINNICK

NELSON CURRENT

A Subsidiary of Thomas Nelson, Inc.

Published in Nashville, Tennessee, by Nelson Current, a division of a wholly-owned subsidiary (Nelson Communications, Inc.) of Thomas Nelson, Inc.

Nelson Current books may be purchased in bulk for educational, business, fundraising, or sales promotional use. For information, please e-mail SpecialMarkets@ThomasNelson.com.

Library of Congress cataloguing-in-publication data on file with Library of Congress.

ISBN 1-5955-5019-4

Printed in the United States of America

05 06 07 08 09 QWK 5 4 3 2 1

This book is dedicated with love to my family:

my parents,
Louis and Wilma

my sister and brother-in-law,
Holly and David

my children,
Jane and Greg

and to my husband,
Mike
who made it all possible

TABLE OF CONTENTS

CONTENTS

PART I

DE-SANCTIFYING HUMAN LIFE

1

SCIENCE ON TRIAL

She was seventeen, of West Indian descent, and hoped, as teenagers do, that the problem would magically disappear. It didn't. Now, on September 21, 1973, she was between twenty and twenty-four weeks pregnant—and terrified. So the young woman—later known only as "Alice Roe"—dragged her heavy body to the outpatient department of Boston City Hospital. A senior physician examined her and scheduled an abortion the following week. It seemed so simple.

IN SEPTEMBER OF 1973, just as Alice Roe was trying to end her pregnancy, a woman in Florida had the opposite problem: she was trying to become pregnant.

Then almost thirty, Doris Del-Zio of Fort Lauderdale, Florida, already had a ten-year-old from her first marriage, and John, her second husband, had two grown children. Now they wanted a child together. But because her fallopian tubes were blocked, the fertilized egg—the zygote—couldn't travel to her uterus, where it would attach itself and grow to term. After three unsuccessful operations to clear her tubes, doctors urged her to get a hysterectomy, but she refused. Doris wanted another child.

In a last-ditch effort, the couple contacted the infamous Dr.

Landrum Brewer Shettles at Columbia Presbyterian Hospital in New York City. Shettles was famous in the popular press for his amazing ability to seemingly "make babies"—and even select their gender.

To date, there had been only whispers from abroad that babies could be made in a test tube. But the mad scientist was sure he could do it. The couple was thrilled.

THOUGH ALICE ROE had first been seen on September 21, she was not admitted to the hospital until September 30, when she was somewhere between twenty-one and twenty-five weeks pregnant. For research purposes, doctors injected her with a substance called aminoglutethamide, designed to increase the hormonal output of the placenta. The abortion had to be postponed for several more days in order to allow the drug to take effect.

Alice Roe met Dr. Kenneth Edelin for the first time on October 2, the date finally scheduled for her abortion. A thirty-five-year-old senior resident in obstetrics and gynecology at Boston City, Edelin, a stocky, light-skinned black man, had been offered a permanent position at the hospital when he completed his residency. Now he was an overburdened resident, working in an inner-city hospital, one of only six residents performing abortions in the wake of their legalization ten months earlier.

Edelin attempted the saline method first. He placed a long needle into Alice's abdominal wall and attempted to inject two hundred cubic centimeters of saline solution into the amniotic sac. But he couldn't get the needle in. He tried again, and then again and again, but the needle still wouldn't go in. Finally, Edelin sent Alice back to her room and consulted his supervisor. The two decided that Edelin should perform a hystereotomy (a "mini-Caesarian"), a procedure in which the fetus is removed through an incision in the woman's abdomen.

Because the procedure delivers an intact fetus, it is valuable for medical research.

IT WAS ALMOST like a drug deal, the way the mad doctor set about creating the Del-Zio baby.

While Doris was waiting in New York Hospital on East 68th Street—she had been taking hormones for six months in order to pump up her ovaries—her husband shuttled her eggs uptown to Columbia Presbyterian. Shettles didn't have an office; he lived and worked in a cubbyhole upstairs where he kept a collection of clocks all set at different times. After a quick trip to the men's room, John gave the oddball doctor a test tube filled with fresh sperm.

The miracles of modern science would, they prayed, finally bring them a child.

WHILE AWAITING THE procedure, Alice agreed to participate in a second study, this one comparing the effects of two antibiotics on the developing fetus. Because of the study the abortion was postponed for yet another three days; now she was somewhere between twenty-three and twenty-eight weeks pregnant, hovering at the twenty-eight-week limit imposed by the Supreme Court. Finally, on October 5, she was again placed under general anesthesia and carried on a stretcher into operating room number two. Edelin made a low transverse incision in her uterus, separated the placenta from the fetus, and then watched the large hand of the clock as it slowly clicked to five minutes. When he slid the fetus out of Alice's body, it was still alive, its heart beating like the wings of an injured bird, until, after three to five seconds, it died from lack of oxygen. A male, he weighed 1.54 pounds and measured 13 inches in length.

Had the fetus been aborted *in utero*, there would have been no problem. Instead, it had still been alive outside the mother's womb. Though technically alive at delivery, it was not yet capable of living outside the mother for more than a few seconds; its lungs were too undeveloped to breathe on their own. In the 1970s, technology was not yet available to stabilize such babies until they can breathe on their own. Some would later argue that Edelin should nonetheless have tried to save the baby, paradoxically the very being he was trying to destroy. There didn't seem much point trying to save the fetus.

Alice never saw her son. She was still under anesthesia when he was placed in formalide, a preserving solution, carried in a cardboard box across Albany Street, and delivered to pathology. There, along with thirty-two other fetuses, he became part of a much-praised study published in the prestigious *New England Journal of Medicine:* "Transplacental Passage of Erythromycin and Clindamycin."

The aborted fetus had a purpose, after all.

WHEN DR. RAYMOND VANDE WIELE, head of obstetrics and gynecology at Columbia Presbyterian—and obstetrician to Greta Garbo and Faye Dunaway, among others—learned of the strange brew that Shettles had concocted, he was instantly suspicious. Despite his fame, Shettles was held in low regard by colleagues because he "failed to show an ability to organize a systematic long-term research project." Indeed, Vande Wiele had been ordered by the hospital's board to fire Shettles but, out of pity, had merely demoted him to a position equivalent to an admitting nurse.

Vande Wiele looked at the test tube, wondering whether it was a real human life or a mere clump of cells that should be disposed of. Should he allow it to be implanted in its mother's womb on the off-chance that it would develop into a full-born infant? Or should he dispose of it like the product of any other lab experiment?

Vande Wiele summoned Shettles to his office and motioned to the tube on his desk, trying to restrain his rage.

"What are you trying to do, create a monstrosity in this world?"

ALICE'S BABY LAY in the morgue, preserved in a jar, where it remained for two months. It was small and shriveled but had all the features of a full-term infant. Tests on its lungs showed that it had drawn a breath; it had been alive outside the womb, if only for a few fleeting seconds. This was not an ordinary abortion—the fetus died outside the mother's body—but still, it had been too young to live on its own. Destined to die anyway, the fetus had served an important medical purpose by measuring the effects of antibiotics on the fetus.

"Since the fetuses of the women who were coming to Boston City Hospital for abortions were going to die anyway, why not give the pregnant woman, before her abortion, a medication that might be used to treat other pregnant women?" wrote one physician, reflecting the consensus of medical researchers and ethicists.

But Boston's Catholic community didn't see it that way. Human life was human life, not to be destroyed or used as guinea pigs for medical research. To mollify the community, Boston City Councilor "Dapper" Albert O'Neil initiated open hearings to investigate practices at Boston City.

"The . . . prospect that this life may be used for experimental purposes . . . is rather frightening," Sister Sheila, who worked with the poor in South Boston, testified during one hearing.

Paul Harrington invoked the concentration camps of Nazi Germany where inmates had been used for medical research before they were packed into ovens. "Such experimentation is immoral, totally objectionable, and an unspeakable crime," he said.

Herbert Gleason, representing the hospital, said that no experiments were performed on live fetuses at Boston City; he knew this because fetuses taken from abortions could not survive the trip from the Ob-Gyn building to the pathology lab.

When the hearings were over, O'Neil delivered the transcripts to Assistant District Attorney Newman Flanagan. Flanagan consulted his boss, District Attorney Garrett Byrne, who said "be guided by your conscience." A Catholic himself, and the father of seven, Flanagan would be accused of succumbing to pressure from the Irish Catholic community. (He denied the charge.) In any event, on April 1, 1974, the grand jury of Suffolk Country, Massachusetts, indicted Edelin, charging that he "[d]id assault and beat a certain person, to wit: a male child described to the said jurors as Baby Boy, and by such assault and beating did kill the said person." Four researchers involved in the experiment were indicted under an 1814 Massachusetts statute that prohibited "grave robbing."*

Colleagues at Boston City Hospital formed a "Kenneth Edelin Defense Fund" to pay for Edelin's high-priced legal counsel, William Homans Jr. Throughout the country, the medical research community was up in arms, incensed by the intrusion of religion into medical practice and further fearing limitation on their use of fetuses for research. "Anti-research elements"—the code phrase for the religious—could do what they pleased inside their churches, but they had no right to inflict their views on science and block cures for the countless diseases that had beleaguered mankind for millennia.

"The Edelin trial is a fiasco," said the *New England Journal of*

---

*All four were foreigners and were able to escape the jurisdiction before their cases went to trial.

Medicine, expressing a near-consensus among researchers who were jittery about "anti-abortion activists."

"Most physicians, lawyers, and advocates of civil liberties . . . feel strongly that politics and emotionalism are playing a major role," said another medical journal. Another referred to the case as a "rampage of 'know-nothingism'" and went on to accuse the religious of launching "an organized assault on medical science."

AFTER DORIS LEFT the hospital without the child she longed for, she sank into a deep depression. Already plump, she gained still more weight and barely left home except to pick up her daughter. Her marriage suffered. She couldn't stomach sex. "I could not look at my husband as a man," she said. "I thought that sex was a mockery of our relationship. I wasn't a whole woman. I haven't been able to live with myself since." At night, she had a recurring dream of a baby crying: it was wrapped in a blanket, but when she approached it, the blanket was empty.

The couple had read that some doctors were having success creating a "test tube baby." In Britain, there were reportedly three babies who had been conceived in a "test tube," successfully implanted in the womb, and eventually born full-term and healthy. This added salt to the wound; had it not been so thoughtlessly disposed of, their embryo might also have turned into a child. Doris and John filed papers in the United States District Court in Manhattan, suing Columbia Presbyterian and Dr. Vande Wiele for $1.5 million.

THERE WAS AN audible sigh in the courtroom as Assistant District Attorney Newman Flanagan held up exhibit nine: a photograph of "Baby Boy" in the jar.

"Take a look at the picture of the subject," Flanagan said. "Is this just a specimen? You tell us what it is. Look at the picture. Show it to anybody. . . . Are you speaking about a blob, a big bunch of mucus [or] . . . an independent human being."

Both at the beginning and at the end of trial, Superior Court Judge James P. McGuire denied the defense's numerous motions to dismiss the case under *Roe v. Wade*, the U.S. Supreme Court's January 22, 1973, decision permitting abortion for the first two trimesters of pregnancy. If a fetus is not a person, the defense argued, then how can it be "murdered"? Recognizing that *Roe* could determine the outcome of the case, the judge instructed the jury that it was bound by the Supreme Court's decision.

"Whether you like that decision or not . . . I charge you that you must accept the law. . . . A fetus is not a person."

But the jury disagreed. To them, the fetus in the jar, its features shriveled from months of storage, was a human life. Even if it could not have survived for long outside its mother's body, Edelin should have tried to save it.

"It looked like a baby," said juror Liberty Ann Conlin.

UNLIKE THE FETUS in the Edelin trial, the strange concoction brewed by Dr. Shettles didn't look like a baby; indeed, it was invisible to the naked eye, consisting of several hundred cells at most.

But the public, believing that procreation could only take place through intercourse, was astonished. Each day, reporters and television crews awaited the Del-Zios as, weary from the trial, they made their way down the long steps of the courthouse onto Foley Square in downtown Manhattan. It was the stuff of science fiction.

"Test tube ma's spirit was destroyed along with the embryo," said one New York tabloid.

The couple, though Catholic, did not come out and say that the clump of cells in the test tube was an actual "person"; the lawsuit alleged that the defendants had inflicted "severe emotional distress," a catch-all civil tort used when others fail. None-theless, all through the five-week trial, the vision of the couple's much-wanted child hovered in the air of the dreary courtroom like Banquo's ghost.

The jury deliberated for thirteen hours, often sending written requests to see the exhibits again. Finally, it returned with a verdict, finding Vande Wiele guilty of "atrocious behavior" that was "utterly intolerable in a civilized community," while awarding the Del-Zios $50,000, a mere fraction of the $1.5 million they had sought. Still, Vande Wiele was devastated; he had never imagined it would come to this.

Even a strange brew of cells in a test tube was a "person" for the jurors in *Del-Zio v. Columbia Presbyterian*.

EDELIN, LOOKING "DRAWN and anxious," took his usual seat at the defense table in the drab courtroom when the jury was charged on Valentine's Day, February 1974. The courtroom was packed with scientists clothed in white, some from across the ocean. All through the indictment and trial, the research community had held their collective breath, waiting to learn what the jury believed was human life.

Outside, feminists held up pictures of women in chains, chanting their support for the doctor they saw as the scapegoat for anti-abortionists. The notion of the fetus as a person was an assault on women's newfound right to abortion; if a fetus was a "person," the shaky right to abortion would collapse. After the jury was sent into deliberation, Edelin supporters held a candlelight vigil outside the courthouse.

On the first day of deliberation, the jury voted 8-4 in favor of conviction, 11-1 in the next vote, and finally reached a unanimous verdict at noon the next day. When the foreman defiantly announced the guilty verdict, the courtroom simultaneously broke out in applause and hisses. Whatever the Supreme Court's fuzzy views of the fetus, the jury had seen a picture of the fetus and saw it as a person worthy of life, however abbreviated.

"That baby should have had a chance to prove his viability," said juror Paul A. Holland.

Edelin supporters held protests on the steps of the Massachusetts State House. He was given a one-year suspended sentence, which was overturned by the Massachusetts Superior Court in 1975 on technical grounds. Though relieved that the case was over, Edelin and his supporters continued to blame the ordeal on small-minded jurors and Boston's "anti-science" Catholic community.

"I don't think it's possible for a jury of *people like those* . . . to really understand the issues, especially some of the scientific and medical problems encountered at the trial," Edelin said. "We attempted to educate them, and I guess we failed."

It was a refrain that would be heard from the scientific community again and again in the months and years that followed.

2

REDEFINING LIFE

As the Edelin and Del-Zio cases show, advances in reproductive technology and changing attitudes towards abortion spawned a radical, but shaky, redefinition of "human life." *In vitro* fertilization—the union of egg and sperm outside the womb—brought hope to infertile couples. But it also produced more embryos than necessary for implantation, "extra" embryos that are either used for another pregnancy, frozen indefinitely, donated to science, or destroyed outright.* What is the status of these spare embryos? Are they actually "human"? Or are they no more than another form of human tissue? These were questions that hadn't been widely asked until the 1970s.

In addition to reproductive technology, abortion politics of the late 1960s and early 1970s, the *realpolitik* of the women's movement, required the diminution of fetal rights. From the outset, abortion was presented as a zero-sum game: only one side could win. On the seesaw of relative human worth, the fetus had to be kept down in order to prop up a woman's right to abortion. If the fetus is given status as a human, then obviously its intentional destruction could not be permitted any more than the destruction of a fully formed life. But

---

*A conceptus is an embryo until about two months when it is referred to as a fetus.

if human life does not begin until a fetus becomes viable, then a woman can dispose of her pre-viable fetus without restriction—and, presumably, so could anyone else. The depersonalization of the fetus not only permitted abortion but also, theoretically at least, extended to justify the use of fetuses—dead or alive—for research purposes.

Historically, as abortion supporters long argued, society accorded little value to fetal life. Thinkers in the Middle Ages and the Renaissance and English common law believed that life begins at "quickening"—the first kick and the first external sign that the fetus is really alive. Theological thinking appeared to agree: Thomas Aquinas identified "movement" as the pivotal juncture in gestation. Early Christian theology and canon held that the fetus became a person when its soul comes into being, a point then defined as "animation."

But these views were as unscientific as the pre-Copernican view that the sun revolves around the earth. Back then, no one could actually see the fetus inside the mother's womb. Aristotle watched and recorded the development of chicks in eggs to understand human life. In 1490, Leonardo da Vinci actually drew the human fetus, relying on autopsies from pregnant women; his anatomical notebooks show the fetus—its age indeterminate—huddled in the mother's womb.

But by the twentieth century, science revealed that within hours of conception, parental chromosomes divide and reshuffle to form a creature that is unique in nature. The technology of the 1970s—most notably, the sonogram—enabled doctors and parents to see the embryo in its early weeks. As the obstacles to knowledge were removed, it increasingly became clear that the fetus was human, at least biologically.

But the increased knowledge of fetal development was at odds with the political and practical need to depersonalize the fetus in order to legalize abortion, control population growth, and further medical research. Because of the highly contentious scientific and religious issues presented by abortion, its legalization would have been better considered in state legislatures, and not the courts. But political pressures of the early 1970s made the issue of abortion so acute and immediate that in 1973 the U.S. Supreme Court mistakenly decided to step in, leaving the complicated issue—what is "human life"?—up to nine unelected officials with lifetime tenure, guided only by legal briefs and arguments with no live expert testimony or public input.

Lacking these resources, the Supreme Court was sinking in quicksand, grasping on to whatever rationale it could create to depersonalize the fetus. *Roe v. Wade* was, by all accounts, a victory for women. But it was a legal disaster, inviting even more confusion around the status of the unborn.*

DURING ORAL ARGUMENT and in the briefs, the Court and the litigants recognized that society could not respect *both* the fetus and the mother. The Court asked Roe's lawyer: "If it were established that an unborn fetus is a person ... you would have almost an impossible case here, would you not?"

"I would have a very difficult case," she agreed.

Writing for the 7-2 majority, Justice Harry Blackmun again acknowledged, "If ... personhood is established ... the appellant's case ... collapses ... for the fetus's right to life would ... be guaranteed" by the Constitution.

---

*This is not a criticism of abortion itself, but of the U.S. Supreme Court's faulty reasoning and dubious jurisdiction.

For critics of the decision—and there were many—the question itself was dangerous, an invitation to carve out categories of humans who were not "persons." This exact rationale had been used by the Court in its 1857 decision upholding slavery. In the infamous *Dred Scott* case, Chief Justice Roger B. Taney asked whether a slave, though human, is actually a "person." "The question is simply this," he wrote, "can a negro, whose ancestors were imported into this country, and sold as slaves, become a member of the political community . . . ?" Taney, like Blackmun, recognized that to reach his desired result, he had to strip certain human beings of full "personhood." And so Taney spun out of thin air a fictionalized category of human being known as "the class of people imported as slaves."

"In the opinion of the Court, the legislation and histories of the time, and the language used in the Declaration of Independence . . . the class of people who had been imported as slaves . . . were not acknowledged as a part of the people," Taney concluded.

Justice Blackmun was far more dishonest than his predecessor; he never quite came out and said what a fetus really is. Instead, he casually sprinkled the opinion with the terms "potential life" and the "potentiality of human life" and similar language to implicitly discredit the fetus. These phrases had already been in vogue for several years among abortion supporters and ethicists who struggled to find an ethical way to discount fetal humanhood, seemingly unaware of the parallel to *Dred Scott.*

In *Roe v. Wade,* the question of a fetus's humanhood was asked in a way that guaranteed the desired result of legalizing abortion. Blackmun reviewed the many contexts in which the Constitution uses the word "person": qualifications for public office, extradition treaties, public censuses—all contexts in which it was physically impossible for the fetus to be considered a person. Not surprisingly, the Court, having already relegated the fetus to the status of "potential life," concluded that in the Constitution "the use of the word [person] has application only post-natally."

In order to legalize abortion, the Court also took upon itself the legislative task of defining the point—right down to the day—in which the fetus becomes a "person." Because pregnancy is a continuum, the question had to be resolved arbitrarily: one day the fetus is not a person, the next day it is. Based loosely on the point at which a fetus becomes viable—then about twenty-eight weeks—the Court selected the third trimester—the 180th day—as the magic point in which the fetus changes instantaneously from "potential life" to an actual "person." But even as it selected the exact day on which life begins, the Court went on to admit its own befuddlement about the very issue it had already decided.

"We need not resolve the difficult question of when life begins," Blackmun wrote. "When those trained in the respective disciplines of medicine, philosophy, and theology are unable to arrive at any consensus, the judiciary, at this point in the development of man's knowledge, is not in a position to speculate as to the answer."

For its leaps of logic, for its expansive reading of the Constitution to include the right to abortion, for its restrictive reading of "person" to exclude the fetus, for its usurpation of the democratic process, for its dangerous endorsement of the notion that some humans are less than human, *Roe* drew ire from legal scholars and physicians alike, including those who otherwise supported abortion. "That learned men have reached no consensus about when 'life' begins . . . argues for judicial restraint," wrote Columbia Law School professor Harold Edgar, one of many scholarly critics of *Roe v. Wade*. "Few problems are less suited for the judicial process than those which require explanation of why 180 days is constitutionally significant and 175 is not."

Some scholars, medical and legal, honed in on the legal fiction of "potential life," a term they believed was used to sidestep the reality of abortion. "The Court's use of the concept of 'potential life' to describe the nature of the prenatal organism creates an interesting legal fiction which has no basis in fact," wrote one legal commentator. "Scientifically speaking, an organism is either alive or it is dead; before it exists—when there is only the potential to create an organism—there is no organism. No meaningful scientific justification can be found for describing the prenatal human organism as a potentiality."

"The Court reversed the inquiry," wrote law professor Robert M. Byrn, "deciding first that the right of privacy includes a right to abort, then deciding that the unborn child is not a person . . . and finally refusing to resolve the factual question whether an abortion kills a live human being.

"The refusal to resolve the threshold question of the fact at the outset is the crucial error in *Wade*."

Dr. André Hellegers, director of the Joseph and Rose Kennedy Center for the Study of Human Reproduction and Bioethics observed that "we know very well when life begins and it is at conception. It becomes clearer by the day as we begin to get into the business of in vitro fer-tilization. . . . I and many others have resented the fact that this question of when life starts has been totally falsified. . . . It's purely a biological term or category but unfortunately . . . the word human is being confused with such things as 'value,' 'dignity,' 'soul,' or 'worthiness of protection.'

"So I don't think there really is a biological debate as to when life starts, but there is a *value debate* . . . as to when life starts."

David W. Louisell, a law professor at the University of California at Berkeley, went even further, lambasting "the Court's invocation of the specially constructed legal fiction of 'potential' human life, its acceptance of the notion that human life must be 'meaningful' in order to be deserving of legal protection, its resuscitation of the concept of partial human personhood, which had long been thought dead since the demise of the *Dred Scott* decision. . . ."

ACTUALLY, THE SUPREME Court knew full well that there was no such thing as "potential life" and that leading authorities were in full agreement that the depersonalization of the fetus was *political,* not *scientific.* More than two hundred doctors from prestigious institutions all over the country, including Harvard Medical School and the Mayo Clinic, filed a seventy-nine-page amicus, "friend-of-the-court" brief in *Roe v. Wade,* detailing and illustrating each and every stage of fetal development from conception to birth and concluding that "[m]odern obstetrics has discarded as unscientific the concept that the child in the womb is but tissue of the mother. . . . From conception the child is a complex, dynamic, rapidly growing organism."

Outside the context of *Roe,* many other prominent physicians in the 1970s agreed that a fetus is a person. According to Dr. Jerome Lejuene, a French geneticist and Nobel laureate who discovered the extra chromosome involved in Down Syndrome, "From its very beginning the 'thing' we started with is a member of our kin . . . the same human being from fecundation to death. The very fact that we have to develop ourselves during nine months inside the bodily protection of our mother does not change anything."

To New Zealand obstetrician Dr. A.W. Liley, distinctions between the unborn fetus and the newborn infant "are just semantic distinctions and somewhat arbitrary.

"Biologically at no stage can we subscribe to the view that the fetus is a mere appendage of the mother. Genetically, mother and baby are separate individuals from conception.

"One hour after the sperm has penetrated the ovum, the nuclei of the two cells have fused and the genetic instructions from one parent have met the complementary instructions from the other parent to establish the whole. . . . By 25 days the developing heart starts beating. . . . By 30 days . . . the baby has a brain of unmistakable human proportions, eyes, ears, mouth, kidneys, liver, and umbilical cord and a heart pumping blood . . . by 45 days . . . the baby's skeleton is complete . . . and he makes his first movements of his limbs and body. . . . He is responsive to pain and touch and cold and sound and light."

TO PLANNED PARENTHOOD and other abortion supporters, the idea that a fetus is a person was "merely" a religious construct. "Whatever the findings of science and embryology . . . whether a fetus is a person . . . derives from matters of a '*religious* philosophy and *religious* principle,'" Planned Parenthood argued. The National Abortion Action Coalition argued that abortion laws are "actually a means of enforcing the *religious* concept that the soul is present in the body from the time of conception and therefore must be saved. The use of criminal statutes to enforce the views of one or more particular *religious* groups is of course proscribed by" the Constitution (emphasis added).

In the years before *Roe*, medical societies had begun to change their views on abortion. By 1970, the New York Academy of Medicine, the California Medical Association, and the American Medical Association all supported abortion—less for scientific reasons than because of the woman's right to control her own body for health and other reasons.

In concert with the Supreme Court, a rising secular movement groped for ethical ways to minimize fetal rights. Many compared the human fetus to the gametes (sperm and egg), arguing that both were "potential life." Dr. Sissela Bok, a lecturer of medical ethics at Harvard

Medical School and a prominent bioethicist, observed that "the ovum cell and the sperm cells are certainly both living and human even before they meet" and that "this group of cells [the embryo] cannot suffer in death, nor can it fear death." Revealing her subjective view of when life has "value," she wrote of the fetus, "Its experiencing of life has not yet begun; it is not yet conscious of the loss of anything it has come to value in life and is not tied by bonds of affection to other human beings."

Although the gamete analogy was seductive, it was intellectually unsound and completely unscientific. Though technically alive, a gamete is not organic; it is incapable of growing into complexity and dies if unfertilized. A fertilized egg immediately undergoes cellular division and, unless destroyed, grows into a full-term infant.

Seymour Siegel, a professor of theology and ethics at the Jewish Theological Seminary in New York City, agreed with the U.S. Supreme Court and many ethicists that the fetus is a "potential life" that grows closer to humanhood each day. Recognizing that the "bias for life" is the "foundation of the Judeo-Christian worldview" and that "this century has seen the consequences" of devaluing human life, Siegel nonetheless succumbed to the morally dubious arguments that he claimed were consistent with rabbinical tradition. "The fetus does not seem to be identical with an infant. . . . The fetus has no independent life-system. . . . It has not developed the social and personal qualities generally assumed to be part of being a full human being."

It might have been more honest simply to acknowledge that a fetus was a human life and then decide whether it was worth preserving at all costs—a morally troublesome question that should have been tackled head on. Some did admit that the fetus is a *human*, but found other philosophical constructs to minimize its value as a *person.* Some compared the unborn life to an adult who had to be hooked up to another person in order to survive. The healthier of the two, the analogy went, clearly had the right to terminate the symbiotic relationship. Again, the logic was tempting for those determined to diminish the fetus, but it was also as flimsy as the others. Because the two adults in the analogy have no biological relationship, the dependent one can go on to find another person capable of supporting his life. In pregnancy, the mother is the *only* human biologically capable of sharing her body with a fetus; without her, the pre-viable fetus dies. And, unlike the parasitic adult, the fetus will eventually live on its own.

Some in the scientific-ethical community—all of them men— often invoked the right of abortion, as though the woman's right enabled *them* to minimize the fetus. "The Supreme Court decision . . . asserts a priority right over the living entity in the womb. . . . [B]ut the decision says nothing about the disposition of an abortus or the uses to which it may be put," one commentator observed.

Some scientists attempted to support the semantics of "potential life," though they never actually used this unscientific phrase. "Scientifically, we cannot answer the question of when life begins," said Dr. Norman Zinder, professor of genetics at Rockefeller University. "There is no generally accepted scientific proof that a fetus has consciousness in the sense of self-awareness," said Nobel Laureate Gerald Edelman during congressional hearings on a proposed pro-life amendment. "If one somehow attempts to glorify a fertilized egg or even an early embryo one must confront questions that are not capable of scientific answers."

He concluded, "It is an infringement upon the rights of a woman to tell her what to do with her eggs, fertilized or not."

To Australian philosopher Peter Singer, then a professor at Monash University in Melbourne, the question of fetal personhood needed to be answered honestly, not in the verbal gymnastics played by clever bioethicists. "Advocates of legal abortion cannot remain neutral about when the developing human being acquires a right to life. If they advocate abortion on request, they are implicitly valuing the claim to life of a fetus as less important than the claim of a pregnant woman. . . . This may be justified, but it is a substantive moral position because it rejects the idea that all human life is equally sacrosanct."

As California's official medical journal observed at that time, "The very considerable semantic gymnastics which are required to rationalize abortion as anything but taking a human life would be ludicrous if they were not often put forth under socially impeccable auspices."

DOCTORS IN NAZI GERMANY found that concentration camp inmates were ideal research subjects. Though biologically "human," these inmates had already been condemned to death, already judged to be "life unworthy of life." Young surgeons got their training by performing arbitrary surgery on inmates. Women would wake up to find their female parts missing. Others were used as guinea pigs to test new drugs before they reached the general public. Joseph Mengele, obsessed with twins, kept a special table for their autopsies. These experiments were conducted to further medical knowledge and were morally acceptable because these people "were condemned to death anyway."

Almost three decades after the revelations of the Nazi German concentration camps, Americans were shocked to learn that their own moral high ground was not so elevated after all.

In 1972, an Associated Press report revealed that more than six hundred black men in Tuskegee, Alabama—all of them poor and uneducated—were being used by the United States Public Health Service as unwitting subjects for medical research. The study began in 1932 with four hundred subjects afflicted with syphilis and two hundred healthy men serving as a control group. For more than forty years, even after penicillin was identified as the cure for syphilis, treatment was deliberately withheld from these impoverished black men. The purpose of the study was to determine *post mortem* what the disease does to the human body.

Tuskegee was hardly an isolated case. Soon it was revealed that many other human subjects—all of them in some way helpless or incompetent—had been used for medical research. A New York cancer specialist had injected live tumor cells into elderly patients. The hepatitis virus was given to mentally ill patients at Willowbrook State Hospital in Staten Island, New York. Mexican women in San Antonio, Texas, were being used to test the impact of contraceptives on psychological health; the control group wasn't told that they were given a placebo and therefore could become pregnant. Experimental brain surgery was performed on patients confined in institutions. In a Los Angeles hospital, forty-five infants died in a study designed to reduce the high mortality rate among premature infants.

Dr. Joan Hodgman, the physician in charge of that study, said she was "proud" of the research, that it had been a "good scientific study" until it was questioned for "political purposes."

Shortly thereafter came revelations of research on yet another category of "subhuman": the fetus.

IT HAD BEEN done beneath the veil of secrecy, known within some medical circles and fully sanctioned—and, in some instances, paid for by the National Institutes of Health, the federal body that supports most medical research in the United States. No one outside the cloisters of science—not Congress, not the public—knew that live fetuses were being deliberately tortured in the name of science. Though the NIH later claimed that it "has no way of knowing everything that is being done under training grants or institutional grants," in 1971, it had explicitly approved such research. "Planned scientific studies of the human fetus must be encouraged if the outlook for maternal and fetal health is to be improved," the NIH said in a report that was not made public.

The information reached the general public on April 10, 1973, with a front-page story by *Washington Post* reporter Victor Cohn: "Live-Fetal Research Debated." The gruesome details shocked the public, including those who supported abortion.

Before abortion was legal in the United States, some medical researchers traveled overseas to experiment on human fetuses. The chief of pediatrics at Cleveland Metropolitan Hospital, Dr. Robert Schwartz, traveled to Finland where, for "research purposes," he removed the brains, lungs, livers, and kidneys from living fetuses. For someone who evidently did not view the fetus as fully human, the doctor's defense was curious: he'd severed the nerves, he said, "to make sure the fetus will feel no pain."

Supported by the NIH, a team of three Finnish and one American investigator, Dr. Peter A.J. Adam of Case Western Reserve University, described how they'd severed the heads of twelve fetuses of between twelve and twenty weeks gestation. When they described their work at a meeting of the American Pediatric Society held in San Francisco, no one in the audience of researchers even "raised an eyebrow." But outside the research community, the reaction was one of shock. "It is the making of a new Frankenstein," said pro-life Congressman Angelo D. Roncallo, a Republican from New York. "These people cut the heads off living human fetuses while they still had a heartbeat and stuck them up on tubes."

The death on August 7, 1963, of Patrick Bouvier Kennedy, the premature infant born to President John F. Kennedy and his wife Jacqueline, created an enormous momentum in the medical community to treat pre-term infants. Some of this research was performed on living fetuses.

In a 1968 study called the "Artificial Placenta," a twenty-six-week-old fetus, weighing more than a pound, was obtained from a fourteen-year-old girl, presumably from a therapeutic abortion. Along with fourteen other fetuses, it was immersed in a liquid containing oxygen and kept alive for a full five hours.

> For the whole 5 hours of life, the fetus did not respire. Irregular gasping movements, twice a minute, occurred in the middle of the experiment but there was not proper respiration. Once the profusion [pumping in of oxygenated blood] was stopped, however, the gasping respiratory efforts increased to 8 to 10 per minute. . . . After stopping the circuit, the heart slowed, became irregular and eventually stopped. . . . The fetus was quiet, making occasional stretching limb movements very much like the ones reported in other human work. . . . [T]he fetus died 21 minutes after leaving the circuit. . . .

The study won the Foundation Prize Award from the American Association of Obstetrics and Gynecology. But the public was less laudatory. Ethel Kennedy, wife of the slain Robert Kennedy and a devout Catholic, placed a personal phone call to her friend André Hellegers, director of the Kennedy Institute for the Study of Biomedical Ethics. Soon hundreds of young Catholic school girls—including Maria Shriver, another Kennedy—descended on the NIH to protest the research.

Opposition to fetal research often came from those who also opposed abortion. "It is dangerous to the common good . . . when individuals assume control and authority over the very lives of others—a right and an authority which they do not have—because authority over humans belongs to God alone," said Monsignor Paul Harrington of Boston, articulating the Catholic consensus on both abortion and fetal research.

To Paul Ramsey, professor of religion at Princeton University, fetal research was merely a "balm for our consciences," a way to justify the evil of abortion. But, he wrote, "an established harm possesses no tendency to justify later harm, two wrongs do not make a right, a greater wrong does not justify a lesser one." A bad act cannot be redeemed by attempting to make good of it.

But a new breed of self-anointed ethicists found ways to bypass the moral qualms. "The biological potential of the fetus becomes irrelevant the moment the decision to abort is irrevocable," wrote Australian philosopher Peter Singer, implicitly holding that a fetus's status as a person depends solely on whether it is wanted. Singer preferred fetal research to its alternative, animal research, lamenting that opponents of fetal research "are accepting that thousands of perfectly healthy animals will be subjected to experimentation involving suffering as well as death."

But not all fetuses were "going to die anyway." In 1974, one researcher asked the federal government to fund a three-year study in which he would take 450 eggs from women undergoing gynecologic surgery, fertilize them in vitro, keep them alive for about six days, and then perform a biopsy. His goal was not to create healthy babies but quite the opposite: to kill those that weren't healthy, a practice that was almost unheard of within the general public in the early 1970s. In the future, said the researcher, at-risk women, particularly older women, could have their eggs fertilized in vitro and then biopsied; the "defective" embryos would be destroyed. The request for funding, though initially approved, was ultimately denied—likely for political reasons. In the early 1970s, the public was not ready to create embryos in order to destroy them. (This reluctance would slowly fade thirty years later.)

André Hellegers likened the "it's going to die anyway" philosophy to the Nazis. "Since we're going to put all those Jews in the gas chamber anyway, let's get some good out of them by doing medical experiments first." Dr. Leon Kass, then a young ethicist (and later head of President George W. Bush's Council on Bioethics), agreed with Hellegers that a fetus was still alive and should be treated with dignity and respect.

The issue was more complicated for those who otherwise supported abortion. Willard Gaylin and Marc Lappé, both doctors and secular ethicists, acknowledged that the distinction between abortion and fetal research was spurious; nonetheless, they supported the first, but not the second. "Such an absolute and complete defense of the dignity and autonomous rights of the fetus seems bizarre, when . . . in abortion, we condone procedures which subject the fetus to dismemberment, salt-induced osmotic shock, or surgical extirpation," they wrote, conceding the intellectual inconsistency of their position.

Opposing the Catholic "pro-life" views were the utilitarians, those who insist there is no intrinsic right or wrong, that all moral decisions should be guided by what is best for the "greater good." A mere clump of tissue, even if biologically human, was less important than the millions of lives that might be saved by its destruction.

Fetal research did appear to accomplish a "greater good."

During the 1960s, a wave of children were born with stumps instead of arms and legs because, it was later learned, their mothers had taken the sedative thalidomide while pregnant. Hoping to avert such disasters in the future, researchers were now using "spare" fetuses to study the effects of medications on the unborn.

There was yet another moral problem with administering drugs to fetuses *in utero*: they sometimes were given as long as thirty days before the abortion. This meant that once the woman agreed to the experiment, the abortion was a *fait accompli*; she couldn't change her mind and have the child because the experimental drug may have already harmed it. Did the woman have a right to change her mind? If the fetus was going to be destroyed, shouldn't that happen as early as possible in the pregnancy? The delay in abortion occasioned by research also meant that the fetus remained alive for an extra thirty days and would be that much closer to full personhood when finally aborted.

Still, fetal research was often necessary. Though many vaccines were tested on animals before they were administered to humans, animals did not always respond the same as humans. Tests of both the rubella and mumps vaccines in monkeys had suggested that the vaccine virus did not cross the placenta, but studies of the vaccine on live fetuses *in utero* showed that it did, demonstrating that theses vaccines should not be given to pregnant women.

Polio had been the scourge of the 1930s, 1940s, and early 1950s, relegating thousands of children to iron lungs, wheelchairs, and sometimes death; President Franklin D. Roosevelt had contracted it in adulthood and spent the remainder of his life in a wheelchair. The polio vaccine wiped out the scourge in one fell swoop. Parents could rest easy thanks to the polio vaccine, which, like most, had been tested on fetal cells.

But proponents of fetal research overlooked a critical distinction. Vaccines are tested on live fetal *cells,* not on the fetus itself.

In 1975, a congressionally created committee commissioned a study from a private research firm, the Battelle Institute in Columbus, to study the benefits of fetal research. Not surprisingly—because resolution of the problem was predetermined and because the institute had been commissioned by proponents of fetal research—the report found that many benefits accrued from fetal research. According to Albert B. Sabin, creator of the oral polio vaccine, the report provided "the most striking evidence we've heard yet on the potential future importance of fetal research." To the medical research community, opposition to such research was ridiculous—destroying a potential life in order to save thousands of actual lives was a moral imperative.

If a pregnant woman gets German measles, her infant is likely to be deformed. Thanks to the rubella vaccine, the report said, the disease was on the decline: from 47,500 cases in the late 1960s to 11,836 cases in 1974. More fetal research was necessary for "treatment of blood diseases in newborns . . . the study of fluid from the womb to detect birth defects, and new treatments for the breathing problems that killed a child of John F. and Jacqueline Kennedy."

Perhaps to deflect attention from themselves, some proponents of fetal research went into default mode: using euphemisms like "emotional" and "anti-research," they attacked religion for blocking scientific progress and stampeding on women's rights. Congresswoman Bella Abzug of New York City, a leftwing Democrat, referred to "scientific know-nothings" who "are using the issue of fetal research to generate emotional heat without compensatory enlightenment." During congressional testimony, one researcher referred to "sectarian interpretations and prejudices."

"The most important thing in the debate," said the American Pediatric Society, "is the infringement curbs offer [sic] to human rights by imposing standards on all of us."

In a speech to a group of secular humanists, James W. Prescott, a researcher employed by the Department of Health and Welfare (later renamed the Department of Health and Human Services), referred to the "politics of abortion." "Fetal research had been a traditional form of medical inquiry, without public dissent, until the issue of abortion was interjected into the practice," he said.*

---

*A secular humanist, Prescott advocated "post-birth" abortion, promoting the killing of "defective newborns." He was not alone. See Chapter Five.

Joseph Fletcher was one of many who supported fetal research—and denounced interference from the religious. A one-time Episcopal priest, he renounced belief in God in the late 1960s and created a humanist morality known as "situation ethics." Fletcher was among the most vocal anti-religionists, often referring to the religious as "anti-research elements." "Many people's belief propositions are entirely visceral, nor rational," he said.

Some didn't concern themselves with right or wrong. The fetus was mere tissue, "potential life," a blob of cells destined for disposal.

"The products of conception during the first three months of gestation should be treated like any other bodily tissue," said one.

"I don't think it's unethical," said another. "Rather than being immoral to do what we are trying to do, it is immoral—it is a terrible perversion of ethics—to throw these fetuses in the incinerator as is usually done, rather than to get some useful information."

Within days of the *Washington Post* story, likely with considerable pressure from the Kennedy clan, the NIH announced that live fetal research would come to a halt. Dr. Robert Berliner, deputy director for science, told an assembled group of Catholic girls that the NIH "does not contemplate approving the support of such research." A committee appointed to study the issue was likely to endorse the ban, he said, ending such research for good. The September 3, 1974, NIH Guide for Grants and Contracts announced a moratorium on fetal research.

Despite the temporary setback for medical research, the stage was set: the invention of "potential life" would give researchers moral *carte blanche* to destroy, desecrate, and replicate human life.

Virtually unnoticed at the time was the *sub-rosa* dismantling of the Judeo-Christian ethic, the "bias for life" that, at least in theory, holds each life dear. Likely the country and the world at large has never practiced that ideal: war, slavery, racism, capital punishment, and poverty—each degrade the sanctity of human life. But the ideal's

29

subtle erosion in the hands of newly fledgling bioethicists—the country's best and brightest—was even more devastating than an honest and outright denunciation of the principle. Constructs such as "potential life" and "criteria of humanhood," the elevation of one life to the detriment of another, were very dangerous, inviting an increasing number of categories of human life that do not rise to the level of full personhood and empowering the intellectual elite to decide who among humanity is a "person."

Among the philosophers, one stood above the rest in his honesty—and brutality. Philosopher Peter Singer called for an outright abolition of religion in favor of a new set of commandments and an abandonment of any notion that human life is sacred. "[T]he sanctity of human life is today in deep trouble," he wrote.

Singer went on to call for a "revolution against a set of ideas we have inherited from the period in which the intellectual world was dominated by a religious outlook."

Medical science, with its promises of saving many lives, did not have the luxury of blessing every human life. "The traditional view that all human life is sacrosanct is simply not able to cope with the array of issues that we face," Singer wrote.*

Other than extremists such as Singer, few at the time would outright acknowledge that scientific technology and changing political attitudes had brought humanity to a new threshold. With *in vitro* fertilization, abortion, and the perceived necessity of fetal research, a human life would now be judged according to its value to others, not on its own merits.

"The traditional Western ethic has always placed great emphasis

---

*As is so often the case, the elite do not apply their "ethics" to themselves. When Singer's elderly mother contracted Alzheimer's disease, he and his family kept her alive until her natural death.

on the intrinsic worth and equal value of every human life, regardless of its stage or condition," observed one medical journal. "This ethic has had the blessing of the Judeo-Christian heritage."

"What is not yet so clearly perceived is that . . . [i]t will become necessary and acceptable to place relative rather than absolute values on such things as human lives. . . . This is quite distinctly at variance with the Judeo-Christian ethic. . . .

"The process of eroding the old ethic . . . has already begun."

3

FOR THE GOOD OF MANKIND

On December 29, 1968, 2,600 scientists, including four Nobel laureates, published a petition in the *New York Times*, the *Wall Street Journal*, and the liberal Catholic magazine *Commonweal* urging Catholics to withhold contributions from collection plates. Calling Pope John Paul VI "unenlightened," they went on to state that "[t]he world must quickly come to realize that Pope Paul VI has sanctioned the deaths of countless numbers of human beings. . . ."

They were referring to the pope's recent encyclical prohibiting artificial birth control. "Pope denounces birth control as millions starve," read a typical poster from that era.

The statistics cited by the over-population community were indeed frightening: world population had jumped from 2.5 billion in 1950 to 3.7 billion in 1970. In a mere two decades, there were more than one billion more mouths to feed on planet Earth. Soon there wouldn't be enough food to go around.

By the late 1950s, most Christian denominations had eased their restrictions on birth control. In 1958, the Anglican World Conference of Bishops advised that couples should decide for themselves the number of children they want, that the decision "has been laid by God upon the consciences of parents." In 1960, Episcopal leaders sanctioned not just "family planning" but the broader concept of "population control."

"There are many lands today where population is increasing so fast that the survival of young and old is threatened. In such countries population control has become a necessity. Abortion and infanticide are to be condemned, but methods of control, medically endorsed and morally acceptable, may help the people of these lands to plan family life without a likelihood of starvation."

While many Catholics advocated and practiced artificial birth control, the Catholic Church wouldn't budge, no matter how hard the lobbying. On July 29, 1968, Pope John Paul VI issued *Humanae Vitae*, reaffirming the Vatican's opposition to artificial birth control. In the "tasking of transmitting life," the Vatican said, married couples were not free to proceed "completely at will" but must "conform their activity to the creative intention of God." Nonetheless, by 1970, 68 percent of all Catholic women in the United States practiced birth control.

Spearheading the anti-Catholic movement was Paul R. Ehrlich, a young biology professor at Stanford University with a specialty in natural butterfly populations. His interest in population growth among humans had been spiked during his freshman year at the University of Pennsylvania where he fell under the influence of professor William Vogt, author of the 1948 *Road to Survival,* which warned about the dire consequences of unfettered population growth—and sold three million copies.

Twenty years later, Ehrlich was following in his professor's shoes, his message particularly appealing to a generation engaged in all-out rebellion against the Vietnam War. Now, in addition to "End the War" buttons, students began sporting buttons that read "ZPG": Zero Population Growth. Not only was Ehrlich hip, cool, and very leftwing, he also had impeccable scientific credentials. His 1968 *The Population Bomb* shot up like a helium balloon to the top of the bestseller lists, and he quickly became a hot item on the lecture circuit and late-night talk shows. If a biologist predicts doom and gloom, it must be so.

Behaving more like a fire-and-brimstone preacher than a calm scientist, Ehrlich preached that the end of the world was imminent and that man himself was to blame. In 1968, he wrote that in the 1970s "the world will undergo famines—hundreds of millions of people are going to starve to death. . . . We must realize that unless we are extremely lucky, everybody will disappear in a cloud of blue stream in twenty years."

There was only one path to redemption: "fertility control."

While population increases geometrically, resources such as food could never keep up with the exploding population. With their gas-guzzling Cadillacs and air conditioners churning at full blast, Americans were to blame for overconsumption. But the unenlightened in the developing world were even more at fault because they had too many children, far above the "replacement rate" of 2.1 children-per-family. Just twenty-three years before, the great minds of science had devised the atomic bomb in order to *destroy* humanity. Now, a younger generation of scientists would find a way to *save* humanity—even if humanity did not want to be saved. To save the world by limiting population growth, wrote Ehrlich, scientists would need more clout.

"Biologists," said Ehrlich, "have to have very good contacts in the political arena."

Biologists could be helpful in another way. "Biologists must promote understanding of the facts of reproductive biology. . . . They must point out the biological absurdity of equating a zygote . . . or fetus . . . with a human being. . . . They must also point out that in many cases abortion is much more desirable than childbirth."

Ehrlich himself lived and worked in tony Palo Alto, California, home of the prestigious Stanford University. In the Bay Area around San Francisco, as in much of the state, freeways were clogged and real estate pricey—all because Americans had too many children. But it was far worse in the developing world where overpopulation had already caused the collapse of civilization. Looking back on a "stinking hot night," he and his family spent in New Delhi, Ehrlich's disgust for people was almost palpable.

"[T]he streets seemed alive with people. People eating, people washing, people sleeping. People visiting, arguing, and screaming. People thrusting their hands through the taxi window, begging. . . . People, people, people, and people. . . . Would we ever get to our hotel? All three of us were, frankly, frightened."

Unlike many population-control hawks who themselves had five or six children while preaching family-planning to others, Ehrlich was no hypocrite: after one child, he had a vasectomy. But it was harder to convince others to do the same. Ehrlich believed that there had to be a way to force people to control their "fertility"—without their knowledge or consent, if necessary. One of his plans was to deny aid to impoverished countries and let them all die—until they agreed to shape up by curbing population growth. At a UNESCO conference, Ehrlich also urged the U.S. government to put sterility drugs in reservoirs and in food shipped to foreign countries. He would save the world, whatever it took.

But saving the world did not meaning saving the *entire* world. During times of war, military physicians used the concept of "triage" to allocate medical care to those most likely to survive. Incoming casualties are placed in one of three categories: those who will *die* no matter what, those who will *survive* no matter what, and those who will survive *only* if promptly treated. Extrapolating from the military analogy, Ehrlich argued that America should withhold aid from those countries "that are so behind in the population-food game that there is no hope that our food aid will see them through in self-sufficiency."

Another disciple of the population movement was Garrett Hardin, a father of four who believed others shouldn't have as many children as he. A professor of human ecology at the University of California, Hardin was a member in good standing of the American Eugenics Society, an organization devoted to improving the human race by controlling procreation among the genetically "inferior." In a 1971 *New York Times* opinion piece, Hardin argued against the "right to breed," suggesting that procreation be regulated by the government, that couples be licensed to reproduce, and (he and his wife excepted) couples be limited to two children apiece. He went on to giddily recall a time not long before when infanticide was an accepted means of limiting family size.

In another writing, Hardin posed yet another novel solution to overpopulation: teach little girls, girls fresh out of kindergarten, that promiscuity is much more fun than motherhood.

"By young I mean first, second and third graders. . . . We need to introduce into the Dick and Jane readers some characters other than Jane's mommy and daddy, and the couple next door whose children are named Carol and Jack and Tom, and the neighbors across the street with their three or four children. Perhaps we need to show Dick and Jane's Aunt Debbie, a swinging single of 40, who's as pretty as a picture. . . . [W]e don't need to tell these first graders what kind of fine time she is having. . . . They need only see the smile on her face."

Kingsley Davis, another population zealot and member of the American Eugenics Society, agreed that women needed to be trained in directions other than motherhood. "Since the female reproductive span is short and generally more fecund in its first than in its second half," he wrote, "postponement of marriage to ages beyond 20 tends biologically to reduce births." He went on to suggest that "women could be required to work outside the home, or compelled by circumstances to do so."

"If at the same time," he continued, "women were paid as well as men and given equal educational and occupational opportunities, and if social life were organized around the place of work rather than around the home or neighborhood, many women would develop interests that would compete with families. . . . [T]his policy is now followed in several Communist countries. . . ."

Others agreed with Hardin about the need to indoctrinate children as early as possible. In 1973, the Population Council's assistant director Stephen Viederman urged wide distribution of a poem written by two sixth-graders in a suburb of Washington D.C.: "If we didn't have people/We would have no pollution/Get rid of the people/That's the only solution."

While some population-control advocates were more extreme than others, nearly all advocated a "strings attached" approach to overseas aid: money must be contingent upon the recipient's agreement to provide abortion, birth control, and consensual sterilization. In the lifeboat of humanity, not everyone could or should be pulled aboard. Many argued that all economic aid—including free daycare centers and financial "allotments"—be denied to those with too many children. Because the alternative to population growth was "massive starvation," it was "morally justified" to use "fertility control agents," a chilling solution to the population problem that was never quite explained.

Concern over population was hardly new. Aristotle had feared "unrestricted increase." "The question arises whether children should always be reared or may sometimes be exposed to die. . . . The proper thing to do is to limit the size of each family."

In 1798, Reverend Thomas Robert Malthus had likewise pushed the panic button: population would double every twenty-five years, while resources would hold steady, he wrote. His predictions were known to be wrong by the twentieth century. Indeed, by 1970, the world population was 3.6 billion, not the 60 billion that his calculations suggested. Still, in the mid-twentieth century, population control topped the list of government and private priorities. John D. Rockefeller III and the Rockefeller Foundation created the Population Council in 1952, eventually persuading the government to get involved. President Lyndon B. Johnson quietly included family planning in his War on Poverty in the mid-1960s. Elected in 1968, President Richard M. Nixon agreed that "population growth is among the most important issues we face," though he tiptoed around Catholic voters.

Coercive solutions to population had been accomplished before. Forced sterilization had been one of Hitler's first edicts when he rose to power in the 1930s. In Nazi Germany, "undesirables"—the mentally infirm, the blind, the deaf, among many others—would be taken to a "health court" which would decide their reproductive fate. Millions were sterilized against their will.

American practices had long been the envy of the Germans just before the rise of Nazism. In early twentieth-century America, thirty-five of the (then) forty-eight states had mandatory sterilization laws for "imbeciles" and other "defective" individuals. Through the early 1970s, the federal government sterilized at least twenty thousand on Indian reservations. In 1968, one-third of the women in Puerto Rico underwent "la operación," because the medical establishment believed that "contraceptive methods are too difficult for lower class Puerto Rico women."

Overseas, the U.S. government likewise funded the sterilization of thousands of women in Hispanic countries where the Catholic populace did not approve of contraception or abortion. According to 1975 hearings before the United Nations Committee on

Colonialism, hundreds of thousands of young women in Puerto Rico, Colombia, and Mexico had been lured into the operation, only a very few understanding that they would have no more children. From the mid-1960s through the mid-1970s, the Indian government, likely prodded by U.S. foreign policy, forcibly sterilized its people, forcing men into "vasectomy camps," threatening to imprison couples who failed to be sterilized after their third child.

"We should have volunteered logistic support in the form of helicopters, vehicles, and surgical instruments," Ehrlich wrote.

Few in the scientific-intellectual community or in the media challenged Ehrlich's preposterous claims or the coercive methods he suggested. Those who did were treated like heretics. In a series of columns in the *San Francisco Chronicle* in 1970, columnist Charles McCabe was one of the few to identify Ehrlich as a "dangerous man." "This guy has to be read to be believed," he wrote. "These are the views of a zealot, not of a rational man."

In response, the chairman of Stanford's biology department and fifteen other members of the faculty wrote a joint letter dated February 5, 1970, excoriating McCabe for questioning Ehrlich's "professional qualifications," affirming that the insect specialist had "excellent credentials for speaking authoritatively on questions of human population growth and environmental quality."

Another heretic was Julian Simon, an economist at the University of Maryland, who, unlike Ehrlich, viewed population as an *asset*: the more people, the more resources—in effect, a secular version of the Judeo-Christian notion of abundance and respect for individual life. In 1980, Ehrlich entered into a bet with Simon: in ten years, Ehrlich wagered, each of four named resources would be gone. It was the easiest thousand dollars Simon ever made. By 1990, those resources were not only still around, they'd actually *decreased* in price by 40 percent.

But perhaps Ehrlich's most formidable opponent was the writer Allan Chase, whose carefully researched 1975 book, *The Legacy of Malthus: The Social Costs of the New Scientific Racism*, stripped away all of Ehrlich's liberal pretensions and showed them for what they were.

"There is nothing in biology in general," Chase wrote, "or in genetics and population genetics in particular, that gives a young, healthy, well-paid American in Palo Alto, California, the moral, scientific, or political right to blandly and not too blandly urge the termination of food, medicine, and all other aid to India and various other countries whose birth policies offend him. . . . There is nothing biological or scientific about such suggestions. They are based on subjective moral judgments about the intrinsic value of a human being other and poorer than oneself. . . ."

THOUGH HE WAS a hit on the college campuses, in the book stores, and lecture circuits, though he pushed all the right liberal buttons—environmentalism, concern for the poor, opposition to war—Ehrlich had a terrible problem: he was a total fraud. Had there been a courtroom trial on the "population explosion," Ehrlich would not have survived five minutes of cross-examination by a first-year law student. Had he been a stock promoter, peddling the Population Bomb Inc., he would have spent years behind prison bars.

Ehrlich was a fraud, not just viewed with the perspicuity of 20/20 hindsight, but from the very beginning. Just as he was preaching his Armageddon prophecies under the intellectual armor of the scientist, just as he lectured young students, breathing fear into the gullible youths, and as his book went into thirteen printings, making him a millionaire many times over, he knew he was wrong. The evidence was there. But the very scientists who preached the scientific method, who glorified the study of science for its objectivity, these were the very men and women who chose to ignore the data there in front of them. These were the folks who pushed their political agendas at the expense of fact.

There was no population explosion, not then, not now. In 1967, a year before the *Population Bomb* hit the presses, the America Census Bureau had already begun to revise its forecasts—*downward.* By 1968, fertility in the United States had not only decreased but in fact had reached a dangerous *low* that resulted in many of our present crises, such as Social Security deficits. Nor were resources diminishing; world food production was actually increasing at a greater rate than population.

In *The Nonsense Explosion,* a 1970 article in the *New Republic,* demographer Ben Wattenberg laid out the numbers, all of them readily available to scientists like Ehrlich. In 1957, "live births per thousand"—one of the best measures of growth—was 123, up more than 50 percent in two decades. From there, it plummeted steadily. By 1960, live births per thousand fell to 98; in 1968 (the year of the *Population Bomb*), it fell again to 85.7; in 1970—just as baby boomers themselves hit their childbearing years—it remained the same as in 1960 when the baby boomers were still in elementary school. The annual percentage of growth in the United States was a mere 1 percent, including immigrants. Indeed, the downward trend of population growth was viewed as dangerous by many demographers and could be compensated for only by massive immigration.

The facts were there, but for whatever reason, Ehrlich and the media and the scientists failed to acknowledge them. In 1968, the very year that the *Population Bomb* was published, population growth was on the decline in the United States, predictably so because, as demographer Ben Wattenberg put it, "the baby boom has ended."

Perhaps Ehrlich, the high priest of population control, was too busy autographing books to read the census data. Perhaps he was too caught up on the lecture circuit and the nightly television talk shows to read the newspapers. By the early 1970s, the media was bombarded with stories about declining birth rates, a trend that a generation later would produce an aging population that spelled disaster for the labor markets, social and entitlement programs, and health-care costs.

"[T]he new baby boom has not materialized," wrote Jack Rosenthal in a 1973 article in the *New York Times*. "In its place has come what is variously described as the 'baby bust' or the 'birth dearth'. . . . The fertility rate—the average number of children born to a family—has dropped so steeply that, for the first time it is now below the 2.1 child average needed for the population simply to replace itself. . . ."

Actual live births, another measure of population growth, painted a similar picture. Most demographers agree that 2.1 children per family are needed merely to replace population. In 1957, Americans produced 3.8 children per family. By 1968, the number had plummeted to 2.2 children, barely above replacement. The "nation's population growth is turning rapidly and dramatically downward," said a 1971 article in the *New York Times*, quoting a fertility study released the year before.

Declining fertility rates did not mean that there would be *more* to go around but actually *less*. In the 1930s, when President Franklin Roosevelt created Social Security, there were more than forty workers per elderly person. By 2004, the number had dwindled to three workers per supported person, in part a consequence of the low birth rates of the 1970s and thereafter. Likewise, medical insurance requires young, healthy people whose insurance premiums subsidize the less-healthy, older generation. And the labor market requires young people to shore up the economy.

While the United States had enough immigrants to make up for low birth rates, the picture was even worse in Europe. Growth rates were so low in France that in 1967 Charles De Gaulle called on the French people to have at least three children apiece. A 1971 study in Europe showed that birth rates were falling below replacement in at least seven countries.

Far from "exploding," population growth was spiraling downwards not just in the United States, but in the so-called overpopulated world as well. In the late 1960s, world-population growth declined from a high of about 2.3 percent to just above 2 percent, and after 1970 slid precipitously downward to 1.7 percent in 1980 and just slightly more than 1 percent in 1980. These numbers do not take into account the high mortality rates among the poor, particularly in the developing world: deaths from violence, war, and AIDS. Moreover, because population was difficult to measure in developing countries (imagine conducting a census in an African village), the alarmist numbers propagated by Ehrlich and his followers were likely inflated to suit their ends.

Likewise, Ehrlich's predictions of world famine were dead wrong. While wars, despots, unfair trade practices, and subsidies can block the flow of food—serious problems not remedied by population control—actual food production is another matter. In 1967, crop yields were at an all-time high, according to the United Nations Food and Agricultural Organization. Two years later, in 1969, worldwide wheat yields were at an all-time high at 305 million tons, which, along with the high production of other grains, created a "food glut."

In 1978, a mere decade after publication of the *Population Bomb*, the *New York Times* wrote in an editorial, "The Population Bomb, Reconsidered," that the sky-is-falling predictions had been wrong.

"The neo-Malthusians have for some time dominated discussions of world population. In their gloom, some even calculated a date by which the planet would have so many people that there would be no room for anybody to lie down. . . . The Rev. Thomas Malthus was mistaken in his conclusions two centuries ago, and so, it appears, are his successors."

In 2003, the *New York Times*' editorial page went even further, announcing that the total world population (not just birth rates) would *decline* by the middle of the twenty-first century, producing "the mirror image of what Paul Ehrlich once warned about."

But the trends had been there all along. Ehrlich, the expert in butterfly populations, had always been wrong—at least about humans.

EHRLICH AND HIS cohorts were, however, right in *one* respect: population within one segment of humanity was indeed "exploding."

In 1973, International Planned Parenthood issued a report on the changing color of humanity. In 1920, Africans made up 7.7 percent of the world population; in 1970, it was 9.1 percent; by 2000, it was 12.6 percent. By contrast, population was headed in the opposite direction in North America: in 1920, North Americans were 6.6 percent of total world population; in 2000, their numbers were down to 5.1 percent. Europeans likewise declined from 18.2 percent in 1920 to a mere 8.8 percent in 2000. Population in Latin America rose from 283 million to 369 million.

The same racial trends were apparent in the United States. Between 1920 and 1940, birth rates were equal among blacks and whites. After 1940, blacks began to surpass whites, and Hispanics surpassed both blacks and whites. In 1970, black couples had 3.7 children on average, compared to 2.2 children for whites. According to the U.S. Census Bureau, in western states, whites increased by 11.9 percent from 1960 to 1970. By contrast, immigration and rising fertility rates produced a drastically different demographic for non-whites: between 1960 and 1970, the black population grew 19.9 percent; American Indians, 51.4 percent; Chinese, 83.3 percent; and Filipinos, a whopping 94.9 percent.

"[T]he WASP and the Jewish population of this country are already reproducing very close to the replacement level," observed a University of Chicago demographer at an annual meeting of the American College of Obstetrics and Gynecology. But such "high-fertility remnants" as "the Negro population and the Spanish-speaking population . . . and a few segments of the Roman-Catholic population" were, he lamented, "rapidly reproducing."

As two other social scientists wrote, "[T]he high rates for Negroes underscore the magnitude of the unwanted burden of dependents. . . ." Under the guise of science, the writers went on to urge the "development of more efficient systems of distribution of contraceptive methods among all Americans, including low-income couples. . . ." Within the context of the article, it is fairly obvious to guess the racial identity of these "low-income couples" in need of "efficient systems."

"Many of the white race and many of the developed countries are beginning to calculate their proportion of the world's total population in fifty years," wrote another commentator in 1975. "Their loss of numbers and power will become politically more evident when we realize that the presently under-developed areas are progressing rapidly." Referring to the "liberal death wish," the writer went on to note "the remarkable fact that the people most unlikely to have children are those evidently most capable of supporting them from an economic point of view."

Even the otherwise liberal *New York Times*, an ardent supporter of civil rights, revealed its own latent fear of "white peril." A blood-chilling sampling of headlines from the 1970s includes: "Birth Curb

Gains in Mexican Study," "Blacks and Puerto Ricans Up Million Here [New York City] in Decade," "White Population in City Fell by 617, 127," and "Every Birth in Asia Limits Hope."

"[T]he minority areas grew to two and three times their former size in Brooklyn, the Bronx, and Queens," observed a 1972 front-page story in the *Times.*

When slavery reigned, blacks were counted as property, biological human beings who were not "persons." By focusing on non-white populations, the population zealots accomplished the same goal as the slave owners, declaring that certain populations are property, not persons, to be manipulated according to the needs of the elite. In the *Population Bomb*, Ehrlich went beyond population control to the sinister essence of the population movement. "If over perhaps five generations, those at the lower end of the genetic intelligence scale far outbred those at the upper end, the average I.Q. in population could be expected to be reduced by a few points. . . . If such a change were detected, *average I.Q. could be returned to its previous level by the proper breeding program*" (emphasis added).

The propaganda worked. By the 1970s, "population control" had indeed accomplished its unstated goal of restricting population growth among blacks. Thanks to the Supreme Court, which had noted the "population problem" in *Roe v. Wade,* the number of black women having abortions was disproportionate to their numbers.

Not surprisingly, the racist underpinnings of population control were bitterly resented by the non-white world, both in the United States and abroad. "Fertility control" was just another form of imperialism, a way to maintain the supremacy of white Americans. "The opportunity to decide the number and spacing of children is a basic human right," declared the heads of twelve states in a United Nations declaration on population control issued by Secretary General U. Thant in 1965. When the World Bank offered to make loans to Argentina contingent upon its adoption of a "population policy," Argentinean president Carlos Ongonia declared that population control was "decadent," that Latin American countries need more, not less, population for "greater prosperity" and "greater liberty."

The left wing in Latin America was likewise suspicious of the imperialistic oppression of "population control" imposed by the industrialized countries, echoing Julian Simon's prediction that more population equals more prosperity and production. As three Colombian university professors said,

> Birth control is dangerous because it can become a distraction, or a justification for the bourgeoisie to reject change. . . .
>
> With our system of production we can support about ten million. Since we have seventeen million we are overpopulated, but if our pattern of production were altered we could support fifty million or more. The reason why they want birth control is that they don't want a technical revolution.
>
> Birth control is being proposed as a panacea, which is utopian, false, and treacherous.

Leftwing Brazilians agreed. "*The reactionary attitude is not that of the Catholic Church but of the family planners* . . . for commercial reasons, out of North American geo-political interests (so there will not be a prevalence of underdeveloped populations). Brazil, lacking in mechanical resources, depends for her economic progress on her working force . . ." (emphasis added).

Militant black groups in the United States likewise attacked the racist motives of population control. In 1962, Malcolm X accurately noted that "family planning" programs were directed against "colored nations." "Birth control is just a plot just as segregation was a plot to keep blacks down," said another radical group. "It is a plot rather than a solution. Instead of working for us and giving us rights—you reduce us in numbers and do not have to give us anything."

One American black woman put it particularly poignantly.

> Having a baby inside me is the only way I feel really alive. I know I can make something, do something, no matter what color my skin is, and what names people call me. . . . The children and their father feel it too, just like I do. Even without children my life would still be bad—they're not going to give us what *they* have, the birth control people.

Religion—not only Catholic opposition to birth control, but also the Judeo-Christian notion of the sanctity of human life—was supplanted with a new religion, one that crusaded against organized religion, while becoming one itself. Calling population control an "ill-conceived mandate from the well-to-do," one demographer wrote in 1969, "What has happened is that pressure groups for family planning, like the Catholic hierarchy they have been opposing, have been acting as self-designated spokesmen for 'public opinion.' *By developing a cause as righteous as that of the Catholics . . . the family planners have used the American way of influencing official opinion*" (emphasis added).

While the Vatican held that all life is precious and therefore should not be stopped, others in the religious community placed population control in the larger context of human history, warning of the dangerous tendency of the elite to remove resources from the poor and disabled.

"How can any 'optimum' number for the population of a country or a world be determined? What objective standards could be used? How much land, space, food, and other material goods should each person have? The ultimate question is *who will make these decisions?*

"The answer of the population planners is an elite group, usually composed of scientists, using expertise from the 'objective' . . . world of science."

4

BREEDING A BETTER RACEHORSE

Between 1890 and 1920, eighteen million immigrants set foot on America's shores: German Lutherans, Irish Catholics, Russian Jews, Slavic Orthodox. They built the railroads; they toiled in the factories, the coal mines, the steel mills; they worked seven days a week, for the lowest of wages and under the most hazardous of conditions; they took jobs that "real" Americans didn't want. They were the backbone of American industry.

But they weren't wanted.

"[F]oreigners who have come in hordes have brought with them their ignorance of hygiene and modern ways of living and . . . are handicapped by religious superstitions," complained Planned Parenthood cofounder Margaret Sanger in her 1920 book, *Women and the New Race.*

Hampered by religious beliefs and foreign customs, these foreigners were having too many children, their huge families threatening the supremacy of the Anglo race. "We have a natural pride in our country . . . but we leave it to our foreign-born to have the babies," bemoaned Dr. Royal S. Copeland, New York City's health commissioner, in 1921.

"[W]hite people are increasing at a rate of less than ten per thousand a year," the *New York Times* complained in 1922.

White folks at the top of the social stratum fought on many fronts to take back their position as the most populous race. In the early 1920s, powerful Anglo-Saxons pressured Congress to restrict immigration from Eastern and Southern Europe, because such folks—particularly the Jews—were not as intelligent as "real Americans." "The primary reason for the restriction of the immigration stream," remarked one member of Congress, "is the purifying and keep [sic] pure the blood of America."

By the early twentieth century, the Land of the Free had already begun to take down its welcome signs: the 1892 Chinese Exclusion Act and a 1908 "gentleman's agreement" with Japan slammed doors on Asians.

"Why should the Americans, who would act upon altruism by Christianity, prove so cruel?" asked one Japanese official in 1924.

In a 1924 letter to the Federal Council of Churches, former ambassador to Japan, Ambassador Cyrus E. Woods, referred to this restriction as a "humiliating race discrimination," "an international disaster of the first magnitude," as well as a "disaster to religion."

"Congress has thrown away one of the most important assets in solving the problems of the Pacific and has, at the same time, created utterly needless feelings of mortification, humiliation, and distrust, with fresh and as yet unknowable potential factors of difficulty in maintaining the permanent peace of the Far East."

On May 24, 1924, President Calvin Coolidge signed the Immigration Act of 1924, which placed firm quotas on immigrants from Eastern and Southern Europe while opening the doors to Nordics. The new law allowed 50,000 Germans, 50,000 British and Northern Irish, and 30,000 Free Irish into the country each year. But immigrants from other areas were effectively excluded, the reforms limiting entry to only 2,000 Russians, 3,000 Poles, 3,500 Italians, and a mere trickle of Africans, Arabs, and Mideasterners. In 1900, nine million immigrants arrived in the United States; by 1930, their numbers had dwindled to 500,000, nearly all of them from "desirable" parts of the world.

Jews were hit hardest. Though the quotas did not exclude Jews outright, the tight quotas on immigrants from Russia and Poland accomplished the same thing. The exclusion was intentional. During hearings on the immigration law, expert witness Lothrup Stoddard warned Congress about "Jewish money" and "Jewish guile" and the existing network that eased their transition into the United States.

"[T]he Jews belong to those classes of the community which everywhere are more desirous of coming to America; that is, the lower middle class and peddling classes generally. Then also there is the fact that Jewish emigration has been assisted by various immigrant aid societies. . . ."

As Samuel Dickstein, a Jewish congressman from New York, remarked, "[Y]ou could not help but understand that they did not want anyone else in this country except the Nordics."

"The point about the whole proposition is the fear of the large number of Jews coming in," said another Jewish congressman from New York.

In 1924, returning from a trip to Europe, Louis Marshall of the Emergency Committee on Jewish Refugees reported that fifty thousand Jews—some *already* holding U.S. passports—were stranded in Eastern Europe and Cuba because the United States would not admit them. Marshall went on to refer to "a carnival of massacres of which the Jews were victims . . . pogroms and mass murders, theft and pillage . . . famine and thyphus . . . the most abominable indignities and atrocities . . . by which the Jews alone were martyred.

"The doors of opportunity which had remained open for a

century . . . which had enabled God-fearing men and women to seek their happiness on our blessed soil, which they had enriched by their labor, their industry, their love, their culture, and their patriotic devotion, were slammed in their faces."

His message went unheeded—intentionally so. Two decades after immigration "reform," eight million Jews and countless other "less intelligent" human beings perished in Nazi concentration camps.

THE IMMIGRATION QUOTAS grew out of a broader movement to "purify" the human race, a movement known as "eugenics"—literally "good birth"—a phrase coined by Sir Francis Galton in 1883. A cousin of Charles Darwin, author of the 1859 *The Origin of Species,* Galton and his enthusiastic followers believed that "survival of the fittest" should be left not to nature, but to man—*certain* men, that is. Among the American founders of eugenics, some, such as biologist Charles Davenport, were also animal breeders who sought to apply their knowledge to better mankind.

"The essence of evolution," said one eugenicist, "is natural selection; the essence of eugenics is the replacement of 'natural' selection by conscious, premeditated, or artificial selection in the hope of speeding up the evolution of 'desirable' characteristics and the elimination of 'undesirable ones.'"

From its inception, the eugenics movement was driven by "science," a science that was often conveniently linked with "progressive" politics and the pretense of promoting the "betterment of mankind." While some eugenicists were clear in their goal to "purify" the human race, others cloaked the same goal with murky language about alleviating poverty by "helping" certain sectors of humanity limit their family size. The liberal pretense of "helping the poor" laid the foundation for the population zealots of the late 1960s who likewise buried their racism in leftwing rhetoric.

Driving the scientific justification for eugenics was the newfound knowledge of genetics, a science that began to move to the forefront of biology at the turn of the century. By the early 1900s, this knowledge catapulted scientists into leadership positions in the eugenics movement, where they increasingly linked all human behavior into discrete genetic units, without regard to circumstance or environment. Animal-breeder Charles Davenport, founder of the American Eugenics Society, identified "pauperism" and "mental inferiority" as genetic traits that must be removed from the human gene pool. With scientific authority, Davenport wrote in numerous scientific and medical journals that 85 percent of the offspring of such inferiors were destined to follow in their parents' shoes; indeed, that poverty itself was primarily attributable to bad genes. Because nearly all traits have their basis in genetics, and not the environment, society should discourage the transmission of bad genes, which, he estimated, cost society hundreds of millions of dollars a year. Medical science was prolonging the lives of such undesirables by focusing "too exclusively . . . on germs and conditions of life." Driven purely by concern for society, eugenicists set about finding a genetic basis for every single trait they deemed undesirable, including external conditions such as poverty.

Darwin's theory of evolution by natural selection, all but dead in the early twentieth century, was revived in the 1930s through a "synthesis" with the emerging field of genetics. The "neo-Darwinian synthesis" was the brain child of the best scientists in America, including many Nobel laureates, who restated Darwinism as "natural selection working on random mutations." For whatever reason—coincidental or not-so-coincidental—many of those neo-Darwinists were also active members of the American Eugenics Society, most notably

Theodosius Dobzhansky (chairman of the board of the AES in 1956), J.B.S. Haldane, and Richard G. Lewontin.* Because of its emphasis on genetics, neo-Darwinism was an ideal ally for eugenics. The two walked in tandem for decades, influencing science and ethics well into the present.

By the turn of the twentieth century, the eugenics movement had become all the rage in Britain and the United States. It was hardly a fringe movement; for years, words like "breeding" and "race better-ment" fell from the lips of such notables as Winston Churchill, George Bernard Shaw, Theodore Roosevelt, and Justice Oliver Wendell Holmes,** along with college presidents and professors from America's best universities—and, of course, scientists.

By the 1930s, as Hitler came to power, American eugenicists looked on with envy as the Nazis stripped away from certain "unde-sirables" the capacity to have children. Returning from a 1935 visit covering more than fifteen thousand miles in Germany, one eugeni-cist described the Nazi Heredity Health Courts set up to "improve the biological and racial qualities of the German people" and "diminish the transmission of qualities making for lower standards of health, and for lower degrees of competence and well-being among the German people."

The science of eugenics came up against one obstacle: religion—at least some religions. At a 1926 conference on birth control, one par-ticipant blamed religion—the "still arrayed power of darkness"—for perpetuating "human misery."

> We still have among us Bishops . . . who regard with comfort-
> able complacency the irrational, reproductive activities of

---

*Remarkably, these men held themselves out as leftists, while also promoting racism.
**"Three generations of imbeciles are enough," wrote Holmes in *Buck v. Bell,* a 1927 Supreme Court decision upholding the forced sterilization of an "imbecile."

improvident slum dwellers with their ever increasing output of wretched souls and diseased bodies. 'The Lord will provide,' they declared. . . . They denounce the sinfulness of birth control but the arguments . . . are usually those of Noah's time . . . when Providence provided manna for the hungry, and a multitude could be fed with five loaves and two fishes. . . .

When ecclesiastical organization or authority gets in the way of human need, human suffering, and the possibility of alleviating human suffering, that ecclesiastical authority doesn't stand a chance . . . whether . . . the ecclesiastical authority is in Rome, or in Canterbury or in Tibet.

A participant at the 1936 Eugenics Conference made clear that religion must take the backseat to science if the eugenics program was to accomplish its desired ends. He reduced religion to "basic feelings" that "may well have a genetic basis" and noted the collapse of religion that occurred in the aftermath of Charles Darwin's *The Origin of Species*. He went on to note the "responsibility to keep our altruistic urges intelligently in accord with the latest scientific discoveries. . . ."

Because the eugenicists themselves played God and disregarded some members of the human races, their philosophy directly opposed the Judeo-Christian tradition of charity for all and respect for individual life, as well as the opposition to birth control among some denominations.

Many mainstream Protestant denominations, easily accepting the atheist findings of modern science, went on to promote eugenics, stamping their approval on "playing God" and blaming charity for helping the unfit. One even went so far as to find support for eugenics in the Bible.

"For the past forty-five years a large element in the churches in

America have stressed not merely the reaching of the individual with the Gospel but also the ideal of a better society, a world-wide family of the children of God. Following the teachings of the Hebrew prophets and of Jesus, they have dared to dream of a new social order, a Kingdom of God among men, in which the will of the Heavenly Father should be done on earth as it is done in Heaven," wrote a pastor in an award-winning essay in the early 1920s.

Though they themselves were the target of eugenics, some naïve Jews likewise supported eugenics. At the 1926 conference, prominent New York Rabbi Sidney Goldstein, a liberal theologian, spoke giddily of "purifying" mankind, evidently unaware of the tragic irony of his words.

"Eugenists [sic] are prepared to cleanse and purify all of the stream of life and then to do whatever they can to cleanse the banks of the stream in order that the stream itself may not be defiled," he said.

The Catholic Church held firm. On December 30, 1930, Pope Pius XI issued an encyclical condemning eugenics as a power illegitimately seized by the state, "a power over a faculty which they never had and can never legitimately possess." "That pernicious practice must be condemned," he wrote, "which closely touches upon the natural right of man to enter matrimony but affects also in a real way the welfare of the offspring. For there are some who . . . put eugenics before aims of a higher order . . . and by public authority wish to prevent from marrying all those whom, even though naturally fit for marriage, they consider, according to the norms and conjectures of their investigations, would, through hereditary transmission, bring forth defective offspring."

There were many ways to "better" the human race, eugenicists believed. Just as they were closing the borders to undesirable immigrants, they were also finding ways to halt the procreation of undesirables who were already inside America's borders. As of 1923, thirty-five American states required sterilization of certain categories of humans: criminals, the "feeble-minded," the "poor," the deaf, and the blind. (In some cases, their family members, though themselves "normal," were also forcibly sterilized.) Laws prohibiting intermarriage between blacks and whites likewise protected the "purity" of the human—i.e. the white—race.

The "race-saving" hysteria of the early 1920s "united" the birth control and eugenics movements, though, in reality, the goals of these two movements were virtually identical. Birth control was eugenics wrapped in progressive language, almost always clothed in phrases like "alleviating human suffering" (though it was unclear exactly who these "suffering" humans were).

"[W]e sought first to stop the multiplication of the unfit," wrote Sanger, herself a participant in many eugenics conferences. "This appeared the most important and greatest step towards race betterment."

The spurious use by progressivism concerns as a pretext for eugenics was not lost on all. Just as others at the 1926 conference were congratulating themselves for their social concerns, one demographer attacked their underlying assumptions.

> Your propaganda to date has emphasized almost altogether the necessity for population reduction as though there could be no doubt of over-population in the United States. . . . [T]he population problem can be attacked only through long and intensive study of our present composition with due regard to the natural resources of the country . . . to the organization of industry, the improvement of our channels of distribution, the training and direction of our labor supply. . . .
>
> Such an approach is a hopeful and constructive one. It is a

far cry from the hasty and rather depressing assumptions which have determined the policy of your organization. Without much hesitation, you have ascribed most of our social and economic troubles to over-population and have proceeded to remedy them by striking at the very root of our procreating capacity.

The demographer went on to accuse the eugenicists of engaging in an "emotional reaction and not on a scientific analysis," going on—ominously and presciently—to warn against state control of reproductive capacity. "The very life of the state is involved as soon as we begin to tamper with who shall and who shall not be born." The warning went unheeded, and eugenicists—many of them scientists themselves—continued to engage in "emotional" reactions at the expense of "scientific analysis," presumably because "scientific analysis" did not suit their political ends, including their desire to obliterate religion.

As the pioneer of birth control, Margaret Sanger was, not surprisingly, at loggerheads with Catholics who then, as now, opposed artificial birth control. In a familiar refrain, Sanger accused the Catholic Church of blocking the alleviation of "human suffering," again wrapping eugenics in virtually the same progressive language used by the population zealots of the 1960s.

In a particularly biting exchange in 1921, Archbishop Patrick J. Hayes condemned Margaret Sanger's efforts to control population. "Children troop down from Heaven because God wills it," he said in a Christmas pastoral read in more than three hundred churches of the diocese. "He alone has the right to stay their coming. . . . [S]ome little angels in the flesh . . . may appear to human eyes hideous, misshapen, a blot on civilized society. . . . [But] within such visible malformation . . . there lives an immortal soul to be saved and glorified."

But the religious talk, the notion that "children troop down from Heaven," that even physically and mentally deformed children are worthy of life, did not sit well with Sanger. Livid, she attacked Hayes for "enforcing" his opinions and interfering "with the principles of this democracy" and—as was always the case—standing in the way of the "betterment of humanity."

> I do not care to answer the Archbishop's rhetorical statement concerning the will of the Almighty. His arguments are purely those based on assumption. He knows no more about the fact of the immortality of the soul than the rest of us human beings. What he believes concerning the soul after life is based upon theory; and he has a perfect right to that belief; but we who are trying to better humanity fundamentally believe that a healthy, happy human race is more in keeping with the laws of God than disease, misery, and poverty perpetuating themselves generation after generation.

MARGARET SANGER AND other progressives in the birth control movement sought birth control across the board, for all women of all social classes. But, perhaps to appease their allies in the eugenics movement, they also spoke of eliminating "undesirables," particularly immigrants. One of the aims of the Birth Control League, Planned Parenthood's predecessor, was the "sterilization of the insane and feebleminded and the encouragement of this operation upon those afflicted with inherited or transmissible diseases." Among the feebleminded, Sanger wrote, "only a small percentage were born of native parents." In other words, immigrants produced the greatest number of undesirable children.

In 1942, Sanger cofounded Planned Parenthood with Dr. Alan F. Guttmacher (in translation, "the maker of good"), a well-known obstetrician. If Sanger was the crusading feminist, Guttmacher was her dignified alter ego, described as "white haired and well dressed," a member of the "prep school circuit," his Jewish ancestry notwithstanding. In 1969, at the age of seventy, he still played tennis and walked to work from his large Fifth Avenue apartment in New York City. A one-time chief of the department of obstetrics at Mount Sinai Hospital and a father of three, Guttmacher traveled to sixty-five countries worldwide, warning of the dangers of "overpopulation," with intra-uterine devices (I.U.D.s) and other contraceptives at the ready.

"Every half-second while I stand here a woman is giving birth to a baby," Guttmacher warned his audiences (to which one listener responded: "We must find and stop that woman at once").

A gushing 1969 article in the *New York Times Magazine* called the father of three an "evangelist" of birth control and a "missionary." But like most population zealots, Guttmacher had a hidden agenda—whether he was aware of it or not: to focus population control on non-whites and the poor. Although he correctly observed that such groups lacked access to birth control, he and others failed to grasp the subtle racism of asking non-whites to limit their family size.

In the late 1960s Planned Parenthood strategically began "crash programs" in areas with the highest concentration of blacks. The latent goals of the birth-control crowd soon were accomplished: in Lincoln Parish, Louisiana, birth rates dropped a whopping 32 percent from 1966-67; in Washington D.C., birth rates were cut by 24 percent in three years; in Baltimore, they were down 38 percent in three years. Combined with high infant mortality—black babies at that time were twice as likely to die as white babies—such reductions in birth rates could virtually wipe out the black population in targeted areas. Not surprisingly, black militants accused Planned Parenthood of being "genocidal," as did some whites.

"What it all comes down to," said one dissenting Planned Parenthood board member, "is that we want the poor to stop breeding while we retain our freedom to have large families. It's strictly a class point of view."

Throughout the United States, black women bore the brunt of the abortion "rights" won for them by the white elite. According to U.S. census data, in 1975, white women had a 17.2 abortion rate per 1,000; blacks had a 49.3 abortion rate per 1,000. When abortions were at an all-time high in 1990, white women had 21.5 abortions per 1,000 women, compared to 54.4 per 1,000 among blacks. Fertility rates among black women fell from more than 4 children each in 1960 to about 2.1 (replacement level) in 1980.

"Admit it or not," said an official of the Population Council, "the genocide faction has a lot of evidence on its side."

The concentration of birth control clinics in black neighborhoods and the precipitous drop in black birth rates is hardly surprising. In addition to being a cofounder of Planned Parenthood, Alan F. Guttmacher was also a vice president of the American Eugenics Society.

COMMON WISDOM HOLDS that the eugenics movement ended shortly after World War II, when the revelations of Hitler's concentration camps shamed the eugenicists into quiescence. "Within the smoke of Nazi eugenics . . . many saw a frightful image," says a recent book about eugenics, which, though scholarly, adroitly overlooks the eugenicism of the overpopulation zealots of the late 1960s.

In 1947, the American Eugenics Society agreed that "the time is not ripe for aggressive eugenics propaganda."

But that didn't mean eugenicists were out of business. The American Eugenics Society was alive and kicking well into the early 1970s, remaining preoccupied with both race and "undesirable" characteristics. Increasingly, members were less vocal about their desire to protect the white population and more obsessed with alarmist messages about the overall decline of the human race occasioned by unbridled population growth and "differential reproduction." In a 1951 biology textbook,* Garrett Hardin—a biology professor, population zealot, and eugenicist—warned students that "people of low I.Q. are reproducing at a faster rate than those with high I.Q." He went on to instruct American youth that "[s]ooner or later ... human popu-lation will reach a limit. ... Sooner or later, not all the children that humans are willing to procreate can survive. Either there must be a relatively painless weeding out before birth or a more painful and wasteful *elimination* of individuals after birth . . ." (emphasis added).

Although hailed by the academic left, Hardin made no secret of his disdain for the poor. "Again, consider the matter of charity," he instructed American students in his 1951 textbook. "When one saves a starving man, one may thereby help him to breed more children. ... Some people maintain that very poor people are, on the average, less able and intelligent than the rich. ... [A]id to paupers undoubtedly has genetic consequences. ..."

The same rhetoric was used in the 1970s, fueled by the imminent legalization of abortion and the development of reproductive technology and prenatal testing. As eugenicist-scientist Irving I. Gottesmon and a colleague wrote in a 1971 issue of *Social Biology*: "Even if some of the disorders have no appreciable genetic loading, the reproductive behavior of such individuals and the characteristics of their offspring will influence human ecology by increasing social costs. ... [W]e must affirm that attending to the quality of the gene pool is a long-term necessity."

The *Journal of the American Eugenics Society* maintained its name

---

*The use of textbooks to promote eugenics was legion. See Chapter Seven.

until 1973, when it was renamed the *Journal of Social Biology*. But, said the journal, "[t]he change of name of the Society does not coincide with any change of its interests or policies."

Indeed, it didn't.

The renamed journal remained obsessed with "differential reproduction," code for the seemingly unlimited reproductive capacity of nonwhites. Among the articles in the *Journal of Social Biology* were "Fertility Patterns within the Mexican-American Population," "Reproduction and Inbreeding among the Samaritans," "Historical-Demographic Analysis of Indian Populations in Tlaxcala, Mexico," and "Demographics and Genetic Structure of Reservation Populations." Needless to say, there were no corresponding studies of the reproductive habits of Anglo-Saxons.

In 1956, another prominent scientist-eugenicist, William Shockley, co-winner of the Nobel Prize for physics, conducted scientific "studies" proving, he claimed, that blacks were "less intelligent" than whites. Blacks are not to blame, he said, because their "failings" are inborn. Reducing intelligence to genes alone, Shockley, like Hardin and others, argued that taxpayer money should not be wasted on programs designed to improve education in the inner cities because nothing would improve intelligence among blacks.

Like many of his scientific colleagues, Shockley also feared the "decline" of the human race, blaming the "poor" for reproducing in greater numbers than the middle and upper classes. He advocated *selective* sterilization with financial inducements for the economically deprived and those with I.Q.s of one hundred or less.

Shockley was immediately rebuked both by Stanford University and the National Academy of Sciences, among others. But other scientists, equally racist, escaped notice because they used more cagey words. "We have learned that when we locate the blacks we locate the centers of poverty with all their evils," wrote Grant Bogue of the department of sociology and anthropology at Western Illinois University.

"[R]ace is extremely important," he continued. "Not only have extremists in our midst pointed for years to the importance of racial differences . . . but social scientists also assert such significance. I, for example, confess that in several years of teaching elementary population courses I have been unable to finish one without at least one lecture on *racial differences* (although of course I do assert the *appropriate* assertions that the differences are culturally induced)" (emphasis added).

As outright racism became increasingly unacceptable, leftwing scientists began to speak in code: "poor" was substituted for non-white, "rich" for whites. "[E]ach rich nation amounts to a lifeboat full of comparatively rich people. The poor of the world are in other, much more crowded lifeboats. Continuously, so to speak, the poor fall out of their lifeboats and swim for a while . . . hoping to be admitted to a rich lifeboat," Garrett Hardin wrote.

The reproductive technology of the 1970s was a boon for eugenicists, permitting the selection of genes *before* a baby was even conceived. "[T]he techniques of artificial insemination that have been well developed by the cattle breeders offer possibilities . . . with respect to the human populations," remarked a eugenicist at a symposium on "hereditary counseling." Because *in vitro* fertilization produces multiple embryos, parents could select the "best" for implantation. Tests administered before and during pregnancy identified "undesirable" fetuses, such as those afflicted with Down Syndrome, which could then be aborted.

Neo-Darwinist Dr. H.J. Muller urged parents to construct their children from the "best available egg and sperm cells," recommending that a complete dossier be kept on all egg and sperm donors. A biologist envisioned the day "when parents will be able to select from one-day-old frozen embryos, guaranteed free of all genetic defects, with sex, eye-color, probable I.Q. and other traits described in detail on the label."

Those scientists who promoted genetics as a new way of manipulating the human genome were hardly on the fringe. Many were Nobel laureates; many had been elected to leadership positions in national science bodies; many were on the faculties of top American universities.

Phil Handler was so respected by his colleagues that in 1969 he was elected president of the National Academy of Sciences—the most prestigious scientific association in America. "Cruel as it may sound," he wrote in the early 1970s, "if the developed nations do not intend the colossal all-out effort commensurate with this task, then it may be wiser to let nature take its course."

Geneticist H. Bentley Glass was likewise respected by his colleagues and was, also in 1969, elected president of the American Association for the Advancement of Science. His credentials were impeccable: a renowned geneticist, he was the vice president of the State University of New York at Stony Brook.

In 1958, Glass argued that "the techniques of artificial insemination that have been well developed by the cattle breeders offer possibilities again with respect to the human population." Twelve years later, in his 1970 speech as outgoing president of AAAS, he went further: "It can no longer be affirmed that the right of the man and woman to reproduce as they see fit is inviolate. . . . [N]o parents will . . . have a right to burden society with a malformed or mentally incompetent child."

Glass was not only a respected scientist and liberal. He was also a member of the American Eugenics Society.

5

THE BOAT IS FULL

Theresa waited in a hotel room for her baby to die. "Baby Fae" had been born with a fatal heart defect known as hypoplastic left heart syndrome—only half of her heart worked. She had two weeks to live. An observant Catholic, Theresa had the child baptized, then settled into a hotel room, waited, wept, and prayed.

Then, in the middle of the night, the young mother's prayers were answered—or so it seemed. The baby might live, after all, her doctor said. A heart was available for transplant.

It belonged to Goobers, a baby baboon.

Human hearts were in very short supply: only 2 percent of potential recipients could get one. As of October 1984, those fortunate enough to get a human heart still faced overwhelming odds; few lived beyond five years. This was an improvement over the first human heart transplant performed by famed heart surgeon Dr. Christiaan Barnard on December 3, 1967; that patient lived eighteen days. Just a year later, out of 105 heart transplants: twenty-four lived for three months; two lived for six to eleven months; one lived for almost a year. But in 1980, a breakthrough changed everything: a drug called cyclosporin was shown to stop immune rejection of a foreign organ. Heart transplant recipients were living longer.

Still, animal organ transplants were another matter. Cyclosporin, the miracle drug for human organ transplants, did not work for cross-species transplants. The use of a baboon heart, said one experienced heart surgeon in Houston in 1984, was at most "a temporary measure to extend the life of the individual until a human transplant can be found." And, even if animal transplants did work, Dr. Leonard Bailey was not the right surgeon to perform this high-risk operation. Chief of pediatrics at Loma Linda Hospital, a Seventh-Day Adventist hospital near Riverside, California, the forty-one-year-old doctor had experimented with animal-to-animal organ transplants but hadn't published the results of his studies in any of the peer-reviewed medical journals where research is scrutinized by medical colleagues. Loma Linda had set aside enough money for five animal-to-human heart transplants, but—until the publicity surrounding Baby Fae—no one in the medical community knew that such an operation would soon be in the works.

Theresa signed the necessary forms, and on October 19, 1984, the infant was checked into the hospital and placed on a heart-lung machine, her temperature lowered to enable the transplant to take. At the same time, three floors below, Goobers' heart was removed and placed in an ice-filled cooler. On October 26, Dr. Bailey removed Fae's heart, replaced it with Goobers', reattached the veins and arteries, then told one medical journal that Fae might live "to see her twentieth birthday."

The world was watching. Fae appeared on national television, the size of a doll, her tiny body enveloped by the surgeon's hand. On day one, the hospital announced, she was doing "just fine." On day two, she was making a "remarkable recovery." On days seven through ten—at a time when transplants are typically rejected—Fae was, according to the hospital, "showing no signs of rejection." The doctor was still "encouraged" on day fifteen.

But by day nineteen, the baby's new heart was not beating "fully."

She was less active and alert. On day twenty, she died of heart block-age, having lived a record length of time with an animal heart.

"No doubt there has been tremendous victory," Bailey told the press. "It was a very encouraging thing for me both in human and scientific terms."

Nevertheless, the day after Fae's death, the hospital opted not to do another such transplant on a baby named James, who was sent on to Boston for a different procedure.

Despite the failure, Dr. Bailey said Fae was "a ray of hope . . . for babies to come."

THE RESPONSE FROM the media and medical community was impas-sioned, mostly against Bailey. Animal rights advocates were livid, pick-eting the hospital, calling the operation a violation of the baboon's rights. "Like us, Goobers was somebody, a distinct individual," said one, adding that animals should be "treated with respect."

It was not an uncommon response. The animal rights movement had sprouted in the early 1970s, and was in full-swing in the 1980s, an offshoot of the diminution of human life that resulted from repro-ductive technology and abortion. Animal rights activists were not all from the fringe; many ethicists in academia likewise argued that ani-mal life was equally valuable as human life. In part, this was an offshoot of increased knowledge of animals and their modes of expression. But more fundamentally, this shift of values was made possible by mod-ern science, whose findings were directly opposed to the Judeo-Christian belief that man was created in God's image.

"With the disproof of the Hebrew myth of creation, the belief that human beings are specially created by God, in his own image, was . . . undermined," observed philosopher-ethicist Peter Singer.

Outside the increasingly vocal animal rights movement, many

were more concerned with the *baby's* rights. Had she been used as a guinea pig? Had she been unnecessarily subjected to excruciating pain and suffering? Had she been sacrificed for the benefit of future infants? Was this Tuskegee all over again?

Dr. Thomas Ryan, president of the American Heart Association, called the operation a "bold experiment." He cautioned that a full assessment could not be made until the operation was written up in medical journals and reviewed by the medical community.

But Dr. Lewis Burrows of Mt. Sinai Hospital in New York City called the operation an "ignoble experiment" that could never have succeeded because the anti-rejection drug didn't work for animal organs. London-based medical ethicist Dr. Raanon Gillon cautioned that the medical community needs "more scrutiny" from the general public and that ethicists need to make a distinction between research that benefits the patient himself (therapeutic research) and research that benefits only future patients (non-therapeutic research).

All along, mostly unspoken, was the real problem: money. The wealthy could always buy themselves premium health care, while the lower classes were expendable. Theresa had no job, no husband, no health insurance, no social status. Had she, a desperate mother lacking in sophistication, been seduced by the promise of a "free" operation that might "save" her dying child?

Dr. Bailey, perhaps realizing he had a perfect human subject in this lower-class family, didn't tell Theresa that a human heart was available—not in the distant future, but on the very date set for Fae's surgery. Surely, this was a far better option than the untested animal transplant.

Nor did Bailey tell Theresa that there was a less invasive surgical option, the Norwood procedure, available at children's hospitals in Philadelphia and Boston. With this procedure, Fae's heart would have been repaired, not removed. Though it was not always success-ful, the Norwood procedure's success rate—40 percent—far exceeded the miniscule success rate of the highly speculative baboon transplant. Dr. Burrows argued that the procedure should have been used to keep Fae alive until a human heart was found. Dr. Ryan pointed out that the second baby, the one the hospital sent away, had received the Norwood procedure and died the next day. But, what-ever the options, at the very least Theresa should have been fully informed before she signed the consent form. The hospital declined to provide a copy of the consent form, so no one really knew what Theresa had been told.

How different it would have been had Theresa been wealthy or middle class, had she possessed a Ph.D. or been a high-powered execu-tive or at least had health insurance, which would have encouraged the less-invasive procedure. Had she not been poor, Theresa might have had her child transferred to a hospital in a major metropolitan area, which would have offered an array of treatments and more skilled physicians.

"I think that they did not make any effort to get a human infant heart because they were set on doing a baboon," said Paul Teraski, the director of a regional organ procurement agency.

Decisions made in desperation are rarely informed, as none other than Dr. Christiaan Barnard himself had noted. Such patients and their families are fair game, the great heart surgeon knew, because they'll agree to almost anything.

"If a lion chases you to the bank of a river filled with crocodiles, you will leap into the water convinced that you have a chance to swim to the other side when you never would accept such odds if there were no lion," wrote syndicated columnist Ellen Goodman, repeating Dr. Christiaan Barnard's description of the terminally ill.

"All of the medical evidence in this case . . . suggests this infant had no chance to survive," Goodman wrote. "Given that, we have to con-clude that Baby Fae's body was donated, alive, to science. . . .

"The rationale, that she was 'going to die anyway,' implies that it is open season on the dying, that we can try even the most outlandish experiment on these human beings. . . . It may be difficult to stop at the shoreline when the lion is gaining on your child. But when the crocodiles are hungry and the baby can't swim, there is no mercy in throwing that child in the water."

Goodman added that even Dr. Christiaan Barnard himself had admitted in his memoirs he'd lied to his transplant patients, offering hope that wasn't there, taking advantage of their vulnerability to fur-ther his own medical research and credentials.

The Baby Fae case raised the most serious ethical issue of medi-cal science, then and now: Should the life of one individual, whether it be a fetus or a terminally ill baby, be sacrificed in the theoretical interest of millions of babies yet to be born? Under the Judeo-Christian based philosophy of Immanuel Kant, an eighteenth-century philosopher and Christian, each human life is valuable in and of itself and as such must never be used to serve another pur-pose, no matter how noble. As a spiritual and physical being, man is intrinsically superior to animals who lack the ability to reason and exist only to serve man. In no case should a single life be sacrificed for a presumed "greater good."

Citing Kant's philosophy, syndicated columnist Dr. Charles Krauthammer agreed with Goodman on what seemed to be a never-ending battle between the dignity of a human being and the overall "good of mankind."

"Civilization hangs on the Kantian principle that human beings are to be treated as ends and not means," he wrote. "So much depends on that principle because there is no crime that cannot be, that has not been, committed in the name of the future against those who

74

inhabit the present. Medical experimentation, which invokes the claims of the future, necessarily turns people into means."

PRESUMABLY, CONGRESS HAD already dealt with the use—and misuse—of humans for medical research. In 1972, the federal government required that all institutions engaging in human research and receiving federal funds establish Institutional Review Boards (IRBs) to review proposals for human experimentation. In 1973, in the wake of Tuskegee and other revelations of research abuses, Congress held extensive hearings on human research, eventually passing the 1974 National Research Act.

As Senator Walter Mondale knew, scientists don't like public scrutiny. In 1968 and each year until 1973, the Democratic senator from Minnesota attempted to introduce a modest resolution to establish a National Commission on Health Science and Society, only to find himself blocked at each turn. Scientists at the hearings were "overtly hostile," a commentator later remarked, to government regulation and oversight.

"I do not think the public is qualified to make the decision," said Dr. Christiaan Barnard, referring to such life and death decisions as organ transplants during testimony before the United States Senate. At times, medical researchers were hostile to the point of utter pompousness, particularly when religion was raised. "If we are to retain a place of eminence in medicine," said Dr. Owen Wangensteen, a surgeon from the University of Minnesota, "let us take care not to shackle the investigator with unnecessary strictures, which will dry up untapped resources of creativity. . . . If you are thinking of theologians, lawyers, philosophers and others to give some direction . . . I cannot see how they could help. . . . [T]he fellow who holds the apple can peel it best."

"I was frankly taken aback by the spirited opposition expressed by many prominent men in the health sciences," Senator Mondale later remarked. "I sense an almost psychopathic objection to the public process, a fear that if the public gets involved, it is going to be anti-science, hostile, and unsupportive."

But by 1974, the public was fed up with the ethical transgressions of those who thought they knew better. Two years earlier, the press had reported on the use of human subjects in Tuskegee, and a year before, the media had exposed the gruesome experiments performed on live human fetuses. Now the Kennedy family loaned its name to the cause: Senator Edward Kennedy of Massachusetts led the Senate hearings, spurred on by his sister, the deeply religious Eunice Shriver, who had been particularly shocked by live fetal research.

The National Research Act, signed by President Richard Nixon on July 12, 1974, ostensibly banned all human research. In reality, Congress established the National Commission for the Protection of Human Subjects of Biomedical and Behavioral Research, consisting of eleven individuals appointed by the secretary of health, education, and welfare, who were "distinguished in the fields of medicine, law, ethics, theology, the biological, physical, behavioral and social sciences, philosophy, humanities, health administration, government and public affairs." The use of committees, panels, and special commissions to resolve morally troublesome issues would become standard fare over the next thirty years.

Composition of this committee was, as would almost always be the case in the next three decades, stacked in favor of medical sciences, with only a token few representing the religious community. Five of the eleven members were "engaged in biomedical research," giving the medical science community a hefty minority position. In selecting these and the remaining members, the secretary was to give "consideration" to the recommendations of the National Academy of

Sciences, Congress's official adviser on scientific matters. In other words, the scientific community would virtually control the selection of all the members.

The National Research Act was particularly fuzzy in its protection of the fetus. One version offered in the House by a pro-life Republican senator from New York would have directly banned "all research activity on a human fetus which is outside the womb of its mother and which is alive with a beating heart." But the final bill deftly removed any such restriction. The Senate was no place in which to answer "complex" questions, Senator Kennedy remarked. A ban on fetal research was imposed for six months, satisfying the public while actually giving the commission the final say. Soon after, the secretary issued regulations *temporarily* (that is, for six months) banning research on live fetuses until the commission reported back with its recommendations.

The commission's mandate was to "conduct a comprehensive investigation and study to identify the basic ethical principles which should underlie the conduct of biomedical and behavioral research on human subjects." The use of "blue-ribbon" panels to recommend public-policy issues was not uncommon in other arenas, but their use here—to identify (and in reality decide) core ethical principles—was a first, though hardly a last. Why shouldn't Congress—which routinely passes laws containing minute economic and legal detail, and which has at its disposal virtually limitless ability to explore the most complicated of issues, and which, most important of all, is accountable to the American public—why shouldn't that body itself address core ethical issues such as fetal research?

Even more scandalously, there were a mere six senators present on June 27, 1974, the day of the Senate vote, and the law was passed after no more than a half-hour of discussion. "[T]he legislation at hand is extraordinarily important," remarked Senator James Buckley, a Republican from New York. "It involves defining and clarifying matters of deepest ethical and moral importance in dealing with human lives and human beings.

"[B]ecause of its importance, I wish once again to express my sense of frustration at the rules of this body which make it possible to take up a matter within hours of the time that the print is dry on the [conference] report. The report on this bill was available only a half an hour ago. . . .

"Unfortunately, as only a half dozen Members are present, the vote that will take place shortly will not in any sense be an informed vote."

Thus was important legislation rushed to a vote by Senator Edward Kennedy, legislation that bequeathed congressional power to eleven "distinguished" individuals, including five who had a direct stake in the outcome and others recommended by the National Academy of Sciences. The Senate floor was no place to make "complex" distinctions, claimed Senator Kennedy, whose constituents included major medical centers in Boston, including Children's Hospital and Harvard Medical School.

The eleven members were sworn in on December 3, 1974. Heading the commission was Dr. Kenneth J. Ryan, chairman of the department of obstetrics at Harvard Medical School, who would go on in the following years to become a leading advocate of fetal research. As one member later recalled, "[M]ost of the commissioners and staff were of a liberal bent." From the start, it was clear that ethical questions would be readily resolved in favor of the medical research community.

In the ensuing months, the unelected commission held a series of public meetings on practices involving human subjects. Speakers trickled in from the religious community, but the overwhelming majority hailed from the research community which did not want to see its work stunted by public ignorance. The commission produced voluminous reports and recommendations, including *Fetal Research* (1975), *Research Involving Prisoners* (1976), *Research Involving Children* (1976), *Psycho Surgery* (1977), *Research Involving Those Institutionalized as Mentally Infirm* (1978), and *Institutional Review Boards* (1978). Over a period of four months and seven meetings, the commission studied the problems of fetal research, hiring Dr. Maurice Mahoney of Yale Medical School to survey the world's medical literature. At the fifth meeting on the subject, Commissioner Albert R. Jonsen distributed his view of the ethical differences between two different types of research: 1) a fetus that was going to be brought to term; and 2) a fetus that was destined for abortion. Jonsen made no distinction between living and dead fetuses, the very issue that had attracted public attention to begin with. But a few others did seem troubled by research on live fetuses. "The question was, on the face of it, distressing: should a living fetus be used for research. It was also perplexing because the research done on fetuses was aimed at the health of future fetuses," Jonsen recalled, suggesting that the "health of future fetuses" should govern. Specialists in moral philosophy and theology called in by the commission "bent their analytic skills to the task," Jensen wrote.

The "analytic" skills did little to protect the living fetus. Attached to the commission's 1975 "Research on the Fetus," was an opus as thick as the New York City phone book, Mahoney's voluminous study of research on the fetus, including studies performed on living fetuses of as much as twenty-six weeks in gestation, a practice Mahoney later called "repugnant to civilization." Among the appendices to the report was one commissioned from Battelle-Columbus Laboratories detailing all the supposed benefits that flowed from fetal research.

In fact, the Battelle report, commissioned by those who were already committed to a certain result, asserted a wide range of "benefits" that came from fetal research, most notably the rubella vaccine and tests for the Rh factor. But these treatments were the result of research on living fetal cells, derived from fetuses who were already dead. Respiratory distress syndrome was another condition that was supposedly studied using live fetuses. In reality, that condition, which affects premature infants, was studied on fetuses and infants who were *already* dead, not on live fetuses. Indeed, more than thirty years later, a number of treatments have been developed for premature infants with respiratory distress; not a single one of them is the result of research on living fetuses.

"Research on the Fetus" was filled with the moral doublespeak of bioethics, the intellectual shifting, the illogic and the numerous loopholes that soon would typify nearly all writings in the emerging field of bioethics. The commissioners recommended that research on living fetuses be limited to the first twenty weeks of its life, provided the mother gives her consent and the research serves a scientific purpose. In his dissent from this portion of the report, Berkeley Law professor David W. Louisell called the "restriction" a "deft escape hatch."

Despite the virtual lack of restriction on fetal research and the stacking of membership in favor of medical research, so-called "humanists" complained that there had been one Catholic on the commission.

THE COMMISSION'S MAGNUM OPUS was its 1979 "Belmont Report," so named because it emerged out of two years of discussion among the "distinguished individuals" at a "very pleasant 18th century house" in Belmont, Maryland.

The Belmont Report announced three broad ethical principles for scientific research on humans: 1) respect for persons; 2) beneficence; and 3) justice. The first—respect for persons—required that a research subject be fully informed about the experiment and that he give his full consent, a provision designed to prevent future Tuskegees and other instances in which a person has not consented to research. Closely related was the second principle: beneficence, the obligation to "do good," both to the individual and society at large. "Beneficence" included research "without direct benefit" to the individual—suggesting, in other words, that future Baby Faes could be sacrificed for other infants.

The third—justice—was the most open-ended and morally troublesome. On one side was the egalitarian philosophy of John Rawls, which holds that all goods and services be distributed equally to all, regardless of economic inequalities. Everyone should have equal access to "basic" healthcare, but the wealthy can purchase "luxury" healthcare, including private rooms with the extra fees derived from there to be reallocated to the general public. But when resources are scarce, when there wasn't enough to go around, "justice," the Belmont Report made clear, can also translate into triage—the distribution of medical care only to those patients who have a chance for survival.

What exactly is "justice"? And who decides? In the United Kingdom, as in other countries with socialized medicine, basic healthcare is accessible to all, but elderly people suffering from end-stage kidney disease, for example, cannot receive dialysis or transplants, an implicit judgment that the elderly are less valuable than the young. "[T]he necessity of selecting patients under the condition of scarcity is common," observed bioethicists William Beaumont and James F. Childress. "The question can escalate into 'who shall live when not everyone can live?'"

"Justice," therefore, boils down to a single question: Who is worthy and who is not?—a judgment that is inevitably eugenic. Where resources are scarce, where there's not enough to go around, someone must be sacrificed. Not everyone who needs an organ can actually get one; extraordinary surgical interventions are too costly to be given indiscriminately to everyone—or so it was said, without any countervailing principle holding that society should strive to make extraordinary care accessible to all.

In a broader sense, the principle of "justice" asks whether it is fair to devote economic resources to extraordinary medical care, at the expense of other priorities, such as education, healthcare, and basic medical research. Theologian Paul Ramsey, a strict Christian, was left with no choice but to recognize the near impossibility of distributing optimal care to everyone, even as he argued for an egalitarian approach in his 1970 *The Patient as Person*.

"To say that we can do anything we decide to do is . . . simply to say that we have the opportunity and the forced necessity of choosing what shall be done from among the many things that are possible, but not all possible together. This is the question of setting priorities which—tragically, perhaps—must be faced and thought through by the medical profession and by society in general. . . . [T]here can be no good reasons and no good moral reasons for decision by indecision, for allowing medical priorities and social priorities to be determined by who has the most spectacular therapy or the loudest voice in the land."

In practice, "justice" was even more eugenic than in theory. In a 1969 study of eighty-seven dialysis centers, investigators found that 91 percent of kidney dialysis patients were white. In deciding who should receive the treatment, doctors took into account a patient's intelligence and "social worth."

Likewise, in the early 1970s, a Seattle hospital appointed an anonymous "life or death" committee to select "suitable" candidates for kidney grafts. Before permitting the procedure, the committee took into account the recipient's marital status, his income and net worth, educational background, social and professional status, and "future potential."

"Committee decisions reflected the middle-class prejudices of its members," observed two law professors at the University of California at Los Angeles.

"Society 'invests' a scarce resource in one person as against another, and is thus entitled to the probable prospective of 'return' on its investment," wrote University of Pittsburgh philosopher Nicholas Rescher in a blood-chilling piece in the journal *Ethics*.

No doubt the Belmont principles prevented much abuse by over-zealous researchers, protecting prisoners, fetuses older than twenty weeks, mental patients, and the poor. But implicit in the Belmont principles is the age-old notion that some humans are more "worthy" than others, that the welfare of the politically and economically vulnerable is incidental to the good of the "worthy" segments of society. How these decisions should be arrived at, or who should decide that certain humans were more valuable than others, remained unclear. But the never-ending manifestation of eugenics in its many "progressive" guises should have raised some moral red flags.

In 1979, the Belmont Report was codified in federal regulations, implicitly enshrining eugenics as the law of the land.

UNDOUBTEDLY, THE NATIONAL Research Act and the National Commission took their cues from the bioethics organizations that cropped up in the late 1960s and early 1970s, increasingly replacing religion as the arbiter of morality.

In 1969, Dr. Willard Gaylin and philosopher Daniel Callahan founded the Institute of Society, Ethics, and the Life Sciences, later renamed the Hastings Center. Gaylin was a prominent psychiatrist and a professor of law and medicine at Columbia University, already well known for his sensitive writings on criminal law. Callahan, a former editor of *Commonweal* and a director of the Population Council, was an energetic man with a Harvard Ph.D. in philosophy. Credentials aside, he knew his way around the world of private foundations. He already knew the Rockefellers from his days at the Population Council and the Ford Foundation (which had funded his four-year international study of abortion) and was adept at raising money. The two men worked from Callahan's home in Hastings-on-Hudson, an affluent suburb of New York City, and were soon joined by a constellation of philosophers and theologians with wide-ranging views.

Just as the Hastings Center was getting off the ground in New York, another organization was created in Washington D.C. by Dr. André E. Hellegers, a Dutch-born, Jesuit-trained professor of obstetrics and gynecology at Georgetown University School of Medicine, an advisor to the Vatican, and a signatory on the amicus brief of the pro-life physicians in *Roe v. Wade*. A close friend of Eunice Kennedy Shriver, Hellegers persuaded the Kennedy Foundation to fund the Joseph and Rose Kennedy Center for the Study of Human Reproduction and Bioethics. The center, later renamed the Kennedy Institute of Bioethics, opened its doors on July 1, 1971.

All along, there was a hurdle to bioethics: religion. With each new scientific advance—*in vitro* research, genetic research, and a host of others—religion erected roadblocks by raising the pesky question of the "fundamental nature of human life and the dignity and worth of the individual human being."

"The first thing that . . . bioethics had to do—though I don't believe anyone set this as a conscious agenda—was to push religion aside," said Callahan.

Most secular bioethicists, joined by liberal theologians, believed that not everyone should live; not everyone should receive medical care; not everyone was worthy of life. In pushing religion aside, they argued that antiquated beliefs could not address the complexities of modern medicine and needed to be displaced by more "flexible" rules. The Bible spoke of life and death, but in contemporary science those markers were no longer clear—life in the womb was mere "potential," and "death" was expanded into a twilight zone of "brain death," and later various "vegetative" states.

Clearly, there are complexities in the varying states of human life, not easily answered by the age-old wisdom that all human life is worthy and must be saved at all expense. But what was most troubling about the Hastings Center was its overlap in membership and assumptions with a movement then believed to have ended long before.

In attendance at the first meeting of the Hastings Center on January 10, 1970, at the Hotel Westbury in New York were a number of individuals who also were or had been prominent in the American Eugenics Society. Over time, they were joined by two other eugenicists, both outspoken in their denigration of human life: Joseph Fletcher and the ubiquitous population zealot Garrett Hardin (who committed a double homicide with his ailing wife in 2003).

Certainly not all of the secular bioethicists were eugenicists—in fact, most were not. Hastings Center founders Gaylin and Callahan and most of the center's fellows were, by all accounts, genuinely searching for ethical principles that addressed the changing climate of the medical sciences. A very few, such as Dr. Leon Kass and theologian Paul Ramsey, viewed ethical issues in a theological light.

Nonetheless, there was a troubling overlap between bioethics and eugenics. According to Hastings Center archives, the organization's funders, most notably the Rockefeller family, had also been active in eugenics. Topics addressed at the center's meetings were those dear to the eugenics movement: genetic counseling, population control, and the general subject of "who shall live and who shall die?"

Some studies were commissioned by the very groups with a financial interest in reducing medical costs.

As with the Belmont Report, bioethics assumed a shortage of resources and working from there addressed ways to distribute them "justly." Ironically, much of the shortage was itself created by the same group of population zealots and eugenicists who favored forced sterilization, abortion, and birth control. So driven were some of these bioethicists by the principle of "shortage" that they overlooked the demographics of medical care. Economically, the young and healthy shore up programs such as Medicare, Social Security, and private health insurance, allocating resources to the elderly and infirm. But with a decline in birth rates, a reverse pyramid took effect: if once an elderly individual was supported by ten healthy people, now there would be only two or three healthy individuals to fund his expensive care. This was true in the family as well: once a couple had five children and twenty grandchildren to shoulder the burden of their care, now an elderly couple with just one child and possibly no grandchildren would have to be cared for in an expensive institution and not at home.

The Malthusian terror of scarcity had thus become a self-fulfilling prophecy: fear of shortage itself generated greater shortage. Demographic trends of the early 1970s, a time when many in this group forecast overpopulation, actually showed that by the next generation the elderly population would be propped up by a much smaller base of the young and healthy. Had population growth been unrestricted, there would have been more, not less, to go around. In other words, eugenics produced scarcity and scarcity produced eugenics.

Much attention was given to the financial side of ethical decisions: Who gets maximum care and at what cost? "[T]he new capabilities will not be cheap," noted one report. "It will not be economically feasible to prolong greatly the life expectancy of more than a very small fraction of the human race." Even the Vatican agreed that extraordinary care need not be given to futile cases, but in the case of secular bioethics economic issues were the driving force. In a 1987 report on "imperiled newborns," the center noted that "it is not uncommon for a small preemie [premature infant] to spend months in a neonatal ICU [intensive care unit]. The costs of such care can run into the tens and occasionally hundreds of thousands of dollars per child, and in the aggregate as much as $2 billion a year to society overall."

In 1981, with funding from Blue Cross Blue Shield, the Hastings Center drafted "Guidelines for the Ethical Management of Health Care for the Terminally Ill." The report said that "the ethical responsibility to the person receiving care must be balanced with . . . the institution's necessarily limited resources." Again—and not surprisingly, in view of the report's funding source—the emphasis is on money alone, not the needs of the patient or his family.

The center's communique, the *Hasting Center Report,* revealed a similar focus on the economic cost of seemingly futile medical treatment, with little attention to the other side of the equation: a way in which resources could be expanded.

By the 1970s, it was standard fare to abort abnormal fetuses or, if allowed to go to term, to "allow" the infants to die, even when some might otherwise have led productive lives. Writing about so-called "defective" infants, many bioethicists used the same chilling language of eugenics.

"[W]e can see this as a problem of resource allocation. . . . Given finite resources to spend on newborns, the issue is unavoidable. . . . [W]e can attack the problem of defective newborns . . . by realizing that other obligations force us to restrict the numbers of such children whom we treat," wrote one bioethicist in a 1974 issue of the *Hastings Center Report.*

These were not merely the theoretical wranglings of graying

academics with little to do during their summers off; these principles were employed in actual practice. In the 1970s, twenty-four infants with *spina bifida* were "allowed" to die at Oklahoma Children's Hospital. In the early 1970s, two Down Syndrome babies born in Johns Hopkins Hospital met similar fates. While infants born with these afflictions face a different kind of life than those born "normal," such babies can in most cases live perfectly happy and productive lives. They were "inconvenient" only because they require more attention—and, more to the point, are more expensive.

"It would be unfair to the other children of the household to raise them with a mongoloid," said one mother.

In 1973, two pediatricians at the Yale-New Haven Hospital admitted in an article that they had accepted parents' decisions to forego treatment, and that forty-three "impaired" infants had died under their care. In these cases, the parents alone were allowed to decide the fate of their child, rather than a court or a court-appointed guardian.

"Infant Doe," born in Bloomington, Indiana, on April 9, 1982, had Down Syndrome along with a potentially fatal, but treatable, condition known as "tracheoesophageal fistula." The obstetrician, Dr. Walter Owens, told the parents that such babies are "mere blobs" and that the lifetime cost (to the parents) of treating the child would be $1 million. The parents said they didn't want the child treated, but the hospital and the country prosecutor disagreed, initiating an emergency hearing before a county judge who went on to hold that the parents' "rights" prevailed. The case was appealed to one court, then a higher court. Each agreed with the parents. Infant Doe died when he was six days old.

"The family is at risk of psychological harm and perhaps economic harm," wrote Beauchamp and Childress.

In a 1974 *Hastings Center Report* one author agreed that Down Syndrome children should be allowed to die if "it can be argued that the action is necessary to protect the personal life of at least one specifiable other person." In other words, if the existence of an afflicted infant stands in the way of *anyone* at all, the infant should be left quietly to die.

The rationale appealed to many bioethicists, including Joseph F. Fletcher, a member of the Hastings Center, a lapsed Episcopal minister, and a eugenicist. Deemed a "pioneer" in bioethics, Fletcher wrote that ethical decisions must be made based on what brings the most *happiness* to the greatest number of people, rather than what brings happiness to the individual himself.

Roe v. Wade had already whittled away at the concept of personhood, endorsing the fiction of "potential life" that inevitably would be expanded to other categories of human life. Drawing upon *Roe*'s message that not all humans are "persons," Fletcher established his own criteria of personhood, including minimum intelligence; a sense of time; self-awareness; self-control; a sense of futurity; a sense of the past; capability to relate to others; concern for others; communication; control of existence; curiosity; change and changeability; balance of rationality and feeling; idiosyncrasy; and neo-cortical function. Looking from the outside, how was anyone to determine whether an individual has a "sense of time," a "sense of the past," or "curiosity"? Such labels paved the way for a eugenic approach to human existence, allowing certain individuals to choose the fate of others they deem less worthy.

From merely "allowing" some infant to die, it was an easy jump to the next step in the logical progression: actually killing some infants.

"Defective fetuses, defective newborns, moribund patients—all of these are human lives," Fletcher wrote. "If there is any ground at all . . . for allowing or hastening the end of such lives, it must be on a qualitative ground, that such human lives are subpersonal. What is critical is *personal* status, not merely *human* status. This is why the law does not allow that a fetus is person.

"If one's standard of the good is human well-being, and one's duty or obligation is to seek to increase it wherever possible . . . then it will follow that infanticide is acceptable. . . ."

Australian philosopher Peter Singer—later a professor of philosophy at Princeton University—not only advocated letting deformed infants die but, like Fletcher, advocated infanticide under some circumstances. He also argued that animal life should be placed on par with human life: "People say that life is sacred. . . . But why should human life have special value?" Like Fletcher, Singer proposed that only some members of the human species should be considered "persons": "[T]he most plausible arguments to attributing a right to life to a being apply only if there is some awareness of oneself as a being existing over time. . . ."

To Catholics in particular, the sliding scale of human worth was heresy, all human life being intrinsically precious. "The Catholic/Christian view of the person is grounded in the biblical teaching that all human beings are made in the image and likeness of God." According to Catholic doctrine, "[e]very person is unique and irreplaceable and is called both to human fulfillment and to eternal life. All human beings are equal and all human life, because it originates in God, is sacred." Though less "rigid" than Catholicism on issues such as abortion, Judaism likewise upheld a similar "bias for life." "[W]hatever the status of the life before us," wrote Seymour Siegel, professor of theology and ethics and rabbinical thought at the Jewish Theological Seminary, "the fact that the life is certainly to be terminated, that it is flawed or doomed does not preclude activation of the 'bias.'"

As one Cambridge law professor said, "[M]ost of modern bioethics is clearly subversive of this tradition of common morality.

Rather than promoting respect for universal human values and rights, it systematically seeks to subvert them. In modern bioethics, nothing is, in itself, either valuable or inviolable, except utility."

In order to forge ahead with the new utilitarian approach to ethics, it was necessary to do away with religion altogether, an agenda that secular bioethics was subtly and not so subtly accomplishing. In his book, *Rethinking Life and Death*, Peter Singer announced that ten new commandments would have to replace the Ten Commandments of the Bible. "Thou shalt not kill" and others are replaced with conditional commandments that humans should be killed under certain circumstances, that animals may at times be more worthy of life than humans, that not all human life is of equal worth, that a newborn infant has no greater right to live than a fetus, and so forth.

In Germany and Austria, with their collective guilt about the Holocaust, Peter Singer is considered so repulsive that his writings are banned. But the academic elite in the United States welcomed him with open arms.

In 1998, Princeton University appointed Peter Singer to the position of De Camp Professor in the University Center for Human Values.

PART II

THE POLITICS OF BIOLOGY

6

THAT OLD TIME RELIGION

Clad in a simple cotton dress, her young face strained with distress, Rachel Brown pleads with her fiancé. She is a plain girl in her early twenties and doesn't want any controversy.

"Bert, why don't you tell them it was all a joke? . . . Tell 'em you didn't mean to break the law, and you won't do it again. . . . It's not too late. Why can't you admit you're wrong? . . . Everyone says that what you did was bad."

Bertram Cates is imprisoned—literally and metaphorically—in the Hillsboro jailhouse, along with the drunks and degenerates. He is there for his principles; he believes he should be free to think and teach the truth.

"They can't lock up my mind," he says.

But Rachel doesn't care about intellectual freedom. She cares only about the opinion of small-town Hillsboro and even more about her father, Reverend Jeremiah Brown, a fire-and-brimstone man of religion.

Cates tries to explain that he didn't do anything wrong; all he did was teach a high school biology class about Charles Darwin's *The Origin of Species*, the 1859 book that introduced the theory of evolution by natural selection—and smashed the biblical account of creation. The world wasn't made in just six days, as Genesis teaches, and man wasn't just created out of dust—he evolved from lower forms of life over millions of years. Cates pleads with his beloved to set aside her religious fundamentalism and embrace the beauty of science, the only true account of reality. "All it says is that man wasn't just stuck here like a geranium in a flower pot; that . . . it just didn't happen in six days," he says. "Do you know, at the top of the world the twilight is six months long?"

Rachel doesn't care about the beauty of science. Mostly she is worried about her father, who already has denounced Cates as Satan himself and burned him in effigy. "But we don't live at the top of the world," she says. "We live in Hillsboro, and when the sun goes down, it's dark. . . . Why can't you be on the right side of things?"

Understanding suddenly washes across Cates's face. "You mean your father's side," he says.

Tormented and impossibly conflicted, Rachel tries to get up and leave, but Cates leaps to his feet to console her. He does not condemn; he understands. But Rachel remains torn between her father and her true love. One seeks intellectual freedom; the other condemns anyone who questions the Word of God.

"For all eternity let his soul writhe in anguish and damnation," Reverend Brown preaches, referring to Cates. "The Word tells us that the World was created in Six Days."

The audience applauds and shouts, caught up in the fiery sermon and the condemnation of anyone who shakes their worldview. A gentle voice speaks up, the voice of Mathew Harrison Brady, a famous lawyer who has traveled to Hillsboro to prosecute Cates. Though a man of religion, a defender of Christian fundamentalism, Brady is gentler than the reverend—and deeply sympathetic to Rachel.

"Is it possible to be over zealous, to destroy that which you hope to save?" he asks.

Brady is a hero to the residents of Hillsboro; he vindicates their deeply held beliefs. The aging, three-time presidential candidate has traveled around America to preach against the evils of evolution and the truth of the Bible. When he arrives in Hillsboro, the town folk greet him with parades and applause. But he is a bit of a buffoon, way past his prime, and in failing mental and physical health.

Brady has a formidable opponent, another great lawyer who likewise has traveled from afar to defend Cates and, even more so, the integrity of science. Henry Drummond is an atheist lawyer and defender of unpopular causes. Some years before he had defended two teenagers who had killed just for the sport of it. The residents of Hillsboro remember this and know of his hostility to religion. Though he is a contemporary of Brady and a one-time political ally, Drummond is still in his prime, tough and articulate. When he hits the small town, he isn't welcome.

Unmoved by Brady's gentle rebuke, wedded to his small-minded beliefs and hostility to anyone or anything that challenges his religion, Reverend Brown reflexively quotes the Proverbs: "He that troubleth his own house . . . shall inherit the wind."

HENCE THE TITLE for the 1955 play by Jerome Lawrence and Robert E. Lee, which opened in Dallas on January 10, 1955, and moved to Broadway's National Theater three months later.

"The events which took place during the scorching July of 1925 are clearly the genesis of the play," the authors state in the preface to *Inherit the Wind*. But the play, they caution, "does not pretend to be journalism. . . . It is theater."

The retelling of the Scopes trial on stage and later in film—the wonderful clashes between two great lawyers, the martyrdom of Bertram Cates, the small-mindedness of the religious—is the most popular rendering of the age-old war between religion and science. A beleaguered scientist attacked by the religious, Cates follows in the footsteps of Galileo, the legendary scientist who was prosecuted by the Vatican for rearranging the position of the earth. In American society, even under conservative administrations, scientists yield far more political power than the religious. But the prototype served science well, instilling fear in the secular public.

ACTUALLY, *INHERIT THE WIND* had little to do with science or religion or even the Scopes trial. Postwar America, with its terror of communist infiltration, was not a happy time for the entertainment industry. The play is a commentary on that shameful era.

In May of 1947, under the leadership of U.S. Representative J. Parnell Thomas, the House Un-American Activities Committee (HUAC) established temporary headquarters at the Biltmore Hotel in Hollywood to begin hearings on alleged communist influences in the entertainment industry. The U.S. Chamber of Commerce and the Motion Picture Alliance for the Preservation of American Values had warned that communists were trying to take control of the film industry and already dominated the Screen Actors Guild. The film critic for *Esquire* wrote that the left wing "has a monopoly in Broadway."

It was not the country's finest moment. The constitutional protection of due process—fairness—was cast aside. Careers were destroyed, friendships torn apart. The HUAC was out for blood. "Friendly" witnesses—those who "named names"—included Walt Disney, Gary Cooper, Robert Montgomery, Robert Taylor, and Elia Kazan. The Screen Actors Guild later required its members to take an oath pledging loyalty to the U.S. government. Twentieth Century Fox and others in the motion picture industry publicly stated, "We will not knowingly employ a Communist or a member of any party of group which advocates the overthrow of the government of the United States by force or by illegal or unconstitutional methods."

Even worse, FBI director J. Edgar Hoover acquired approval rights over some television series and films, hardly the free speech envisioned by the country's Founding Fathers. Fearing further recrimination, many screenwriters and playwrights produced works with highly insipid melodramas whose themes reinforced America's superiority over the rest of the world.

Some "unfriendly" witnesses—those who refused to cooperate— served prison terms because they refused to name names. Others were blacklisted by the entertainment industry and worked under pseudonyms or not at all.

Playwrights Jerome Lawrence and Robert E. Lee were not themselves blacklisted, but they, too, were affected by the "red scare" and the censorship of Hollywood. *Inherit the Wind* was actually completed in 1950, but the playwrights waited until 1955 because "the intellectual climate was not right." "I wouldn't have dared write a letter to my congressman," Lee said.

But by 1955, the HUAC had folded its tent, and the two playwrights believed that conditions had changed enough for them to release the play. They told the *New York Times* that *Inherit the Wind* dramatized the plight of "people caught in an intellectual ferment they did not completely understand" and showed that "conformity and thought control are enemies of progress and enlightenment." As Shakespeare used history as a mask for criticizing Elizabethan England and as Arthur Miller's *The Crucible* used the Salem witch hunt as a metaphor for the red scare, *Inherit the Wind* used the Scopes trial to show the evils of "conformity and thought control" in postwar America.

Among the writers blacklisted by the film industry was a talented screenwriter named Nedrick Young. On April 8, 1953, he was summoned by the HUAC to testify about his alleged association with communism. Not only did he refuse to answer, but he went on to refer to the hearings as "a disgusting procedure" and called Congressman Donald L. Jackson a "contemptible man" who had "told outrageous falsehoods in the halls of Congress." For his sins, Young was placed on a blacklist, compiled by the House Committee and the American Legion.

Seven years later, Young—a.k.a. "Nathan E. Douglas"—teamed up with Harold Jacob Smith to write the screenplay for the movie version of *Inherit the Wind*.

IN REALITY, THE Scopes trial was hardly as dramatic, hardly as black and white as portrayed in the play and later the movie.

The real John T. Scopes was never imprisoned for teaching evolution. He had no romantic involvement at the time, no fiancée torn between the forces of religion and science. In *Inherit the Wind* Bertram Cates (Scopes) is arrested and dragged to prison while in the middle of teaching evolution to his high school students. His conflicts with Rachel likewise add drama to the play, but they are not based in reality.

The actual Scopes trial began far more inauspiciously.

"We are looking for a Tennessee teacher who is willing to accept our services in testing this law in the courts," the American Civil Liberties Union announced in the *Chattanooga Times*. The law in question—the Butler Act—made it a crime to "to teach any theory that denies the story of the Divine Creation of man as taught in the Bible, and to teach instead that man has descended from a lower order of animals."

"Our lawyers think a friendly test case can be arranged without costing a teacher his or her job," the ACLU continued. "Distinguished counsel have volunteered their services. All we need now is a willing client."

In the local drugstore in Dayton, a group of men spotted the ad and saw an economic opportunity in a high-publicity trial. So they sent a young boy to dispatch John Thomas Scopes, a quiet, clean-cut twenty-four-year-old teacher and athletic coach at the local high school, who vaguely recalled that he might once have referred to Darwin during a stint as a substitute teacher in biology. Already hostile to the Butler Act, Scopes agreed to be arrested. "America would never be the same again," Edward J. Larson wrote in *Summer for the Gods*, his Pulitzer Prize-winning account of the Scopes trial.

Dayton was abuzz. The post office and telephone company hired additional employees. The courthouse was renovated, repainted, and enlarged to accommodate more than five hundred spectators.

Scopes was defended by the crème-de-la-crème of lawyers, hired by the American Civil Liberties Union, Chicago lawyer Clarence Darrow, best known for his defense of Leopold and Loeb, two privileged teenagers who killed a classmate just for fun—his defense was that the young men were victims of "social Darwinism" (eugenics), which had encouraged them to kill their "inferiors."

Dayton was enemy territory for Darrow who "regarded Christianity as a 'slave religion,' encouraging acquiescence in injustice, a willingness to make with the mediocre, and complacency in the face of the intolerable." He told a group of convicts that the biblical concept of original sin, salvation, and grace was "a very dangerous doctrine—silly, impossible, and wicked. . . . When a person is sure that he is good, he is nearly hopeless; he gets cruel—he believes in punishment." Though he enjoyed science, Darrow did not fully understand Darwin's theory of evolution but "readily embraced [its] . . . antitheistic implications."

Darrow had a formidable opponent in William Jennings Bryan,

later portrayed as the bumbling Mathew Harrison Brady. Bryan had served as secretary of state under Woodrow Wilson and had launched three unsuccessful bids for the presidency. Author of the column "Weekly Bible Talks," Bryan crusaded around the country warning Americans about evolution, which he considered evil because it conflicts with the Bible.

The trial began on July 10, 1925, a Friday. The courtroom was packed, the temperature unbearable. Town folks were impassioned, boycotting a local merchant named Jim Darwin because of his last name. In the barbershop, a fight broke out over this "damned monkey business."

More than two hundred newspaper reporters from all over the country descended on the small town to report on the now-legendary legal face-off. They sneered at the residents of Dayton. The *New York Times* reported that "Dayton believes in a Christ born by a virgin and resurrected from the tomb, a real Adam and a real Eve and a real serpent and a real angel with a flaming sword. Mayor and druggist and school teacher and club women and old men and women of the mountains say over and over again, 'The Book is all we got to tell us how we came and where we're going.'"

Judge John T. Raulston opened the trial with Christian prayer, rousing the audience to reply "amen." Darrow complained about the religious invocation but to no avail; the judge's mind was set. Darrow later asked permission to call scientific experts to testify about the truth of evolution. Again, the judge refused. Finally, Darrow made a shocking request: he called Bryan to the stand as an expert witness on the Bible.

Bryan was indeed an expert on the verses of the Good Book—he had committed many to memory. But apparently he had never thought through its scientific impossibilities.

"Do you believe Joshua made the sun stand still?" Darrow asked.

"I believe what the Bible says." Bryan said, then hesitated. "I suppose you mean that the earth stood still?"

"I don't know," Darrow responded. "I am talking about the *Bible* now."

"I accept the Bible absolutely," Bryan responded. "I believe it was inspired by the Almighty, and He may have used language that could be understood at that time instead of using language that would not be understood until Darrow was born."

The audience got the joke and broke into laughter.

Darrow continued. "If the day was lengthened by stopping either the earth or the sun, it must have been the earth."

"Well, I should say so."

"Now, Mr. Bryan, have you ever pondered what would have happened to the earth if it *had* stood still? . . . Don't you know it would have been converted into a molten mass of matter?"

Eventually, under Darrow's unrelenting cross-examination, Bryan finally caved. Dumbstruck, he fell into the trap that Darrow had made for him: the six "days" of creation could actually have spanned millions of years—a "day" did not necessarily mean a twenty-four-hour day.

"From those people you call 'yokels,' those are the people whom you insult," said a shaken Bryan when he finally emerged from the blitz.

To which Darrow replied: "You insult every man of science and learning in the world because he does not believe in your fool religion."

WHILE MANY REPORTERS covered the Scopes trial, the writings of one rose above all others—those of the acerbic H.L. Mencken of the *Baltimore Evening Sun*. Mencken filtered the Scopes trial through the lens of his atheism, rewriting history to suit his ends.

"History is not always written by the victors, and the losing side [John Scopes] . . . wrote the version of the case that made it into most of the history books—with more than a little help from H.L. Mencken," wrote Terry Teachout in his biography of Mencken.

A committed eugenicist, Mencken hated almost everyone; but he reserved special venom for the "professional kikes"—the Jews, that is—who "got us" into World War II. He didn't like blacks much, either. "The white man is actually superior to a Negro on all counts," he wrote, referring to blacks as "the most unpleasant race" he'd ever heard of. An opponent of World War II, Mencken never wrote about the Holocaust, perhaps agreeing with Hitler's goal to rid the world of Jews.

Mencken also detested religion, seizing upon the Scopes trial as a perfect opportunity to ridicule the small-town "yokels," the "Ku Klux theologians," the "peasants," and the "fundamentalists of the hills." He referred to religion as "degraded nonsense . . . rammed and hammered into yokel skulls." "There is no possibility of reconciling science and religion. . . . If the one is sound, then the other is bilge. . . . The two things are not only different; they are squarely and eternally antagonistic."

In his 1930 essay, *The Beliefs of an Iconoclast*, Mencken used science as the proverbial stick to beat the dog with. "When Copernicus proved that the earth revolved around the sun, he did not simply prove that the earth revolved around the sun," Mencken wrote. "[H]e also proved that the so-called revelation of God, as contained in the Old Testament, was rubbish."

ON JANUARY 10, 1955, almost thirty years after the Scopes trial, *Inherit the Wind* opened in Dallas. It was such a hit that it moved to Broadway's National Theatre on April 21, 1955, a mere three months after its Dallas opening. The Broadway cast was spectacular. Producer Herman Shumlin cast Tony Randall as Hornbeck (Mencken) and Ed Begley as Mathew Harrison Brady (Bryan). For the role of Drummond (Darrow), Shumlin originally approached Orson Welles, who then had other film commitments. His second choice was Paul Muni, then fifty-nine and six years into retirement. Although initially reluctant, Muni read the play and was sold on it. After six months of preparation, Muni played Darrow right down to "the shuffling gait, the unpressed suit, the ruffled gray hair . . . and the stentorian voice of the lawyer rushing in for the kill." "When Mr. Muni is on the stage," the *New York Times* drama critic wrote, "*Inherit the Wind* is gripping and absorbing." The play brought Muni "out of the doldrums" into a "second fling with fame."

Muni's stellar performance notwithstanding, the play was not well-reviewed by the New York theater critics. Lewis Funke of the *New York Times* called Randall's performance "commendable," Begley's "fine," Muni's "magnificent," but the play overall, he wrote, had a "clinical quality" and overall "lack of tension."

The movie version changed all that.

In 1956, the iconoclastic filmmaker Stanley Kramer paid $200,000 plus royalties for the movie rights to the play. Released in 1960, the film version of *Inherit the Wind* was a critical and popular success, far more dramatic than the play and ultimately the most widely accepted account of the 1925 trial.

Kramer was producer *par excellence,* a free thinker whose every film was infused with the plight of an individual standing up to the group-think mentality. His many film credits included *The Defiant Ones* (1958), the drama of two escaped convicts, one white, the other black; *Ship of Fools* (1965), a study of anti-Semitism aboard a ship headed for Germany during World War II; and *Guess Who's Coming to Dinner?* (1967), an examination of the subtle forms of racial prejudice. Kramer's 1959 *On the Beach*, about the nuclear end of the world, was admired by communist countries. But the film riled the State Department and the American Legion because of its allegedly "pro-Soviet" message. Anti-communist groups counseled that Kramer's movies should be viewed with "caution."

"I think I am . . . one who truly believes in the inherent rights of an individual in the world in which I live," Kramer told the *New York Times* in 1961.

World affairs aside, Kramer was also disgusted with the "entrenched management" of large film companies for being "most reactionary and adamant about what sort of pictures should be made and what sort of people should make them. . . . The most exciting things that have stimulated people into coming into theatres . . . are scornfully resisted by the 'control factors' in the American industry."

Kramer's enormous success was due in large part to his choice of actors, especially the much-celebrated Spencer Tracy whom he cast in the role of Henry Drummond (Darrow) and later in *Judgment at Nuremberg* and *Guess Who's Coming to Dinner?* Frederic March played Brady (Bryan), and singer Gene Kelly played the unctuous Hornbeck (Mencken). Perhaps for dramatic effect—or because five years had elapsed since the play had opened—the movie was even more hostile to religion than the play itself.

In the play, *Inherit the Wind* opens with a scene in the prison between Bertram Cates and Rachel. The movie, however, opens on a far more ominous note, as four men march in unison to arrest Cates, then in the midst of innocently teaching evolution to his high school students. The hymn "Give Me That Old Time Religion" punctuates the movie, piped in whenever a person of religion appears particularly stupid.

In the film, the small-town folks are even more antagonistic to

Drummond than in the play. At a rally held for Brady outside the courthouse, they hold up signs that read "The Bible and God," "Don't Monkey with Us," "Doomsday for Darwin," and "Keep Satan Out of Hillsboro." Nor are the motives of these holy folks entirely pure. The banker fears his son won't get into Yale; the local merchants light up at the possibility of visitors. Most of the jurors have never heard of evolution; all are Christian fundamentalists, most of them reflexively so.

One of the best dramatic encounters in both the play and the movie (aside from the courtroom confrontation between the two lawyers) occurs when Brady calls Rachel to the witness stand to testify about her fiancé's antagonism towards religion. As always, she is uncomfortable, conflicted, but this time her tension breaks as she finally tells all. Some years back, Rachel says, a boy named Tommy Stebbins had accidentally drowned while swimming. At the boy's funeral, Reverend Brown had preached that because the boy hadn't been baptized, he was doomed to damnation and would forever "writhe in hell fire." Tommy Stebbins was a budding scientist; he used to visit Cates to peer through his microscope and once told Cates that "he might even be a scientist when he grew up." (No wonder poor Tommy had to die!)

Not a very happy side of religion, condemning an innocent child because his parents had forgotten to have him baptized. Cates leaps to his feet. "Religion is supposed to comfort people. . . . Not frighten them to death."

After Drummond's grueling cross-examination of Bryan on the particulars of the Bible, the ailing Bryan crumbles before us, emptily shouting religious clichés as the spectators leave the courtroom. "You lost them today," his wife later tells him. His wavering about the Bible, his increasing senility and foolishness finally catch up with him. He was once great, but now is a bumbling, Lear-like fool.

Cates is found guilty but receives only a hundred-dollar fine, a token punishment. For all practical purposes, Drummond has won, just as Darrow had all but won in 1925.

The movie version of *Inherit the Wind* opened at the Astor Theater in New York City. *New York Times* film critic Bosley Crowther called the film "a triumph." Kramer, he wrote, "has wonderfully accomplished not only a graphic fleshing of his theme but also has got one of the most brilliant and engrossing displays of acting ever witnessed on the screen."

The accolades aside, Crowther did note the gratuitous stabs at religion. "He [Kramer] has filled his courtroom with yokels. . . . [O]utside, he has pictured Bible-thumpers, a man with a trained chimpanzee, and hymn-singers howling defiantly, 'That old time religion is good enough for me.'"

As New York University professor Carol Iannone later observed, the work "supplies the view that most Americans have of the Scopes trial, and it often surfaces in response to the . . . never-ending quarrels between evolutions and creationists." *Inherit the Wind*, she went on, "flagrantly distorts the details . . . under the color of artistic license [and] . . . amounts to an ideologically motivated hoax."

SINCE *INHERIT THE WIND* was never intended to be factual, its artistic license and anti-religion bias, much of it likely taken from Mencken's reporting, can easily be forgiven. History rarely unfolds in a dramatic fashion, as the *New York Times* drama critic Lewis Funke wrote in his review of the play: "History already written is lacking in suspense and suspense is one of the vital elements of theatrical sustenance."

Undoubtedly, the powerful movie version of *Inherit the Wind* is among the best in the history of film. But its parting message is downright wrong, lulling viewers into the false comfort of believing they can have their cake and eat it, too.

As Drummond leaves the courtroom at the conclusion of the trial, he holds Darwin's *The Origin of Species* beneath his arm. But then, as the stage directions provide, he thinks for a few minutes and "picks up the Bible in his other hand and . . . balancing them thoughtfully . . . slaps the two books . . . into his briefcase side by side." Then, comes the hymn again: "Give Me That Old Time Religion." Drummond is a changed man; he not only believes in science, but in religion, too.

This sugarcoated Hollywood ending works well on stage and screen, but it's completely false: the movie, like the play, never explains what Darwin is really about.

ALTHOUGH CHARLES DARWIN has come to be synonymous with evolution, in fact his contribution to science was not in his discovery of evolution itself. Years before his seminal 1859 *The Origin of Species,* some in the scientific community had already speculated that life may have predated its current forms—that species, including man, had changed over time.

Some geologists drew this conclusion from fossil remains that did not match existing species. Others offered differing explanations of why species change. Jean-Baptiste Lamarck proposed that evolution occurs because *acquired* traits are passed on to the next generation: a giraffe has a long neck because his ancestors had to stretch their necks in order to reach the treetops. Lamarck's archrival Georges Cuvier agreed that Earth had a long history but, in a foreshadowing of Darwin, believed that the planet's inhabitants were periodically wiped out by catastrophe, leaving the few survivors to reproduce.

Darwin's revolutionary theory* of evolution by natural selection provided the most elegant explanation of how species change over time. What made Darwin's theory so attractive to scientists and intellectuals is that it did not require divine intervention; everything was explainable by natural processes. "Darwinism provided the program for a theory which made plausible an explanation of species without recourse to a *deus ex machina* wrote one critic."

Within a given species there are the strong and the weak, Darwin observed. Only the strongest can survive environmental pressures: storms, floods, hurricanes, and the like. These strong survivors then go on to reproduce, and their even stronger ancestors also reproduce, until eventually, over millions of years, an entirely new species emerges.

"Darwin's work [is] . . . revolutionary . . . because he found a plausible mechanism to explain how species can change: by means of natural selection. Darwin's was the first mature and persuasive account . . . represent[ing] the scientific mind at its highest achievement."

This million-year transition of one species to another could not, of course, be directly observed, as Darwin noted: "We see nothing of these slow changes in progress, until the hand of time has marked the long lapses of ages, and then so imperfect is our view into long past geological ages, that we only see that the forms of life are now different from what they formerly were."

But evolution could be inferred from the rapid variations that occur *within* a given species. During his famed five-year voyage aboard the HMS Beagle, Darwin observed these variations first hand. On a stop in the Galapagos Islands, he noticed the different beak sizes and

---

*The word "theory" when used in science is different from its ordinary use. A scientific theory is considered virtually the same as fact.

shapes among the finches that had flown in from the mainland, each settling on a different island. Some had longer beaks, some shorter, and sharper, and so forth—all shaped by natural selection to adapt to the different seeds available in different islands.

Through most of human history—even during the bitter clashes about the earth's place in the cosmos—science and religion were essentially compatible, each often reinforcing the truth of the other. Astronomer Johannes Kepler had used his work to deepen his vision of the divine. And naturalist William Paley inferred the divine from the very intricacy of life, the pattern of design which, like the existence of a watch, confirmed the existence of the watchmaker.

With his radical view that nature is the source of change, Darwin's theory left no room for a God who looks after mankind. At best, this God created life and then threw the dice, allowing nature to work out the particulars. "Other evolutionists spoke of vital forces, directed history, organic striving, [that] permitted a Christian God to work by evolution instead of creation," wrote Stephen Jay Gould. "Darwin spoke only of random variation and natural selection."

Within scientific and intellectual circles, Darwin is almost universally hailed as the most brilliant scientist of all time. There are more books about Darwin than about Galileo, Copernicus, and Kepler combined. But, ironically, Darwin's theory was inspired not by science, but by the politics of his time.

While resting on an island near New Guinea, pondering once again the mysteries of evolution, Darwin suddenly remembered Malthus's *Essay on Population*—that rapid population growth will use up resources.

"Then it suddenly flashed on me," Darwin wrote in his autobiography, "that this self-action process would necessarily *improve* the race . . . that . . . the inferior would inevitably be killed off and the superior would remain—that is, *the fittest would survive.* . . . Then at once I seemed to see the whole effect of this, that all changes necessary for the adaptation of the species to the changing conditions would be brought about. . . .

"The more I thought it over, the more I became convinced . . . that I had found the long-sought for law of nature that solved the problem of the origin of the species" (emphasis added).

Just as Darwin was formulating his own thinking, a non-scientist independently arrived at exactly the same conclusion. In 1852, British socialist Alfred Russel Wallace traveled to the Malay Archipelago where he experienced an identical epiphany.

"[B]ed-ridden by hot and cold flushes one afternoon, he too switched [the Malthusian] logic from man to the animals," wrote Darwin biographers Adrian Desmond and James Moore.

And so it was that two very different men, one a scientist and one a socialist, applied Malthus's shortage theory to evolution and almost simultaneously arrived at the same conclusion. There was nothing particularly scientific about either man's theory: each man viewed nature through the scope of contemporary politics. Some commentators have since argued that both men were influenced by the abrupt changes then occurring in Victorian England, the transition from a society dominated by clerics to an industrial society based on "survival of the fittest."

"Instead of remaining passive with respect to data . . . [w]e favor . . . research programs that are consistent with the values and commitments we express in the rest of our lives," wrote Karl Popper, the great philosopher of science.

"Darwinism sprang up where and when capitalism was most strongly established," Alexander Sandow wrote in a 1938 article in the *Quarterly Review of Biology.*

T.H. Huxley, Darwin's spokesman, certainly had a social and economic agenda in mind when he championed Darwin to the public at large. Huxley had a desire for "progress, meritocracy, a functioning well-run state . . . the diminution of inherited privilege. . . . And he needed a medium in which to effect his ends. Conventional Christianity was not going to serve his purpose."

"Huxley and his friends had therefore to set about creating their own secular religion," wrote philosopher Michael Ruse.

"And evolution . . . was the perfect vehicle."

7

THE FEDERALIZATION
OF SCIENCE

On October 4, 1957, America was shocked out of its postwar complacency. The Soviet Union had launched Sputnik, the first satellite in outer space and, more significantly, a symbol of America's technological inferiority to its archenemy. To the military, this was "the Pearl Harbor of the technological war," the "opening battle of World War III." To scientists, this was a call to arms. They had helped win World War II by developing the nuclear bomb, dropped on Hiroshima and Nagasaki in August 1945. Now, following the launching of Sputnik, they were called upon to save the country once again.

"It is already clear that a historic change is taking place in the position of science and scientists in our society," the *New York Times* observed in 1957.

"The future belongs to the nation with the best technical brains," said John R. Dunning, a professor of physics at Columbia University.

"Scientists Found Rising in Esteem," the *New York Times* headlined a November 1957 report.

"Of all the forces shaping and reshaping life in America, some of the most insistent and powerful spring from science and technology," said the president's scientific advisory committee.

Science had flourished under President Harry Truman, Eisenhower's Democratic predecessor. In the late 1940s, Truman established the Scientific Research Board and the National Science Foundation (NSF) to encourage "a national policy for the promotion of basic research and education in the sciences." Democrats would continuously prove themselves cheerleaders for government-funded scientific research, while Republicans were, over and over again—and to this day—chastised for their "neglect" of science.

The launching of Sputnik under a Republican president was fodder for Democrats still reeling from Eisenhower's reelection the year before.

"We unqualifiedly condemn President Eisenhower for his failure as president to place in effect the great scientific capacity of this country with the result that the Soviet Union launch an earth satellite ahead of the United States," a group of midwestern Democrats charged in 1957.

Government support for science was almost *de rigeur* after World War II, in large part because the end of the war had left many scientists unemployed. From 1948 to 1958, overall spending on science hit $50 billion a year, nearly all of that allocated for the development of aircraft, tanks, and other related military technology. Funding for basic research, non-military work designed to increase overall scientific knowledge, increased from $2.1 billion to $2.7 billion from 1953 to 1957 with the increase eaten up by inflation and the ever-skyrocketing costs of conducting research. "By far the largest amount [of spending on science] goes for development of military weapons," said the *New York Times*.

The Truman-created NSF believed it was poorly treated by the Eisenhower administration. From 1952 to 1957, it received only half of its requested $65 million. With the launching of Sputnik, however, the NSF got a shot in the arm: $140 million in new funds, *triple* the amount it received the year before. But even that wasn't enough. In the aftermath of Sputnik, eminent scientists prevailed upon Eisenhower to promote even more basic scientific research, an endeavor that yielded long-term results and better scientific understanding overall.

Leading scientists and educators agreed that high school education should no longer be left to the vagaries of ill-informed local school boards, that to better shape the young, science education should be directed out of Washington D.C. "[T]he news of the past few weeks gives a new urgency to the problems facing education," a group of leading educators announced on November 9, 1957.

"The Russian satellites may be the price we are paying for a generation of poorly financed schools, of understaffed and over-crowded colleges, of failure to make the best use of all our talent." The schools now had an obligation to produce a scientifically literate population with special emphasis on the "gifted" student. "[W]e have happily awakened to the two-fold need in American education to stress the training of the gifted pupil at least as carefully as the average and retarded one," said one educator. The chairman of the economics department at the University of Chicago complained that bright high school students suffer from "hostile anti-intellectualism among their classmates"—in other words, religion.

As a communist state, the Soviet Union *compelled* its promising students to study science. The United States could only *encourage* theirs. With more than twenty thousand school districts, each locally governed, the federal government would now oversee science curriculum and textbooks. The standards would have to be "*teacher proof,*" scientists argued, in order to overcome the "local prejudices" of teachers and school boards.

Eisenhower reluctantly agreed. As the former dean of Columbia University and a much-celebrated general in World War II, he was a champion of education. But as a moderate conservative, he also believed that the federal government ought not to be involved in local education. In January of 1958, he sent Congress an education-aid plan with a whopping $1 billion (in 1958 dollars) budget. Nearly $9 million would come from the federal government, provided the states came up with $600 million. But the program would last only four years. "This is a temporary program," Eisenhower cautioned, "and should not be considered a permanent federal responsibility."

After many versions in the House and Senate, Congress overwhelmingly passed a revised version of Eisenhower's bill on August 23, 1958—less than a year after the launching of Sputnik. In addition to aiding the schools, the law enabled 100,000 gifted students to attend college with low-interest loans and funded 1,500 "national defense" fellowships. It also authorized $60 million for vocational training designed to work on the Jupiter missile and $8 million to help the general public better understand science through television and motion pictures. Many members of Congress were unhappy with the legislation, for varying reasons. One bemoaned the "massive transfer of education to federal aid." Another wondered why science alone should be funded at the expense of other academic subjects, including the humanities.

Nikita Khrushchev was jokingly nominated as "the man who has done most for American education in 1957."

Despite the millions designated for education, many stakeholders—particularly unions—complained that this was not enough. The National Educational Association wanted the entire $1 billion in the first year, not over a period of fours years. The AFL-CIO wanted more money for school construction. The American Federation of Teachers criticized the focus on science, warning of the creation of "military monsters" and "scientific superman." Democratic senator J. William Fulbright and others wanted as much as $3 billion. Unlike the Democrats, Eisenhower believed that the private sector, companies that benefited from science, should fund science education as much if not more than the federal government.

In any event, whatever the complaints, federal support for education, particularly science education, would soon reach an all-time high.

But the scientific community was still unhappy. In 1959, the president's Science Advisory Committee recommended in a 16,000-word report that educational expenditures for science be *doubled.* The committee proposed strengthening science education in four categories: curriculum, teacher quality, encouragement of students, and development of intellectual leadership. It also recommended that women be brought into the sciences and encouraged more paperbacks about science, better science reporting by the media, and "science caravans" to visit communities that could not afford a science museum of their own. "A democratic citizenry must understand science in order to have a wide and intelligent democratic participation in many national decisions."

UNTIL WORLD WAR II, when much of America depended upon agriculture, physics was by far the most important branch of science, and the most prestigious, attracting the genius of Albert Einstein and his colleagues who solved many of the great mysteries of time and space. With the development of nuclear warfare, it became the most important branch militarily.

The hard sciences were on the top of the government's list. In 1957, with an initial NSF grant of $303,000, a group of physicists in Cambridge, Massachusetts, formed the Physical Science Study curriculum to create standards for the teaching of physics. Chemistry came next, with another NSF grant. But it took biologists another year to persuade the NSF that biology was also a branch of science equally deserving attention in the schools.

Biology was the lowest priority in the post-Sputnik bandwagon of scientific prestige and funding. Although there were some luminaries in biology, in general, the subject biology in the 1960s required far less brain power than physics, which demanded innate mathematical prowess and imagination. So threatened were they by their counterparts in the hard sciences that some biologists feared they weren't getting enough government funds, a worry disguised as "the problems of adequate representation in Washington [D.C.] where they could be in close contact with national granting and policy agencies." So in 1958, a group of leading biologists formed the Biological Sciences Curriculum Study (BSCS) to promote the teaching of biology designed to educate a large number of students—who are "potential voting citizens."

WITH ALL THE emphasis on technology and military defense, and the celebration of the brilliant minds that helped win the Second World War, biologists had good reason to feel inferior. Even before Sputnik, America's agricultural economy required that the hard sciences be stressed in the public schools with scant attention to biology. Darwin's theory of evolution by natural selection was biology's path to prominence and recognition in mid-twentieth-century America.

"Evolutionists . . . really did have to fight for a place in the sun," wrote philosopher Michael Ruse.

In the early decades of the twentieth century, Darwin had faded into obscurity, only to rise again in the early 1930s with the "neo-Darwinian synthesis." While Darwin had postulated "survival of the fittest" without understanding how traits are transmitted, neo-Darwinists explained the role of genes in natural selection. Occasionally, genes make "mistakes"—mutations—which at times are so beneficial that they enhance an individual's ability to survive and reproduce. In turn, the same screening process occurred in ensuing generations, until finally the cumulative effect of all these changes results in a new species.

Apart from clarifying Darwin's theory, neo-Darwinism had the added advantage of elevating biology to a level on par with the hard sciences.

"[The] synthetic theorists were driven by the desire to gain respect for their work as evolutionists," wrote philosopher Michael Ruse. "The theorists wanted to move out of the museums and into the universities and to have all the privileges and benefits of real researchers. . . .

"[T]hey did what they did not just to gain a better understanding of the natural world but for professional respect."

But the neo-Darwinian synthesis actually, in many ways, discredited Darwinism. In the mid-1960s, a group of respected mathematicians—all of them secular—posed the most difficult question in biology: the mathematical improbability of beneficial mutations, rare in number, accumulating to form new species. As historian Gertrude Himmelfarb wrote in her 1959 biography of Charles Darwin:

> [I]t is now discovered that favorable mutations are not only small but exceedingly rare, and the fortuitous combination of favorable mutations such as would be required for the production of even a fruit fly, let alone a man, is so much rarer still that the odds against it would be expressed by . . . an improbability as great as . . . a monkey provided with a typewriter would by chance peck out the works of Shakespeare.

In 1965, during a picnic held after a meeting of the World Health Organization in Geneva, a group of mathematicians and biologists engaged in a heated debate at the otherwise happy event. The mathematicians expressed "a pretty widespread sense of dissatisfaction about . . . so-called neo-Darwinism." In 1966, a prominent mathematician from the Massachusetts Institute of Technology joined by other mathematicians from leading universities throughout the world convened a conference at the Wistar Institute of the University of Pennsylvania to explore the mathematical feasibility of neo-Darwinism.

"We have . . . wondered how it appeared extremely unlikely *a priori* that in the short span of one billion years, due to successive random mutations, all the wonderful things we see now could have appeared," observed Stanislaw M. Ulsam of Los Alamos Scientific Laboratory.

"We believe that there is a considerable gap in the neo-Darwinian theory of evolution, and we believe this gap to be of such a nature that it cannot be bridged with the current conception of biology," said Marcel-Paul Schutzenberger, an internationally renowned mathematician from the University of Paris and a member of the French Academy of Sciences.

Schutzenberger went on to question neo-Darwinism until his death in 1996, but his dissent was ignored by the American media. Perhaps because of science's post-Sputnik prominence, perhaps for political and philosophical reasons, and, mostly likely, because of the stigma that attaches to any view that reinforces religion, the other objectors faded into oblivion and neo-Darwinism went on to thrive, unquestioned, as the only acceptable scientific explanation for the origin and evolution of life.

THOUGH OSTENSIBLY CREATED to further biology education, the Biological Science Curriculum Study (BSCS) was as driven by politics as it was by science, its political agenda seeping into the text-books under the guise of "science."

Although the BSCS included some local science educators, most of its leaders, those who produced the textbooks and other materials, were overtly hostile to the Judeo-Christian religion. Some of the BSCS leaders were outright eugenicists who, in other contexts, had openly promoted the "betterment" of man through selective breeding. This alone should have disqualified these individuals from educating America's youth, but their associations were never exposed by the media, which to this day fails to probe the political and economic agendas of the scientific community.

Heading the BSCS was Bentley Glass, a renowned geneticist and member of the American Eugenics Society, who disparaged procre-ation, promoted population control, and advocated the establishment of genetic "clinics" to weed out the "defective." Joining him was Herman J. Muller, who agreed with Glass about genetic oversight and complained that public school biology was dominated by "antiquated religious traditions." Richard Lewontin, also a member of the American Eugenics Society, headed the "gifted student" committee, a position that dove-tailed perfectly with the eugenic goal of perfecting the human race.

Yet another leading BSCS member was biologist John Moore. While not himself a eugenicist, Moore was avowedly hostile to reli-gion, contemptuously berating the Judeo-Christian worldview in his book, *Science as a Way of Knowing*.

"A fundamental difference between religious and scientific thought," he wrote, "is that the received beliefs in religion are ulti-mately based on revelations or pronouncements, usually by some long-dead prophet or priest. . . . Acceptance of a common dogma is one of the most cohesive forces in society. . . . All belief systems tend to close the mind."

As he unrolled the BSCS curriculum to a group of high school educators, Glass inadvertently revealed his eugenicist bent. "I would certainly suspect," he said, "that before the next thirty years are finished . . . [m]an will certainly have learned to accelerate his own evolution in a desired direction." Those were dangerous words he passed on to American educators: history has shown all too well what happens, and who suffers, when man attempts to manipulate his evolution in a "desired direction." Now this goal, however implicitly, was being promoted under the guise of biology.

In that same presentation to public school educators, Glass went on—with extraordinary condescension—to encourage teachers to brave it out when confronted by the religious and "anti-science" communities.

"We teachers of biology are going to have to meet some opposition," he said. "There are people who do not want us to teach this kind of revolutionary biology. After all, it is upsetting to feel the ways of life changing. . . .

"We will also have to face some opposition in certain places from anti-evolutionists, perhaps a dying breed, and from others—who are more common and more to be feared than anti-evolutionists— who are simply 'anti-science' in point of view. We must steadfastly and courageously support our standard in the face of all such opposition."

Likely everyone in the audience knew that Glass was referring to evolution, a threat to the beliefs of fundamentalist Christians. In the past, evolution had been lightly treated or omitted altogether in most biology textbooks. But now, the BSCS made clear, evolution was central to the study of biology.

"The BSCS program deserves great credit for its frank treatment of so-called 'sensitive areas' in biology: evolution, the nature and origin of life, and human reproduction. . . . The presentation of evolution as an accepted part of biology, rather than as something 'proved' each time it is presented ... frees ... the teacher to concentrate on evolution as a process," wrote one BSCS member in 1961.

When the BSCS held its early meetings at the University of Colorado in Boulder (its headquarters) on February 5, 6, and 7 of 1959, the leadership made clear that its curriculum would emphasize evolution and related subjects. Muller and his colleagues had criticized existing biology textbooks "because they did not contain enough material about evolution," arguing that evolution should be pervasive and presented as a "major embracing theory."

In 1963, the BSCS published three different versions of high school biology textbooks—the "green," the "blue," and the "yellow," each emphasizing evolution as the "warp and woof of modern biology." Though they all shared an emphasis on evolution, each version had a somewhat different focus: the green emphasized ecology and evolution; the blue, biochemistry; the yellow, development and genetics. Heading the Committee of the Content of the Curriculum was John A. Moore, whose hostility to the Judeo-Christian tradition would subtly seep into the BSCS's biology textbooks.

Though publicly funded, the BSCS soon gained an intellectual and economic monopoly on science education, creating a model curriculum that by the 1960s was used by nearly half of all biology students in the country. In the past, commercial publishers produced two versions of science textbooks: one for public schools, another for Catholic schools. In yet another slap at religion, the BSCS refused to cater to the Catholics. Because of its enviable market share, BSCS negotiated a royalty rate that was twice as high as the rate the commercial publishers offered. Commercial publishers soon complained about "unfair competition."

BSCS textbooks reflected the committee's political and antireligious agenda. They characterized human behavior as rooted in "biology" and human beings as "animals," terminology that smacked against the theological view of a species created in God's image. The reduction of humankind to "animals"—terminology that would be repeatedly used in the last half of the twentieth century—was as much philosophical as biological, glossing over science's inability to explain behaviors such as charity that have nothing to do with survival.

There was also a subtle political side to the reduction of man to a mere animal. If man is no more than a creature of instinct, he is malleable to state control; he can be trained and bred like any other species. The reduction of man to animal expressed not only the committee's eugenic agenda, but also laid a foundation for a fascist state which controls human reproduction and family size.

The philosophical leanings of BSCS textbooks had a precedent in a textbook of the 1920s, Hunter's *A Civic Biology*, ironically, the textbook used by John Scopes. Under the guise of biology, that work restated the very core principles of eugenics. "If the stock of domesticated animals can be improved, it is not unfair to ask if the health and vigor of future generations of men and women on the earth might not be improved by applying to them the laws of selection." Referring to epileptics and others, Hunter said, "If such people were lower animals, we would probably kill them off to prevent them from spreading. Humanity will not allow this, but we do have the remedy of separating the sexes in asylums or other places and in various ways preventing intermarriage and possibilities of perpetuating such a low and degenerate race."

Hunter's textbook went on, again in the guise of biology, to instruct students that certain races are superior to others.

At the present time there exist upon the earth five races or varieties of man, each very different from the other in instincts, social customs, and, to an extent, in structure. There are the Ethiopian or negro type . . . the brown race . . . the American Indian, the Mongolian or yellow race . . . and finally the highest of all, the Caucasians, represented by the civilized white inhabitants of Europe and America.

Though unreported, the Scopes trial itself was as much about eugenics as it was about evolution. Ironically, it was the religious, not the so-called "progressives," who took the high road. During the 1925 trial, William Jennings Bryan declared eugenics to be "brutal" and offered it as a reason not to teach evolution. Billy Sunday, a popular evangelist in the 1920s, had used the link between eugenics and evolution to argue in favor of the Tennessee anti-evolution law later used to prosecute Scopes. In planning the BSCS curriculum, the leaders were cagey about their eugenics agenda. Bruce Wallace, a population geneticist, wrote in a BSCS publication, "It is not inappropriate . . . to point out the bearing the above calculations [of the probability of genetic diseases] have on eugenics programs. In the past there have been overzealous eugenicists who advocated the sterilization of genetic unfortunates." But, he added, "This does not mean that eugenicists have nothing to say to couples who through marriage or intended marriage have encountered genetic problems."

The BSCS textbooks themselves were far less outright eugenicist than Hunter's *A Civil Biology*. But by promoting the myth of the "population explosion," they served the same purpose. A 1961 "yellow" textbook, supervised by John A. Moore, stated, "The present explosive increase in human populations, world-wide, represents a completely unstable situation, one with a highly questionable future." It is unclear exactly what this had to do with high school biology itself, but it certainly inculcated students with the false science and racism of population control.

Bentley Glass was more explicit. During a 1968 meeting of the BSCS in Chicago, he spoke about the "social" aspects of biological education, suggesting that "students evaluate their genotype [genes]" and reevaluate the "right of parents to produce children." In other words, students should be told that certain members of the population should not be allowed to reproduce. A 1969 BSCS teachers' manual states that "programs of fertility regulation and family planning help to control population growth and . . . avoid eventual disaster," going on to mention the problem with "religious bodies." In the 1970s, with the help of a generous NSF grant, the BSCS expanded its curriculum to include politics, engaging children in activities that include "growing up politically." Exactly why this should be part of the biology curriculum again remained unclear.

To BSCS leaders, biology wasn't just science; it was politics, *their* politics. Not only did biology now include the functions of living beings, it also included "responsible parenthood." In BSCS parlance, "responsible parenthood" did not mean a parent's responsibility to clothe and feed a child; what it really meant was the "responsibility" to have as few children as possible—or, better yet, none at all. On what basis should a group of biologists, many with links to the eugenics movement, instruct children not to have children? Why is this a goal of science education? Certainly, given the Vatican's views on birth control, the BSCS materials were a gratuitous condemnation of Catholicism.

During the 1960s, the federal government gave BSCS more than $10 million in taxpayer money to "improve" biology education.

AS MANY A toppled totalitarian regime has learned, humans will not put up for long with a centralized directive that tells them how or what to think. It is one thing to teach students about the parts of a cell, quite another to tell them not to have children. Objecting to federal control over science education, some conservative lawmakers recognized exactly this problem. "You do not interfere unless they ask you to interfere," said one U.S. senator in 1958. "I don't want these things rammed down the throat of educators," said another. As a member of Congress said in 1967: "You are not suggesting the *philosophy* that is being taught? This is the option of the school district."

The new emphasis on evolution inevitably invoked the wrath of biblical fundamentalists. While the BSCS was correct in presenting evolution as the scientifically accepted explanation of life, its curriculum extended far beyond science to private matters that some parents believed should be taught inside the home. Though Glass predicted problems with the "anti-science" community, he and his colleagues failed to understand the sensitivities of some communities.

In a 1961 experimental launching of the BSCS curriculum in Dade County, Florida, school authorities demanded that diagrams of the reproductive system be removed from all materials. After the BSCS refused, authorities themselves blackened out the diagrams before distributing the materials to students—within that community, parents and school officials did not want their children exposed to the information about sex. When Texas considered adopting BSCS textbooks, the Reverend Reuel Lemmons of the Church of Christ, a fundamentalist sect of 600,000, called the books "pure evolution from cover to cover." His objections didn't end there. Lemmons said the books were "completely materialistic and completely atheistic."

There was yet another problem: The BSCS curriculum didn't even accomplish its goal of improving biology education.

Ten years after the BSCS developed its curriculum and textbooks, American students began their precipitous decline in academic standing. The BSCS textbooks were not the reason for this decline—but they certainly didn't help. In fact, they weren't very good.

In 1990, after a three-year study, a panel convened by the National

Research Council complained that biology textbooks were, among other things, "inaccurate and outdated," and that students continued to be disinterested in science. "Most students leave the experience [of biology] with the conviction that further exposure to science is something to be avoided if at all possible," the twelve-member panel concluded. "Curricula and textbooks are typically exercises in memorization rather than an intellectual voyage of exploration."

Evidently forgetting the millions of dollars already poured into the BSCS, the panel recommended that yet another federal body be created to "monitor" science education and create model curriculums, textbook standards, and criteria for teacher education.

In June 2000, the American Association for the Advancement of Science examined ten biology textbooks, two of them published by the BSCS. None received a high rating, and all contained "serious shortcomings in content and instruction design."

Exactly what had the BSCS accomplished?

More scandalous, given the post-Sputnik spur to improve science education, American students were getting worse, not better, in science. Americans who had grown up in the 1950s—before the BSCS—had far greater proficiency in science than those who followed. According to the National Center for Educational Statistics, science proficiency among American seventeen-year-olds *declined* from 1970 to 1990—despite the centralization of science education and the use of BSCS textbooks. Throughout the 1990s, studies by the Third International Math and Science Study showed American students lagging at the bottom of twenty-two countries in science proficiency.

While the tragic decline in education occurred in all academic subjects—reading, writing, history—science was the only discipline that had received a massive infusion of federal money, the only discipline with a model curriculum and textbooks produced by "experts."

Science proficiency should have been higher than in other disciplines. It wasn't.

In the mid-1980s, the American Association for the Advancement of Science initiated "Project 2061" designed to improve science education. In 1989, the governors of the fifty states, led by Governor Bill Clinton of Arkansas, wrote national goals for education which President Bill Clinton incorporated in his "Goals 2000," an ambitious program whose goal was to make American students number one internationally in math and science by the year 2000.

Funded by the U.S. Department of Education, in 1995, the National Academy of Sciences published yet another "model" science curriculum, once again invoking a Sputnik-like fear that other countries would surpass America.

"More and more jobs demand advanced skills. . . . An understanding of science and the processes of science contribute in an essential way to these skills. Other countries are investing heavily to create scientifically and technically literate work forces. To keep pace in global markets, the United States needs to have an equally capable citizenry." The standards promised to help students "increase their economic productivity through the use of the knowledge, understanding, and skills of the scientifically literate person in their careers."

NAS president Bruce Alberts told Congress that the new NAS standards represented the "best thinking" of scientists about what is "best" for America's students.

The NAS standards exhibited exactly the same hubris as the BSCS standards, once again using science to advance political agendas. While surfacely "progressive"—the standards urge educators to be "sensitive" to minorities and the disabled—they once again use science as a means of regulating procreative behavior. "Students should understand various methods of controlling the reproductive process," the NAS said. Worse, the NAS standards belittle religion, calling it "useful and socially relevant" but otherwise irrelevant. "Science distinguishes itself from other ways of knowing and from other bodies of knowledge. . . . Explanations on how the natural world changes based on myths, personal beliefs, religious beliefs, mystical inspiration, superstition, or authority may be personally useful and socially relevant, but they are not scientific."

During the 1990s, political correctness pushed science textbooks into further anti-intellectualism. Many textbook publishers employed multicultural review committees to make sure that women and non-whites were represented in the textbooks, but they failed to employ scientific reviewers to review the science itself. A 2001 study produced by the David and Lucile Parkard Foundation documented more than five hundred factual errors in science textbooks used by 85 percent of American high school students. One book misstated Newton's first law of motion. Another confused gravitational acceleration with gravity. And yet another widely used textbook showed the equator running through the United States.

"Political correctness is often more important than scientific accuracy," said the report's author, John Hubisz, a physics professor at North Carolina State University. "Middle school text publishers now employ more people to censor books than they do to check facts."

Many textbooks omitted all mention of white male scientists, condescendingly proffering women and nonwhite "scientists," many of little accomplishment. A 1998 biology textbook suggested to high school students that the evolution of skin color from white to black occurred over "many years," rather than the fifteen thousand years believed to be the time span necessary for this evolutionary change. The suggestion that skin color can change so rapidly was politically correct but absolutely false as science, an ironic distortion of evolution. Somehow it seemed that scientific inaccuracy was perfectly acceptable if it advanced a leftwing agenda but perfectly reprehensible if sensitive to religion.

In 2002, President George W. Bush signed the "No Child Left Behind Act" appropriating millions more for science education: $450 million for math and science partnerships and another $25 million for science and math overall.

In 2002, despite the failure of federal biology education, the National Science Teachers Association complained, without a trace of irony: "Now more than ever the need for a scientifically literate population is essential for our national security."

8

MONKEY BUSINESS

The Tennessee anti-evolution law remained on the books long after the Scopes trial, but it was never enforced. Despite the trial's notoriety and the scorn heaped on religious fundamentalists, evolution received scant attention in the public schools until the BSCS textbooks took over.

The waters remained still until 1967 when Gary Scott, a twenty-four-year-old teacher in rural Tennessee, lost his job because he taught evolution.

Like Scopes, Scott didn't have to pay for his lawyer. The National Education Association, one of two major teachers' unions, funded his lawsuit. Following in the footsteps of the Scopes trial, the NEA engaged the services of a flamboyant, big city lawyer who turned what might have been a local dispute into a political *cause célèbre*, a civil war between atheism and religion, North and South, big city and small town. A local lawyer might have been a better pick, someone who could present evolution in a manner palatable to the residents of rural Tennessee. The NEA's choice of William Kunstler guaranteed national media attention, but it was a bad public relations ploy for science, only increasing the local paranoia that evolution was an atheist plot.

By the late 1960s, the long-haired New York City lawyer was already controversial. Following the assassination of President John

Kennedy in 1963 Kunstler took on the defense of Jack Ruby, the man who had shot and killed Kennedy assassin, Lee Harvey Oswald. In the mid-1960s, Kunstler defended civil rights protester and leader Martin Luther King Jr. But by the late 1960s, the lawyer rejected liberalism in favor of rabid radicalism. He defended the "Chicago Seven," a group that had launched a violent protest on the 1968 Democratic Convention. He went on to defend Malcolm X, the Black Panthers, and radical separatists groups that denounced the Jews.

Scott v. Tennessee likely would have turned into a circus, but it was stopped in its tracks on May 16, 1967, when the Tennessee legislature repealed its anti-evolution law.

But other Southern states took up the mantle.

THE BIG CITY lawyers, however offensive, did, in fact, have the winning legal argument under the Establishment Clause of the First Amendment: the government cannot endorse any particular religion. No matter how creationists protested otherwise, their "science" was theology, one that was uniquely Christian.

The California-based Institute of Creation Research (ICR), prime mover in nearly all the creationist battles, calls itself a "Christ-based ministry"; some biology textbooks published by creationists praise Jesus Christ. The ICR's museum in Santee, California, near San Diego, devotes several walls to Christ and, while respectful of Judaism and Islam, instructs that Christ "must also be their redeemer"—in other words, that Jews and Muslims will not be saved unless they convert.

Ken Ham, a well-known creationist who founded Answers in Genesis, described creationism as a tool of Christian evangelism, a way of "evangelizing" our society. "The Lord," he wrote, "provided us with a phenomenally powerful tool that must be used today—creation evangelism."

Outside the fundamentalist community, many religious groups did not view Genesis as a literal account of creation and did not believe that Earth was created in six twenty-four-hour days. In his wordy 1950 *Humani Generis*, Pope Pius XII said that "the teaching authority of the Church does not forbid that, in conformity with the present state of the sciences and sacred theology, there should be research and discussion on the part of men experienced in both fields, with regard to the doctrine of evolution, insofar as it inquires into the origin of the human body from pre-existent and living matter—for the Catholic faith obliges us to hold that souls are immediately created by God."

The pope's statement is hardly a ringing endorsement of evolution, but it does make clear that Catholicism can coexist with evolution. Catholic theologian John F. Haught argued outright that creationism should not be taught as science: "[T]o teach the doctrine of special creation in the context of the classroom is not merely a violation of scientific integrity, but even worse is an implicit debasement of religion. . . . [T]eaching biblical creation accounts in the classroom implicitly desacralizes revered writings whose intention is to open us to holy mystery."

Like Christian creationists, some ultra-Orthodox Jews in Israel believed that Earth is only about six thousand years old. In America, some of the stricter Jewish congregations took issue with the implicit atheism of Darwin and viewed creation as a mystery that can be explained not by science, but by faith alone. "While science may enhance the comforts of living," said one rabbi in 1959, "it can never create human happiness, nor can it ever exhaust the mysteries of the universe." "Creation is one of the mysteries of the Torah, and if all the statements are merely to be taken literally, what mystery is there?" asked Rabbi Abraham Isaac Kook, former chief rabbi of the Ashkenazic

Community of Israel. Virtually no one in the American Jewish community argued that the Bible should be viewed as science.

However well-intentioned, creationism is a direct attack on those who do not accept Christ.

THE ESTABLISHMENT CLAUSE of the First Amendment forbids exactly this: "Congress shall make no law respecting an establishment of religion, or prohibiting the free exercise thereof," a prohibition that also applies to the states.

This prohibition was vital to the country from its beginning. At the time of the country's founding, residents of the thirteen colonies were already religiously diverse and included Presbyterians, Anglicans, Quakers, German Reformed, Dutch Reformed, Lutherans, Catholics, and many others. The founders recognized that only a religiously neutral country would attract immigrants on the run from religious persecution.

Although the government cannot endorse any particular religion, the concept of a nondenominational God was the country's warp and weave. The belief that God is the author of individual freedom hailed back to the English Revolution and the philosophy of John Locke and is reflected in the archives of American history. The 1775 declaration of war against Britain stated that "a reverence for our great Creator . . . must convince all those who reflect upon the subject that government was instituted to promote the welfare of mankind." The 1776 Declaration of Independence said men are "endowed by their Creator with certain unalienable rights."

In their own bills of rights, individual states went even further. Virginia's 1776 Bill of Rights declared that "it is the mutual duty of all to practice Christian forbearance, love, and charity towards each other." Massachusetts proclaimed "the right as well as the duty of all men in society . . . to worship the Supreme Being, the Creator and Preserver of the universe." Government, said the state, depended upon "piety, religion and morality" and "public worship of God."

In his 1889 *Democracy in America*, Alexis de Tocqueville observed: "Religion in America takes no part in the government of society, but must nevertheless be regarded as the foremost of the political institutions of that country. . . . I am certain that they hold it to be indispensable to the maintenance of republican institutions. . . .

"The Americans combine the notions of Christianity and of liberty so intimately in their minds, that it is impossible to make them conceive the one without the other."

The U.S. Supreme Court relied on the Establishment Clause to strike down the reading of the Lord's Prayer in the public schools, a daily reading of the Bible, the posting of the Ten Commandments, and almost all government appropriations to parochial schools. But the high Court went far beyond banning denominational expressions of religion; by the 1960s it struck down even nondenominational prayer, as though the Constitution forbade all reference to a higher being.

In 1968, on the strength of the Establishment Clause, a unanimous Supreme Court, with little fanfare, struck down an Arkansas "anti-evolution" law, stating that "the First Amendment does not permit the State to require that teaching . . . must be tailored to the principles . . . of any religious sect or dogma."

SINCE THEY COULDN'T teach outright religion, creationists took a different approach: creationism wasn't religion, they said, but science. Though a state cannot teach "religion," surely it can teach "science."

"The creation chapters of Genesis are marvelous and accurate accounts of the actual events of the primeval history of the universe," wrote Henry Morris in 1974. Morris, who held a Ph.D. in hydraulics, argued that Earth had emerged fully formed from the beginning with only the "appearance of age" and that man had been "created directly as man, with a fully human body and brain from the beginning."

Mainstream science had long relied on fossils and radioactive dating to show that Earth was formed 4.5 billion years ago. Fundamentalist Christians believed otherwise. Using seventeenth-century calculations and genealogies from the Bible, Bishop James Usher said Earth was only between 6,000 to 10,000 years old. Now, under the guise of science, creation-scientists said there was actual scientific evidence for a "young Earth."

In 1970, a Baptist organization founded the Institute for Creation Research (ICR), headed by radio minister Tim LaHaye (coauthor of the Christian *Left Behind* series). Teachers at ICR's affiliated Christian Heritage College were required to pledge their belief in the "absolute integrity of the Holy Scripture . . . both Old and New Testament." By 1980, the ICR had published 55 books (some translated into as many as 10 languages), lectured on 400 college campuses, given seminars in at least 350 cities, and appeared opposite evolutionists on hundreds of radio and television debates. Unlike some other creationist groups, the ICR recruited academically credentialed scientists such as Duane Gish (Ph.D. biochemistry, University of California at Berkeley), Henry Morris (Ph.D. in hydraulics from the University of Minnesota), and Lane Lester (Ph.D., P.D. in genetics, Purdue University). In the early 1970s, other creation-science organizations cropped up around the country, including the Creation Research Society, the American Science Affiliation, and Answers in Genesis.

From the outset, creation-scientists were met with scorn by established scientists and their representatives in the National Academy of the Sciences and the American Association for the Advancement of Science. Creationists could not get their work published in official science journals, such as *Nature* and *Science*, which are reviewed by other scientists before publication. "The 'creation-science' explanation of the world is supernatural, untestable, and absolutist," said the NAS.

Despite the sharp rebuke from established science, creationists struggled to get their view of creation into the public schools, if only side-by-side with evolution. In the early 1980s, Paul Ellwanger, a Roman Catholic layman from South Carolina, launched a campaign to pass "balanced treatment" laws, advising colleagues in the creationist community not to mention religion.

"It does the bill effort no good to have ministers out there in the public forum," Ellwanger wrote. "Ministerial persons can accomplish a tremendous amount of work *behind the scenes*, encouraging their congregations to take the organizational and P.R. initiatives. And they can lead their churches in storming Heaven with prayers for help against so tenacious an adversary."

"Please urge your coworkers not to allow themselves to get sucked into the 'religion' trap," Ellwanger told a Christian volunteer. "It would be very wise . . . not to present our position . . . in a religious framework." To another, he warned against "written communications that might somehow be shared with those . . . whom we are trying to convince," he said. "It should exclude our own personal testimony and/or witness for Christ."

In 1980, creationist attorney Wendell Bird drafted a model balanced treatment law that required the teaching of both creationism and evolution in science classrooms. He sent the draft bill on to Arkansas State Senator James L. Holsted, described by the media as "born again."

At thirty-eight, the freshman Republican senator had already used up his nine lives. In 1972, his mother shot his father, also a state senator, then shot herself. After studying business at Vanderbilt University, Holsted stopped attending church. But when he became embroiled in business and marital problems, Holsted turned to Christ. He joined a Christian businessman's committee and attended weekly prayer meetings. In 1978, he ran for state senator and won. In 1981, Holsted was charged with shifting money from one of his businesses to cover losses from another. The setback, however, didn't seem to affect his status in the state senate.

On March 19, 1981, Governor Frank White, himself a Christian, signed Arkansas 509, which required "balanced treatment" of evolution and creation while also prohibiting "religious instruction." On May 27, 1981, the American Civil Liberties Union brought a lawsuit in federal district court charging that the law promoted religion in violation of the Establishment Clause. Its litigation strategy was brilliant. This time, quite shrewdly, it brought suit on behalf of other religions, thereby demonstrating that creationism was a vehicle of Christian fundamentalism, not Christianity overall. Presbyterian minister Bill McLean, the "name plaintiff" (the name appearing on the lawsuit), was joined by Methodists, Catholics, Episcopalians, Presbyterians, Southern Baptists, and African Methodists.

Dubbed by the media as "Scopes II," *McClean v. Arkansas* attracted reporters from the big cities, all of whom approached the controversy with the same disdain expressed by H.L. Mencken forty years before.

Though not quite a circus, at times Scopes II had its share of courtroom humor. A teacher testified that he demonstrates the vast age of the universe by stretching a string across the classroom and sending students to place markers on the origins of life, the dinosaurs, and the beginnings of mankind. On cross-examination, the teacher was asked how he would have taught creationism.

"I guess I'd have to get a short string," he replied.

To prove that creation-science is not science, the ACLU flew in experts from all over the country, using "credentialed" scientists from public and private universities. University of California geneticist Francisco Jay Ayala, a former priest, found proof of evolution in the genetic similarities between man and animals. Evolution does not obliterate God, he said, because "God can create the world in any way He chooses." Geologist G. Brent Dalrymple testified that radiometric dating proved Earth is 4.5 billion years old. Creationism, he said, is "in the same category as the flat earth hypothesis that the sun goes around the earth."

But the ACLU's star witness was Harvard paleontologist Stephen Jay Gould, already a best-selling author of popular science books. Gould testified that creation-science is not science because "it calls on a creator to suspend the laws of nature." His testimony was much like the cross-examination of Bryan elicited by Darrow in the 1925 Scopes trial—the literal Bible would require that nature's laws be violated. The sun cannot stand still.

In their defense, creationists attempted to characterize evolution as itself a "religion," one that inculcated atheism rather than God. Indeed, evolution was synonymous with atheism, one theologian testified. Other witnesses were called to support the scientific basis of creationism. But the judge was not persuaded.

A native of Arkansas and a product of its public universities, Judge William Ray Overton had been appointed to the bench in 1979 by President Jimmy Carter when he was forty, a very young age for a federal judge. By all accounts, he was a thorough, meticulous jurist, described as a "scholar" by his colleagues and praised for keeping the courtroom in control during the controversial trial. Months before the trial, Overton immersed himself in the reams of legal documents submitted by the parties, the pre-trial proceedings, and literature from both the creationist and evolutionist sides.

Overton had little patience with the creationists, repeatedly admonishing them to stick to hard scientific evidence. After listening to an hour of testimony from a biochemist at a local college who complained of the "systematic censorship" of creationism, Overton blew up. "You've expressed all sorts of opinions," he said. "But I haven't heard one single solid basis for any of them."

Overton's decision came as no surprise. On January 5, 1982, he issued a lengthy, detailed opinion that found the creation law unconstitutional because it imposed a religious view in public schools. "There is no doubt that Senator Holsted knew he was sponsoring the teaching of religious doctrine," Overton wrote. "It was simply and purely an effort to introduce the biblical version of creation into the public school curricula." And, because it required supernatural force, creationism was "simply not science." Judge Overton's decision earned him front-page coverage in the *New York Times.*

Creationists urged Arkansas's attorney general not to appeal in order to confine Judge Overton's ruling to Arkansas. A higher court decision affirming Overton would prevent other states in the region from passing laws permitting the teaching of creation-science. Judge Overton's "bias is too subtle to be clearly reversible," the creationists said, and the media had already characterized them as "rightwing kooks and freaks." In any event, the state, then under the leadership of Governor Bill Clinton, did not appeal.

Despite its victory, the science community remained on high alert. "We cannot relax because of a defeat for creationists in one courtroom, nor do we expect creationists to give up," warned William D. Carey, executive officer of the American Association for the Advancement of Science. The election of Ronald Reagan and the rising of the conservative tide frightened them. Frank Press, the new head of the National Academy of Sciences, told the *New York Times* in 1981 that, as "a leading person in American science," he had to take a firm stance against creationism.

Scientists had reason for concern. In such diverse states as Indiana,

Texas, California, Georgia, and New York, creationists were success-fully persuading schools to give "balanced treatment" to science stu-dents—despite the rulings of the country's highest court.

"I mention both sides," said a biology teacher in a suburb of Chicago in 1980. "I refer to God. We may believe there is good evi-dence that organisms adapt to environment over time. But we do not come out strongly for evolution. We just say, 'Here are two views.'"

"Armed with sales techniques, pamphlets, slide presentations, tape recordings, and other documentation, creation proponents no longer limited their campaign to references from the Bible," observed the *New York Times* in a front-page article on April 7, 1980. "Citing biochemistry, physics, and fossil records as documentation for their view, they contend that it is simply impossible for a random process to account for life as it is known today."

Though creationists were gaining ground throughout much of the country, their every advance was met with condemnation from the scientific community and the national media. The *New York Times* routinely gave front-page treatment to local battles over the teaching of evolution.

SOON AFTER JUDGE Overton's decision, creationists took a different tack. Attempting to score a victory in the nation's highest court, they worked together to write a statute which "would have a better chance in the Supreme Court." Such a statute would have to appear to be free of religion in order to avoid the stricture of the Establishment Clause.

Louisiana rose to the challenge. "People are very irritated with Judge Overton and are more determined than ever to win in Louisiana," proclaimed Louisiana State Senator Bill Keith. Omitting any mention of religion, the Louisiana law's preamble stated that "the body of scientific evidence supporting creation science is as strong as that supporting evolution. In fact, it may be stronger." "Students exposed to it better understand the current state of scientific evidence about the origin of life." But J. Kelly Nix, the state's elected superintendent of education, believed that the statute was unconstitutional and refused to enforce it.

The ACLU brought a lawsuit in federal court in New Orleans, *Edwards v. Aguillard,* challenging the law as a violation of the Establishment Clause. The complainants included eight clergymen from Protestant, Catholic, and Jewish organizations, including the Rabbinical Council of New Orleans and the board of the United Methodist Church, each arguing that the law would inhibit "the religion of those who do not accept a literal interpretation of Genesis." The use of other religions again reinforced the legal argument that creationism was uniquely Christian and therefore should not be taught in public schools.

The creationists lost in the lower court and just barely in the Court of Appeals, which ruled against them 8-7, hardly a decisive victory for science.

After the U.S. Supreme Court agreed to hear the case, hundreds of organizations rallied around the evolution side, submitting friend-of-the-court briefs to the U.S. Supreme Court. Briefs came from such luminaries as seventy-two Nobel Prize-winning scientists in physics, chemistry, and medicine (including Francis Crick and James Watson of "double helix" fame), as well as the state attorney generals of New York and Illinois. Numerous political, scientific, and religious groups signed on to the evolution side, including the National Academy of Sciences, Americans United for Separation of Church and State, the American Association of University Professors, and People for the American Way. Both teachers unions, the American Federation of Teachers and the National Education Association, filed briefs along with the AFL-CIO.

But the point was driven home by the briefs of Christian and Jewish organizations. Among those filing briefs for non-fundamentalist religions were the Anti-Defamation League of B'nai Brith, the American Jewish Congress, the American Jewish Committee, the National Council of the Churches of Christ, Americans for Religious Liberty, and the Rabbinical Alliance. Along with the clergy from assorted religions who were part of the original lawsuit, these groups sent a powerful message.

The "balanced treatment" law, said the American Jewish Committee, the National Council of Churches, and the General Convention of Swedenborgian Churches, "favors one particular religious belief—fundamentalist Christian doctrine—over all others." The evolution side was represented by a stellar legal cast, the crème-de-la-crème of legal talent in the United States. Jay Topkis, a commercial lawyer with Paul, Weiss, Rifkind & Garrison in New York, coordinated the overall litigation, enlisting other superstar lawyers and law firms, including: Marvin Frankel, a former federal judge from New York, Burt Neuborne of the American Civil Liberties Union in New York, and leading commercial law firms such as Skadden, Arps, Slate, Meagher & Flom (New York City); Wilmer, Cutler & Pickering (Washington D.C.); and Caplin & Drysdale (Washington D.C.).

The creationist lawyers were outmatched from the start. The principal lawyer, Wendell R. Bird of Atlanta, who had himself played a role in drafting the balanced treatment act, was joined by the attorney general of Louisiana, and friend-of-the-court briefs were submitted by only a few conservative organizations. The case was argued before the Supreme Court on December 10, 1986. First up at bat was Wendell R. Bird, who made the startling concession that "some legislators had a desire to teach religious doctrine in the classroom." Having conceded the lawmakers' religious purpose, Bird probably lost the case on this statement alone. Still, he went on to argue that the Louisiana law was based on "science," not religion, and that "academic freedom" required that teachers teach both accounts of creation. Nearly twenty years later, Jay Topkis still recalls that Bird's arguments "startled me."

"Mr. Bird is a little slender to play Tweedledum, but that's what he's trying to do," Topkis told the Court in what he recalls was a convivial exchange. "He wants words to mean what he says they mean. And that didn't fool Alice, and I doubt very much that it will fool this Court."

The case was not about academic freedom, Topkis argued, not about what *teachers* wanted to teach, but about the rights of students to be free of religion in the public schools. Topkis faced much tough questioning from Justice Antonin Scalia who brought up Aristotle's belief in a first cause and wondered whether teaching Aristotle would be considered religion. Justice Lewis Powell compared balanced treatment to teaching both the Protestant and Catholic accounts of the Reformation. Few lawyers will openly contradict a Supreme Court justice, so Topkis could not point out that science is different from history or philosophy because science is based on fact while other academic disciplines explore a range of opinions.

Six months later, the Supreme Court struck down the Louisiana law, a result that was hardly surprising in view of the prestige behind the evolutionist position. Still, it was not the victory that scientists hoped for. Though seven justices voted to strike down the law, their rationale was splintered, stated in three different opinions with overlapping, but not identical, approaches to the law.

The main opinion was authored by the most liberal judge then on the U.S. Supreme Court. Appointed by Republican President Dwight Eisenhower in 1956, Justice William Brennan was "the most influential justice in the 20th century." The author of more than 1,300 opinions during his thirty-four-year tenure on the Court, Brennan helped solidify the right of free speech, the right of political protest (the Ku Klux Klan's included), and the right against self-incrimination—all fundamental rights explicitly stated in the Constitution. But conservatives saw many of Brennan's other opinions as far in excess of what the Constitution requires. Brennan extended the First Amendment's right of free speech—whose intention, many constitutional scholars believe, was to protect *political* speech—to include virtually any type of obscenity. He voted to overturn the death penalty and sanctioned the use of the courts to require states to increase school funding. Eisenhower said that his appointment of Brennan was one of the "two biggest mistakes" of his two-term, Cold War-era presidency. (The other was his appointment of Justice Earl Warren.)

Joined by six other justices, Brennan held that the Louisiana law was unconstitutional because it embraced a *particular* form of religion. Thurgood Marshall, Harry Blackmun, and John Paul Stevens appeared to agree that religion must be banished altogether from the classroom. "Families entrust public schools with the education of their children, but condition their trust on the understanding that the classroom will not purposely be used to advance religious beliefs that may conflict with the private beliefs of the student and his or her family. Students in such institutions are impressionable and their attendance is involuntary," Brennan wrote.

Still, even those justices left open the possibility that Darwin could be criticized on secular grounds, an opening that would later prove favorable to Darwin critics. "We do not imply that a legislature could never require that scientific critiques of prevailing scientific theories be taught."

But the sweeping opinion of the four justices was not shared by all, even those who agreed with the result. Justice Lewis Powell, a moderate Nixon appointee, wrote a concurring opinion that subtly disagreed with Brennan in key respects. The Louisiana law was "ambiguous," he wrote, not clearly religious on its face. But after examining the law's legislative history and the role of Christian fundamentalists, most notably the Institute for Creation Research, Powell concluded that "the intent of the Louisiana legislature was to promote a particular religious belief."

Still, Powell, joined by Reagan appointee Sandra Day O'Connor, did not believe that religion overall—the belief in God—should stay out of the classroom. Powell noted "an unbroken history of official acknowledgement . . . of the role of religion in American life."

"[T]he Founding Fathers believed devotedly that there was a God and that the unalienable rights of man were rooted in Him [as is] clearly evidenced in their writings, from the Mayflower Compact to the Constitution itself." The Bible itself was not necessarily banished from the classroom, except where "the purpose of the use is to advance a *particular* religious belief." Religion itself can be included in the public school curriculum as long as it is nondenominational. It was an important distinction.

Justice Byron White, a moderate John F. Kenney nominee, wrote his own separate opinion, even more hesitant that Powell's. He relied only on the lower courts' interpretation of the Louisiana law, suggesting that he himself might have ruled differently had he been on the lower court. "Even if as an original matter I might have arrived at a different conclusion based on a reading of the statute . . . I cannot say that the two courts below are so plainly wrong that they should be reversed." In other words, White didn't appear to believe that the Louisiana law was unconstitutional.

On the other side of the ideological spectrum were Justices Antonin Scalia, a Reagan appointee, and William Rehnquist, who was appointed by Nixon and later promoted to chief justice by Reagan. The two solidly conservative justices did not agree with the majority that the Louisiana law had a religious purpose and believed that students are entitled to hear any evidence that contradicted evolution. "The people of Louisiana, including those who are Christian fundamentalists, are quite entitled, as a secular matter, to have whatever scientific evidence there may be against evolution presented in their schools just as Mr. Scopes was entitled to present whatever scientific evidence there was for it." (Actually, the judge in the Scopes trial *didn't* allow scientific evidence that supported evolution.)

Scalia went even further, suggesting that "secular humanism is a religion," and that teaching evolution alone promoted atheism. "By censoring creation science and instructing students that evolution is a fact, public school teachers are now advancing religion."

Although the ACLU emerged the victor, the decision was hardly a resounding victory for the evolutionists or for secularists in general. Brennan opened the way for the teaching of "prevailing" scientific views that did not agree with Darwin. (The meaning of "prevailing," however, was unclear.) Powell and O'Connor affirmed the country's religious tradition. Scalia and Rehnquist suggested that teaching creationism alongside evolution might actually be *required* by the First Amendment.

WHATEVER THEIR VICTORY on paper, evolutionists faced a far more formidable public relations hurdle than the U.S. Supreme Court. Polls conducted from the 1980s to the present reveal that almost half of all Americans believe in the Genesis account of creation—that Earth was literally created in six days—and an even higher number believes that evolution and creationism should be taught side by side. Their beliefs are based more on social class than on religion. Those in the lower economic class are far more fundamentalist in their religious beliefs than those in the upper-middle classes, education being one of the key factors. According to Gallup polls, 65 percent of Americans with a high school diploma or less are in the creationist camp, compared to only 25 percent of the college-educated. Among Americans earning less than $20,000 a year, 59 percent were creationists, compared to only 29 percent of Americans with annual incomes above $50,000.

These numbers suggest that the debate over teaching evolution has much less to do with science than social class, a disconnect that deepens each time the ACLU brings its big-city lawyers into town. Rather than promote public understanding, the gap in social standing between the pro-evolutionists and the creationists leads only to political clashes, not to improvement in science education.

Yet it's not about social class entirely. More than 90 percent of all Americans believe God had a role in creation and evolution, a view directly at odds with Darwin. Many in the American public who say they agree with Darwin evidently accept the sugarcoated Darwinism of *Inherit the Wind,* without comprehending that natural selection excludes the divine. If chance alone governs our lives, there is no room for the divine intervention that is the basis of all true faith.

If left to American voters, science education might have been different; science classes might include some acknowledgement of the divine. But that is not the nature of science, which studies only the natural. Science is not democracy; the law of gravity cannot be repealed by public opinion. Unless and until another theory of evolution gains critical mass among scientists themselves, Darwin and Darwin alone must be taught in science classes. To question Darwin is to raise the possibility of God, a subject forbidden by science.

Evolution has become highly politicized. On the right, conservatives, religious and secular, see evolution as a leftwing plot to abrogate the Founding Fathers and strip America of religion altogether. Evolutionists and liberals fear the opposite: that teaching creationism is merely a ruse for turning a secular country into a theocracy. The battle over the teaching of evolution may be less about religion and more about politics, "an essential front in America's culture war," pitting left against right.

But if America's religious fundamentalists were overly fervent and evangelistic, so were the liberal secularists who flaunt their elite credentials to ridicule the religious in the eyes of the public. Creationism, wrote the late Stephen Jay Gould, is just part of the "long, sad history of American anti-intellectualism."

And Americans, he wrote, should "cringe in embarrassment."

9

CELEBRITY SCIENCE

He was a handsome man, tall and casually dressed, more poet than scientist. As he walked alongside the ocean with its crashing waves, the breeze blowing back his hair, he was very much the Romantic poet—John Keats or William Blake—contemplating the wonder of the universe.

"There is tingling in the spine," he said, "and a faint sensation as though falling from a great height. . . ."

For his role in the thirteen-part series that ran on consecutive Sundays from September until Christmas of 1980, Carl Sagan, already wealthy beyond imagination, received a hefty $2 million advance. A collaboration between Carl Sagan Productions and Los Angeles station KCET, *Cosmos* was the most expensive and glitzy production in the history of public television, whose science programs to date had been limited to the more modest *Nova* and *National Geographic* series. Filmed in forty locations in twelve countries, the production's $8 million budget rivaled that of many movies from that era.

Sagan's subsequent book, *The Cosmos*, was read by 500 million people in sixty countries and remained on the *New York Times* bestseller list for seventy weeks, the most popular science book ever. The video cassette and DVD versions of the series remain widely available.

A foundation operated in his name after his death in 1996 continues to market his products.

Like *Inherit the Wind* before it, the *Cosmos* television series, which won both a Peabody and Emmy (along with many other awards), helped shape the public's perception of science—while also perpetuating the supremacy of science over religion.

By 1980, Sagan, a semi-regular on the *The Tonight Show with Johnny Carson*, was already well known to most Americans. His 1973 *The Cosmic Connection* was a bestseller as was his 1977 *Dragons of Eden*, which won the Pulitzer Prize and sold more than 500,000 copies. "As a science populizer, Dr. Sagan has become a national celebrity and a booming corporation," wrote the television critic of the *New York Times* in 1980.

Born to Jewish parents in New York City—his mother was a garment worker, his father an immigrant from Ukraine—Sagan had little use for religion. He was married three times—his first wife was Lynn Margulis, who would go on to become a famous microbiologist—and had five children, who often wouldn't speak to him. He left his second wife for his third, writer Ann Dunyan, then twenty-eight, a political radical and aspiring writer. Sagan was actively involved in leftwing politics, particularly in nuclear disarmament, but repeatedly snubbed Ronald Reagan's invitations to the White House to discuss space policy.

Though a populizer of science, Sagan was held in disdain by his colleagues. Harold C. Urey, the Nobel Prize-winning chemist who worked with him for some time, regarded Sagan as "a bright but verbose, reckless thinker." Based in part on Urey's harsh criticism, Sagan was denied tenure at Harvard. In 1992, after an unusual and emotional debate, the National Academy of Sciences refused to make Sagan a member, a sharp rebuke from the country's most prestigious science body and a clear message that his scientific credentials were more Hollywood than real. "As Saul despised David for receiving ten thousand cheers to his own mere thousand, scientists often stigmatize, for the same reason of simple jealousy, the good work done by colleagues for our common benefit," wrote the late Stephen Jay Gould, who had also been scorned by some colleagues for his celebrity. "I am . . . sad that many scientists never appreciated his excellence, while a few of the best of us (in a shameful incident at the National Academy of Sciences) actively rejected him."

Even before he crossed the threshold into celebrity, Sagan had long involved himself in the politics of religion, warring against the ever-persistent creationists. As neo-Darwinist Richard Lewontin (a eugenicist who had been involved in the BSCS) later gloated in a piece in the *New York Review of Books*, in 1964, he and Sagan traveled to Arkansas to face off against Governor Orval Faubus (a segregationist as well as a religionist) and the creationist flocks.

"Carl and I then sneaked out the back door of the auditorium and beat it out of town, quite certain that at any moment hooded riders with ropes and flaming crosses would snatch up two atheist New York Jews who had the *chutzpah* to engage in public blasphemy."

Lewontin correctly concluded that "the confrontation between creationism and the science of evolution was an example of historical, regional, and cultural issues that could only be understood in the context of American history."

But to Sagan, the confrontation in Arkansas was the Scopes trial redux, "a struggle between ignorance and knowledge." According to Lewontin, "[T]he struggle to bring scientific knowledge to the masses has been a preoccupation of Carl Sagan's ever since, and he has become the most widely known, widely read, and widely seen popularizer of science since the invention of the video tube."

Sagan thereupon became the priest of science, the evangelist who brought wisdom to the ignorant masses. His intentions were noble—

to educate the ignorant—but the *Cosmos* series was as much about self-promotion as it was about science.

To *New York Times* television critic John J. O'Conner, the *Cosmos* series "could be subtitled 'The Selling of Carl Sagan.'"

> Shots of the various galaxies are alternated with close-ups of Dr. Sagan's face, presumably to suggest awe. Instead we are left with what looks like a succession of decidedly goofy grins. . . . At one point, at the very beginning of Episode Two . . . Dr. Sagan . . . appears rather bizarrely to be sitting at a Steinway.
>
> Sagan tends to play too forcefully the role of "merchant of awe." . . . His favorite adjective is "astonishing." His vocal inflections are nearly always a touch overly dramatic . . .

As O'Conner noted, Sagan often removed his scientist's hat to pump up platitudes of politically liberal ideas such as nuclear controls and feminism, causes that "[are] akin to arguing for Mom and apple pie."

And still the series promoted an even more subtle agenda than entertainment and pompous politics. As he explains the origins of the universe in each episode, Sagan continuously—and gratuitously— sprinkles his narrative with the words "accident" and "random," descriptions that guard against any inference of the divine. To the more "naïve," including the millions of Americans of faith, it might have been equally valid to ponder the beginnings of the universe and rejoice not in the "accident" of existence, but in its miracle.

While randomness is the very stalwart of neo-Darwinism, the concept of a universe created by chance alone is also a judgment call, a philosophy that wears the tenuous mask of science. Indeed, the words "accident," "chance," and "random"—all of them gratuitous— reveal far more about the narrator's own fear of God than they do about the nature of the universe.

It was pretty obvious to many exactly what Sagan thought he was accomplishing. In a letter to the *New York Times*, one viewer wrote that the series could just as easily have been called "The Selling of a Machinist-Materialist Darwinism." "Such determinists," the viewer wrote, "are forever projecting what they consider Earth's experience to be—a predictable materialistic 'process.'"

"Throughout 'Cosmos,' there are certain given propositions," wrote O'Conner. "Foremost among them is that science is infinitely superior to 'religion and superstition.'"

Sagan's constant references to "dark forces" refer not to any force in the universe, but to religion itself, ever threatening to throw its wet towel on the enlightenment of science. In one dramatic reenactment, seventeenth-century astronomer Johannes Kepler sticks to his scientific principles, standing up to entrenched religious thought. That segment appears to imply that Kepler was another great scientist martyred by religion when, in fact, Kepler, who discovered the elliptical orbit of the planets around the sun, was forced to stand up *not* to the "dark forces" of religion but to the hedonistic lifestyle of his patron Tycho Brahe in Prague. Sagan never noted that, to Kepler, religion was not the enemy of science but an ally. Like many of his scientific contemporaries, Kepler viewed the spectacular workings of the material world as a path towards, not away from, the divine, each new discovery only deepening his faith.

"To God," Kepler wrote, "there are . . . in the whole material world . . . the most appropriate order. . . . God wanted us to recognize them by creating us after his own image so that we could share in his own thoughts."

IN THE LATE 1970s, science became hugely popular in America. At about that time, the alignment of the planets simplified a voyage to the outer planets, reducing the time it took to go from one to another. In 1977, two unmanned space crafts, Voyager I and II, shot out of Cape Canaveral heading towards Jupiter and Saturn. (Voyager II went on to Uranus and Neptune.) Voyager I began photographing Jupiter in 1979. It was a heady time for science, and a love affair began with a doting public once again worshiping those who were solving the mysteries of the universe. Produced in 1977, *Star Wars* was among the popular movies of the time. It wasn't just space exploration. Other heroes emerged, even in less interesting fields of science. James Watson, who with Francis Crick discovered the nature of DNA in 1953, wrote the best-selling *The Double Helix* in 1968, a work that whetted public appetite in biology (though it was criticized by scientific colleagues for its brutal portrayal of Watson's colleagues). Beginning in 1978 and continuing to the present, books about science have almost always won the Pulitzer Prize and topped the bestseller lists. In 1981, Harper & Row published fifteen books about science, and the Book of the Month created a new club devoted to popular science books.

"[T]he public cannot seem to get enough books about science," the *New York Times* observed in 1981.

These science heroes themselves became celebrities, often aggressively promoting their "science" to advance their political agendas, while also achieving fame, adulation, and enormous wealth.

If Sagan was at least somewhat subtle in his use of science to advance his personal and political philosophies, his colleague in Britain expressed his own atheism with the zeal (and the faithful followers) that would rival that of any television evangelist.

Married to an actress, and meticulously dressed in tailored European suits, British zoologist Richard Dawkins was, as science writer John Horgan described him, "an icily handsome man, with predatory eyes, a knife-thin nose, and incongruously rosy cheeks.

When he held out his finely veined hands to make a point, they quivered slightly. It was the tremor not of a nervous man, but of a finely tuned, high-performance competitor in the war of ideas."

Dawkins's Oxford accent, his extraordinary command of history, literature, and philosophy combined to exude British contempt for everything American—especially religion. In a 1997 piece in the *New York Times,* Dawkins famously remarked that anyone who doesn't believe in evolution is "stupid, and ignorant and . . . *wicked*" (emphasis added).

Indeed, it was an article of faith for Dawkins that the "uneducated" were the only class of humans who could possibly believe in God; the "educated" had long ago dispensed with religious superstition. From this premise, Dawkins, evidently overlooking the theology department of his own university, took it one step further: anyone who believes in God is *ipso facto* "uneducated."

Dawkins's intellectual stature gave him an almost papal authority to speak upon spiritual matters. His books sold millions of copies, making him an instant millionaire and the intellectual hero of secular humanists. Like Sagan—but more far more explicitly—Dawkins moved Darwinism out of the realm of science into a broader philosophical domain in natural selection applied to every aspect of life. In his 1986 *The Blind Watchmaker,* Dawkins examined philosophies that predated Darwin but found no sound basis for atheism until Darwin. "[A]lthough atheism might have been logically tenable before Darwin, Darwin made it possible to be an intellectually fulfilled atheist."

Dawkins went even further than this. Like the social biologists of that era, he believed that all human life could be explained by biology alone; that, in effect, humans had no souls or higher purpose, but could be understood by biology alone. But Dawkins took it even further than most: all animals, mankind included, exist for no other purpose than to replicate their genes.

Not only did he use Darwin as a pulpit for non-belief, but also he reduced even admirable conduct to the struggle for survival. In his 1976 *The Selfish Gene,* Dawkins argues that all living creatures—man included—are no more than repositories for genes: genes which, in turn, will seek to perpetuate themselves at any cost. Charity is the basis of all Western religion—putting aside one's selfish desires to help another. But to Dawkins, there was no such thing as pure selflessness. Humans, like animals, may *appear* to act unselfishly, but in reality, according to Dawkins, they are merely helping others to remain alive so that their genes might be perpetuated. A mother loves her child only because the child can spread her genes. Mother Teresa might have worked tirelessly with the children of AIDS in Africa, when, in reality, her genes made her do it so that they might—somehow—live on.

> [W]e and all other animals are machines created by our genes. . . . [A] predominant quality to be expected in a successful gene is ruthless selfishness . . . [which] will usually give rise to selfishness in individual behavior. . . . [But] there are special circumstances in which a gene can achieve its own selfish goals by fostering a limited form of altruism at the level of individual animals.

"You have to be an intellectual to believe such nonsense," George Orwell once remarked. "No ordinary man could be such a fool."

The celebrity scientists and the many wannabes launched what appeared to be a competition: Who can be the most absurd? Who can take natural selection to its most philosophically reductionist extreme? Who can most offend religion? Who can make the most outlandish pronouncements about mankind? It wasn't just for sport: the more man could be reduced to a creature of biology, the less he was a creature of God.

"[Y]our joys, your memories and your ambitions, your sense of personal identity and free will, are in fact no more than the behavior of a vast assembly of nerve cells and their associated molecules," wrote Francis Crick in 1994.

So far out of the mainstream were many of these philosopher-scientists that, like the eugenicists and fringe bioethicists, they revered the practice of infanticide. Steven Pinker, a psychology professor at the Massachusetts Institute of Technology, along with fellow "evolutionary psychologists," seized upon the reductionist philosophies of Dawkins, Crick, and others to portray criminal behavior—rape and murder—as products of evolution. Because man had once *needed* to rape and murder in order to survive, these traits, genetic in origin, were passed on to later generations.

In November of 1997, Pinker wrote a piece for the *New York Times Magazine* about two separate cases in which eighteen-year-old girls had brutally murdered their unwanted babies. Pinker, obviously overruling the "selfish gene"—the mother's genes can't be passed on if she murders her offspring—virtually excused the shocking actions by explaining them in terms of biology, not evil. In the past, it was common, Pinker said, for a mother to sacrifice one child for the good of her other children. "Neonatocide [his word for infanticide] has been practiced and accepted in most cultures throughout history," he wrote. "A new mother will coolly assess the infant and her current situation. . . . In those first few days, it would seem that killing an infant would be perfectly natural and appropriate."

"First cousins to the old Marxist economic determinists, the evolutionary psychologists are behavioral determinists," wrote Michael Kelly in the *Washington Post*.

"This view is radical; it seeks to supplant both traditional Judeo-Christian morality and liberal humanism with a new scientific philosophy that denies the idea that all humans are possessed of a quality that sets them apart from the lower species, and that this quality gives humans the capacity and responsibility to choose freely between right and wrong. And it is monstrous."

Calling the *New York Times* the "closest thing we have to the voice of the intellectual establishment," Kelly wrote that it "came out for killing babies."

Kelly might have gone on to note that the evolutionary biologists, and psychologists were no better than the eugenicists, the bioethicists, and the population zealots who debased mankind in order to control it. Like so many of the politically "progressive" population fascists, Pinker and Dawkins posed as liberals. In fact, the implications of their "science" was as inhumane as those who proposed to allow Africans to die of starvation if they wouldn't use birth control. As New York University professor Dorothy Nelkin noted, these views were "especially convenient at a time when governments faced with cost constraints are seeking to dismantle the welfare state. . . . No possible social, educational, or nurturing plan can change the status quo."

Nelkin went on,

Evolutionary psychologists are missionaries, advocating a set of principles that define the meaning of life and seeking to convert others to their beliefs.

Missionaries, inspired by their revelations, often place limited value on empirical evidence. . . . Missionaries also tend to dismiss their critics. . . . They label non-believers as unenlightened, misguided, ignorant, unwilling to learn the truth, deluded, ideological, or politically incorrect.

While represented as a scientific theory, evolutionary psychology is rooted in a religious impulse to explain the meaning of life. (Emphasis added.)

To some commentators, Dawkins was as evangelistic as any fire-and-brimstone preacher.

> [F]or Dawkins there is nothing left to argue; genes are selfish; the watchmaker is blind. . . . Cherished concepts like "free will" and "spirituality" live in the dark, helical shadows of our genes. He has roused the ire of England's religious communities by publicly expressing his view that theology is nothing other than a pseudo-intellectual grab bag of charming myths.
>
> Dawkins is a fiery evangelist for atheism.

NOT ALL PHILOSOPHER-EVOLUTIONISTS were as extreme or as pretentious as Dawkins and the evolutionary psychologists. Another celebrity scientist tried to tone down the anti-religious rhetoric and bring science and religion into some degree of reconciliation.

Harvard professor Stephen Jay Gould was among America's most prominent science writers, his brilliant prose and musings making him the best-selling author of dozens of books. He didn't like Dawkins, referring to the rants of his British colleague and his followers as "Darwinian fundamentalism." These "ultras," as Gould called them, are "fundamentalists at heart . . . [who] try to stigmatize their opponents by depicting them as apostates from the one true way."

Unlike Dawkins, the affable, chubby Gould, who died of cancer at age sixty in 2002, was a regular guy. "Gould is disarmingly ordinary-looking," wrote John Horgan. "He is short and plump. . . . When I met him, he was wearing wrinkled khaki pants; he looked like the archetypal rumpled, absent-minded professor." Perhaps more than any other celebrity science—other than Sagan—Gould brought science to the people.

The intramural disputes among the celebrity scientists-philosophers were often brutal. Many in the Dawkins camp vilified Gould and his colleague Niles Eldridge for departing from classic neo-Darwinism and postulating their own theory of "punctuated equilibrium" which holds that evolution progresses in leaps and bounds, often responding to natural calamities that wipe out all those who can't adapt. Gould had once famously announced that neo-Darwinism was "effectively dead, despite its persistence as textbook orthodoxy." It was the worst act of blasphemy that a scientist could commit.

His views aside, likely Gould's colleagues were as jealous of his success as they were critical of his science. In a particularly biting 1999 piece in the *New Yorker*, philosopher Robert Wright, not content to merely criticize Gould's science, went on to launch a personal attack on the man himself—sadly, just about the time when Gould began his decline from cancer. Wright accused Gould of being an "accidental creationist" who engaged in "rhetorical extravaganza" and "emboldened" the enemy (religion).

"Gould . . . lent real strength to the creationist movement," Wright charged and went on to claim that Gould's colleagues did not consider him to be a "great scientist" and found him so confused as to not be worth bothering with.

In a piece in the *New York Times Book Review*, eugenicist and neo-Darwinist Richard Lewontin likewise launched a personal attack on Gould, calling his work "*an haute* vulgarization of science." Philosopher Daniel C. Dennett likewise pounced on Gould for his divergent views: "Gould's campaigns have had to take the form of calls for revolution. Time and again, Gould has announced from his bully-pit to a fascinated world of onlookers that neo-Darwinism is dead."

Gould fought back against Dawkins and the others, calling their reductionist views "a hyper-Darwinian idea that I regard as a logically flawed and basically foolish caricature of Darwin's genuinely radical intent." He saw Dawkins as a "fundamentalist at heart," not unlike the robotic fundamentalists of *Inherit the Wind*.

"I am no psychologist, but I suppose the devotees of any superficially attractive cult must dig in when a threat arises," Gould wrote, referring not to traditional religion, but to neo-Darwinism. "That old time religion, it's good enough for me."

The infighting aside, Gould stood above the rest in his attempt to reconcile religion and science, introducing in his *Rock of the Ages* the concept of "non-overlapping magisteria."

"I have great respect for religion," Gould wrote. "Much of this fascination lies in the stunning historical paradox that organized religion has fostered throughout Western history, both the most unspeakable horrors and most heartrending examples of human goodness in the face of personal danger."

He evidently saw more nuance in man's behavior than did Dawkins, the capacity for extraordinary goodness that was not explainable by evolution alone. Still, Gould was a bit like the anti-Semite who claims "some of my best friends are Jews." He didn't really approve of religion but knew that if he, like Dawkins, came out shooting, he would only hurt the cause of science. So in his *Rock of the Ages*, he wrote that science and religion could live side by side, science explaining the *how* of the physical world, religion the *why*: "[W]e study how the heavens go; they determine how to go to heaven."

But what was good for the goose wasn't good for the gander. Religion needed to stay in tow; it had to be highly obedient and confine itself to Sunday mornings. Science had no such limits; it was free to question the basic premise of religion.

"One of the first commandments of NOMA [non-overlapping magisteria] might be summarized by stating: 'Thou shalt not mix the magisteria by claiming that God directly ordains important events in the history of nature by special interventions knowable only through revelation and not accessible to science.'"

Not exactly "non-overlapping magisteria," Gould's generous overtures to religion were more like "heads I win, tails you lose."

Dawkins himself recognized this in a piece in *Forbes*. While not actually naming Gould, he called "non-overlapping magisteria" an "agnostic conciliation," which is the "decent liberal bending over backward to concede as much as possible to anybody who shouts loud enough. . . .

"The belief that religion and science occupy separate magisteria is dishonest. . . . [R]eligious apologists try to have it both ways. When talking to intellectuals they carefully keep off science's turf, safe inside the separate and invulnerable religious magisteria. But when talking to a nonintellectual mass audience, they make wanton use of miracle stories—which are blatant intrusions into science. . . .

"To an honest judge, the alleged marriage between religion and science is a shallow, empty spin-doctored sham."

But it was not that religion and science couldn't coexist; until the nineteenth century, they always had. What now stood in the way of their coexistence was the incursion not so much of religion into science, but the reverse: the antireligious pronouncements of Sagan, Dawkins, Gould, and many others.

FOR THE CELEBRITY scientists who relied on their science to promote their often astonishing views of life, there was an elephant in the living room. It was right there in front of them for all to see. It was menacing, all-powerful, able to pounce at any moment and trample on the carefully constructed nihilism of the scientific-philosophers.

"If I were a creationist," wrote John Horgan of *Scientific American,*

"I would cease attacking the theory of evolution . . . and focus instead on the origin of life."

Life's origins, how it all came into being, was central to both religion and science. Religion took it on faith that God created life, while science took it on faith that life came into being through a purely materialistic process in which inorganic molecules somehow evolved into life. Often scientists would ignore or trivialize the enigma of life's origins, claiming that answer would be "simple" once it was found. Many, however, tried to hide the fact that science couldn't figure out life's beginnings; they couldn't just wave the white flag and admit like fumbling fools on the witness stand that the answer was beyond the grasp of science.

One seasoned journalist humorously recounted his many attempts to wrest this admission from scientists he had interviewed. His experience with their word-sputtering defenses has been shared by many other journalists who likewise have been stared down with silent accusations.

"It was like giving a bobcat a prostate exam," wrote Fred Reed. "I got everything but answers. They told me I was a crank, implied over and over that I was a Creationist, said that I was an enemy of science (someone who asks for evidence is an enemy of science). . . . They told me I didn't know anything . . . that I was a mere journalist.

"But they didn't answer the questions. They ducked and evaded. . . ."

Scientists had a reason to be defensive. Anyone who looked at them closely could see that when it came to the metaphysics of existence, they were sinking fast in the quicksand. In laboratories all over the country, they had tried again and again to solve the mystery of life, to discover a process that turns non-life into life. The distance between the two is not a simple step like water to ice; it is a distance beyond human comprehension.

"Between a living cell and the most highly ordered non-biological system, there is a chasm as vast and absolute as it is possible to conceive," Australian biochemist Michael Denton wrote in *Evolution: A Theory in Crisis*, a seminal work, highly criticized, that in the 1990s would inspire a group of other scientists to reexamine the premises of Darwinism.

Even bacteria, among the most simple forms of life, wrote Denton, "are exceedingly complex objects."

"The simplest bacterium is so damn complicated from the point of view of a chemist that it is almost impossible to imagine how it happened," said Harold P. Klein, chairman of a committee formed by the National Academy of Sciences to investigate origin-of-life research.

The origins of the universe itself likewise were unknown to science, Carl Sagan's celebrity cosmology notwithstanding. The huge amount of energy needed to produce the universe surpasses even scientific explanation.

"[T]he universe had, in some sense, a beginning," wrote Robert Jastrow, an astronomer of world renown, "under circumstances that seem to make it impossible—not just now but *ever*—to find out what force or forces brought that into being at that moment. . . . No scientist can answer that question."

In 1953, it looked as though a young scientist had discovered the process by which the inorganic became the organic. Working under the famed Nobel Laureate Harold C. Urey, Stanley L. Miller, a twenty-three-year-old graduate student at the University of Chicago, appeared to have recreated in his lab at least part of the process in which non-life turns into life. Attempting to re-create the conditions of Earth about three billions years before (a billion years after its formation), Miller filled a sealed glass with methane, ammonia, and hydrogen—gasses believed to have been on Earth from the beginning—added water and then a spark of electricity. Within days, the glass was stained with a "reddish goo," which upon analysis was found to be rich in amino acids, the "organic compounds linked up to form proteins, the basic stuff of life."

In the late 1950s, Sidney Fox appeared to have found even more evidence for Miller's conclusion. By heating amino acids, he induced them to coagulate into short protein strands which he called "proteinoids." But there was a problem: these proteinoids couldn't reproduce. Without reproduction, life cannot evolve.

Researchers next believed—some still do—that DNA was the beginning of life. But DNA itself cannot reproduce without enzymes (which are proteins), and proteins cannot reproduce without DNA. "To those pondering the origin of life," wrote Horgan, "it is a classic chicken-and-egg problem: Which came first, proteins or DNA?"

Another theory held that RNA was the first self-replicating molecule that eventually evolved into life. In 1989, two molecular biologists shared a Nobel Prize for experiments that showed that RNA could produce its own enzymes, copy itself, and eventually, through evolution, acquire the other ingredients necessary to form a living cell. But other experiments showed that RNA would have been difficult to synthesize under the conditions on Earth that likely existed billions of years ago. Stanley Miller himself, long after his seemingly successful experiment creating life, could only say that life began when some compound developed the ability to copy itself, eventually making "mistakes" which, in turn, enabled it to replicate more rapidly. In effect, origin-of-life researchers were back to square one.

So difficult was this problem for the continued stature of scientists that many grappled for still other ways to find a scientific explanation for life's beginning, however improbable. Francis Crick, Carl Sagan, and others promoted the idea of "panspermia": that life dropped down on Earth from another planet. The theory begged the question of where the extraterrestrial life came from, but, if true, at least it solved the problem of life on Earth.

he discovery of life on one other planet," Sagan wrote, again _ his fear of the divine, "can transform the origin of life from a miracle to a statistic."

But Sagan and Crick never achieved that much-desired "statistic." Even with the billions of dollars expended on space exploration, no sign of life could be detected outside of Earth, and the hypothesis collapsed.

To British astronomer Fred Hoyle, the origin of life was about as probable as a tornado creating a 747 as it whirled through a junkyard—in other words, so unlikely as to be impossible.

But the ultra-reductionists had an answer in the ready, the same answer they gave to every other troublesome issue raised by evolution: given enough time, they argued, "anything is possible." But that was it. The sum and substance of their science was itself based on religious faith.

And so the answer proved so elusive, the scientific guesses so unsatisfactory, that the great pillars of atheism began to collapse.

One wonders exactly what Richard Dawkins must have thought when a compatriot and one-time Oxford colleague made his public turnabout, cracking the very foundations of atheism. In 2004, philosopher Antony Flew—one of the world's most committed atheists—captured the international limelight with an astonishing announcement: that *because* not *in spite* of science, he was no longer an atheist. In his video "Has Science Discovered God?" Flew said that the investigation of DNA "has shown, by the almost unbelievable complexity of the arrangements which are needed to produce life, that intelligence must have been involved."

Quite a betrayal from a man who for more than fifty years had taught at universities around the world and in lectures, books, and articles that atheism was the only explanation for life.

"This religious faith of the scientist," wrote Robert Jastrow, "is violated by the discovery that the world had a beginning under conditions in which the known laws of physics are not valid, and as a product of forces or circumstances we cannot discover.

"When that happens, the scientist has lost control."

10

OVER THE RAINBOW

On August 11, 1999, calamity struck the state of Kansas. Both the *New York Times* and the *Boston Globe* called it a "tragedy." The *Miami Herald* warned that there would be "real consequences to suffer." The *San Jose Mercury News* predicted that Kansans would soon have "flabby minds." So great was the tragedy that word spread across the oceans, appearing in the *Times Media Limited* (South Africa), the *Scotsman, Agence France Presse*, the *Federal Capital Press of Australia*, the *Toronto Star*, the *Irish Times*, and the *Montreal Gazette*.

Not surprisingly, Kansans were the most upset. The *Topeka Capital Journal* remarked that "the image of Kansas has taken a beating."

On the night of the tragedy, Linda Holloway, a once-obscure special education teacher from the suburbs of Kansas City, appeared on Tom Brokaw's *NBC Nightly News*. The only child of Southern Baptist parents in Georgia, the soft-spoken fifty-year-old woman had never expected this.

With her Southern accent and plastic clip-on earrings, she didn't stand a chance.

IT ALL BEGAN for Linda Holloway in 1996 when a friend suggested she run for the state's board of education. She sought counsel from

her husband and her pastor, the Reverend Ellsworth, hoping they'd
dissuade her. They didn't. She prayed with her prayer group—they
met weekly at the food court at the Crown Center, a shopping mall
near Kansas City—and they, too, encouraged her. Finally, Holloway,
after prayer, believed God Himself was telling her that it was indeed
her duty to serve on the state board of education.

So she tossed her hat into the school board election, running in
a district that included affluent Johnson County, just outside of
Kansas City, plus a sliver of adjoining Wyandotte County. She beat
incumbent Richard Spears in the second district by a conclusive margin of 70,210 to 48,692.

Back then, Kansans took little notice of its board of education.
Fewer than 10 percent of voters even bothered to cast a vote for a
board member. But with school districts now funded by state rather
than local revenues, the state board of education was acquiring more
responsibility for setting statewide standards for what should be taught
in the public schools, a trend that was occurring nationwide.

At her victory celebration on November 5, 1996, at the Doubletree
Hotel in Overland Park, Holloway stood up and told her audience that
she would push "academic excellence and communication with the
public."

As a teacher, Holloway had watched helplessly as progressive
forces tightened their grip on the public schools, force-feeding such
concepts as "self-esteem." A "fuzzy wuzzy" academic credo stroked
tender egos, allowed kids to use calculators during math exams, neglected the basics of education, and approved test answers that were
demonstrably wrong. Holloway believed that progressives were rapidly taking over the classroom, casting out the families, and inculcat-
ing kids into a mindset that said homosexuality, premarital sex, and
abortion were just fine, as were poor test scores.

Particularly irksome was a question on a math exam that asked students to *estimate* how many quarters are in a dollar, as if there could be more than one correct answer. As a teacher, Holloway had been told that she shouldn't use a red pen to correct wrong answers because corrections in red ink might injure a child's delicate self-esteem. The best path to "self-esteem" was getting the answers right, Holloway believed, not teaching kids that their answers were right when they were wrong.

By 1999, conservatives in Kansas had captured five of the ten seats on the state board, giving them the power to deadlock, if not actually defeat, the liberal agendas they opposed. They were part of a national movement by Christian conservatives to better effect their goals at the local level. Groups such as the Christian Coalition, Concerned Women of America, and Citizens for Excellence in Education encouraged conservatives to run for local and state school boards in order to transform education at the grassroots level. They stood resolute against the liberal movement that, along with then President Bill Clinton, was threatening education throughout the country.

The liberal philosophy towards education was summed up by the infamous "Dear Hillary" letter, written to Hillary Clinton by crony Marc Tucker a week after her husband's White House victory. "What is essential," Tucker wrote, "is that we create a seamless web of opportunities to develop one's skills that literally extends from cradle to grave and is the same system for everyone—young and old, poor and rich, worker and full-time student." Based on the German model, American public schools would serve as a "human resources development system."

In 1994, Clinton signed The School-to-Work Opportunities Act, granting federal funds to school districts that implemented "school-to-work" programs designed to steer students directly into a vocation. That same year, he also signed The Goals 2000 Education Act, whose sweeping pronouncements of what kids should learn was clothed in subtle language that reflected Tucker's ultra-liberal vision of public schools as instruments of the federal government.

Dangling federal grants, the new legislation required state governments to "establish challenging academic standards in core subjects." To conservatives, this meant that academic standards would slant leftwards. History students presumably would still learn about George Washington, but they'd also, conservatives feared, be forced to learn about the country's genocide towards Native Americans and its mistreatment of the Japanese during World War II. The legislation also created expensive bureaucracies including the National Education Standards and Improvement Council, the National Education Goals Panel, and the National Skills Council—each required to shape the direction of local education.

Just as science education had been "federalized" after Sputnik, now academic standards in all subjects would be dictated by Washington D.C. It didn't take conservatives long to rise up. To them, the federal government had become the problem, not the solution. America's test scores had plummeted just as federal spending on education soared to an all-time high. The U.S. Department of Education, created in 1979, had increased its annual budget from $14.5 billion to $34.7 billion. (In 2000, the Department of Education would be investigated because it somehow "lost" $150 million.) Per-pupil spending rose from about $900 in 1960 (numbers adjusted for inflation) to nearly $7,000 in 1995. Yet, throwing money at education hadn't moved the dials. SAT scores gradually slid from a combined score of 975 to 900, despite "dumbed-down" SAT exams.

Conservatives cringed at the notion that "government schools"— as they called the public schools—would be stamping out individual potential, parental sovereignty, and local control over education.

"We can no longer hide behind our love of local control of the schools," Clinton said in a speech.

As conservatives gained power in the mid-1990s, winning control of the House in 1994, they moved on to states and school boards. Candidates were often advised to conceal their religion during campaigns and "come out of the closet" only when elected, a strategy that infuriated liberals and moderates.

"It's like guerilla warfare. It's better to move quietly, under cover of night," said Ralph Reed, the leader of the Christian Coalition.

The more liberals fought for politically correct academics, the more conservatives fought back.

In 1994, the Clinton White House gave $2.2 million to a committee charged with developing national history standards. Among other things, those standards eliminated AD and BC in history's calendar. They also presented America as the oppressor of Native Americans and blacks.

"The standards go beyond an honest appraisal of national failures, replacing 'America, Land of Opportunity' with 'America, Land of Oppression,'" said a policy analyst for the Family Research Council. Lynne Cheney, a member of the president's panel, angrily quit the committee, lambasting the history standards for their excessive devotion to multiculturalism and political correctness, their emphasis on America's shortcomings, and scant attention to "the country's heroes, its scientific accomplishments, its legacy of political freedom."

In 1996, a Republican Congress cut off national funding for Clinton's education policies, and Clinton's plans fizzled. But the feud between conservatives and liberals continued to simmer on the backburner. As education became "standards based" all around the country, state capitols took on the paternalistic role of telling local school boards what to teach, often based on recommendations from national authorities.

Mainstream Republicans in Kansas and elsewhere worked hard to distance themselves from the religious right wing that threatened to brand the party as implacably conservative. Governor Bill Graves, a moderate Republican elected in 1995 and reelected in 1998, feuded bitterly with the board from the beginning. In 1996, he proudly issued an executive order establishing a "school-to-work partnership" between businesses and public schools, which would train students to bypass college and go directly into the workforce. In June 1998, he obtained $16.8 million in federal "school-to-work" money.

The five conservatives on the board of education blocked the school-to-work initiative, turning away nearly $17 million in federal funds.

Graves was furious.

As impasse ensued as conservatives dug in their heels to block any initiative they deemed liberal. In November 1998, the board voted 5-5 to block a sex education initiative, while moderates, in turn, blocked a conservative-sponsored initiative that would stress abstinence as the best way to prevent pregnancy and disease.

"Division on the Kansas Board of Education continues to thwart initiatives aimed at student improvement," the *Kansas City Star* opined.

To this oft-stalemated board came the daunting task of developing academic standards in math, reading, and science.

Even math proved controversial as liberals pushed for props such as calculators, while conservatives pushed for academic basics. In what would be dubbed the "math wars" by the *Kansas City Star*, the board, on June 15, 1998, divided 5-5 on how math should be taught, with tempers flaring, a harbinger of the science standards more than a year later. It required six drafts before the board grudgingly approved a set of math standards.

But the math standards, Holloway later joked, were "child's play" compared to science.

MATH WAS ONE thing; science quite another.

Everyone wanted to improve science education, to make it more interesting to students, to teach them to perform experiments, ask questions, become hands-on, instead of just memorizing periodic tables by rote. But conservatives feared the *sub-rosa* agenda of the science establishment. They feared Carl Sagan and Richard Dawkins and the many others who used science to bludgeon religion and debase the sanctity of human life. They knew of the science establishment's disdain for local educators and school boards, their condescension towards anything religious. The stage had been long set, going back to the Scopes trial, *Inherit the Wind,* the Biological Sciences Curriculum Study, and the BSCS textbooks. Their fears were not unfounded. Whether rightly or wrongly, the religious were under attack.

"Most of our school systems are hierarchical organizations that are completely out of step with what we know about creating an environment that fosters continuous improvement," Bruce Alberts, head of the National Academy of Sciences, told Congress in September 1997 during testimony in support of national science standards, an anthema to those, mainly conservatives, who favored local control of education.

The American Association for the Advancement of Science and the National Academy of Sciences had published a series of "model" standards that told local science educators what students needed to learn about science—how it should be taught. Like the BSCS, these groups promoted an expansive—and anti-religious—view of science.

"[S]cience distinguishes itself from other ways of knowing and from other bodies of knowledge," the standards said, virtually dripping in condescension towards religion. "Explanations based on myths, personal beliefs, religious values, mystical inspiration, superstition, or authority may be personally useful and socially relevant, but they are not scientific."

It is difficult to understand why "religious values" were placed on par with "myths" and "superstition." Evidently, to the NAS and other science bodies, religion had about as much validity as reading tea leaves or avoiding the cracks in the sidewalk.

Like the BSCS before it, the NAS enlarged the scope of science to include non-scientific, highly private issues, such as sex and procreation, as though these subjects have anything to do with science itself. "Sexuality," said the model standards, "is basic to the physical, mental, and social development of humans." Science students in grades nine through twelve learn that "sexuality is basic to healthy human development"—AIDS apparently notwithstanding. Though abortion and birth control are not explicitly mentioned, "students should understand various methods of controlling the reproductive process." In addition, the model standards make constant reference to a "population crisis," as though that myth hadn't been debunked. Taken together, the standards essentially tell impressionable students that they shouldn't have too many children, subtly perpetuating the racism of Paul Ehrlich and his followers. The teaching of science is one thing; the teaching of mythology, even leftwing mythology, quite another.

Although labeled "model," the NAS and other science standards are anything but. In a section called "Changing Emphases," the NAS promised financial support to states that developed "new curriculum materials aligned with the standards" but loss of funding to those states that placed "less emphasis" on the standards. Though with one hand, the NAS breezily grants to states the freedom to use the standards as a "model" for their curriculum, with the other, it steadfastly refuses to release its grip.

And, above all, one thing in particular was singled out as an absolute requirement. "Biological evolution cannot be eliminated from the life science standards," the NAS declared.

IN EARLY 1998, a committee appointed by the Kansas Board of Education drafted science standards that were nearly identical to the model published by the NAS. It might have gone unnoticed but for Celtie Johnson, a homemaker in Prairie Village (near Kansas City) who spotted a legal notice in the back pages of a local paper. In fine print and legalese, the notice announced that the state would be holding public hearings on the proposed science standards. Johnson called the state Department of Education, trying to track down a copy of the standards. When she finally obtained and read them, the recently "born-again" Johnson understood exactly what was at stake.

Johnson sounded the alarm to other Christians: the leftwing atheists from Washington were taking over. Over lunch, the group agreed that the writing committee was unlikely to address their concerns. What should they do? One suggested they write their own science standards. And so they did. In contrast to the "liberal" set of standards, the Christians' science standards required students to learn by the twelfth grade that "sexuality is a serious component of being human and it demands strong personal reflection in light of the long-term effect on students."

Working behind the scenes was Tom Willis, head of the Creation Science Association of Mid-America, a regional creationist group. Though the work of creationists, the Christian draft did not go so far as to offer the biblical account of creation, but it did encourage doubts about both evolution and science overall.

At meetings of the full board, some conservative members worried that the national standards overly expanded the role of science in human knowledge, arguing that science was one way to understand the world, but that it should not eclipse religion. The Christian group rewrote the standards to restrict the role of science and to encourage skepticism.

"If something cannot be observed in some way, then it cannot be dealt with scientifically," the alternative standards read in a sharp rebuke of science. "Science cannot prove an historical event."

"Students will learn to identify the assumptions that underlie . . . the theories taught to them," their draft said, suggesting that science is not objective or fact-based at all.

"It is fine," the document went on, in a slap at Darwin's often slavish followers, "to make statements like 'this theory is backed up by a great body of experiments and observations,' but often overlooked is the fact that such claims are meaningless."

More to the point was this: "Students," the Christian document said, "should learn the . . . limits of science."

IN MAY 1999, the Kansas Board of Education had before it two profoundly different sets of science standards: one written by the creationists, the other based on the NAS model. They differed not only in their emphasis on evolution but on social issues such as sex education and, most importantly, the relative importance of science and the limits of its knowledge.

Meetings of the board, normally ignored by the public and relegated to briefs in the back pages of local newspapers, soon became so densely packed that speakers were limited to two minutes. Among them were members of the clergy, who, much to the chagrin of the creationists, preferred to keep Bible study out of the classroom, evidently overlooking the subtle atheism of the NAS standards.

"The Bible of the church and temple was not intended to become a classroom textbook," said Steve Langhofer, pastor of St. Paul's United Methodist Church in Lenexa, Kansas, in written comments. "Yes, it contains for me religious truth about how the world was formed. But that is most faithfully interpreted and expounded in a religious setting, not the secular arena."

"We do a disservice to kids if we give equal time to theories of religion," another said. "There are many benefits to keeping religious beliefs away from schools."

"We need to be tuned into education, instead of agenda," said yet another.

But many speakers also protested the NAS science standards, among them not only creationists but others who normally would not be on the side of the fundamentalists.

Catholics, unlike Protestants, ordinarily do not protest the teaching of evolution, because they do not read the Bible literally and because the Vatican condoned it. Nevertheless, Mary Kay Culp, spokeswoman for the Kansas Catholic Conference, charged that the writing committee's draft was the product of "a small group of people with a certain ideological agenda [that] has given us standards which deify evolution, relegate religion to the status of 'superstition,' censor opposing scientific views and ultimately give more dignity to the environment than to man, even referring to human beings as 'soft machines.'"

Rebecca Messall, a pro-life lawyer who lived just outside Kansas City, went even further. A Catholic, she had once believed that the origin of the species was "a matter of God's choice of methods" and that the brewing controversy in Kansas was merely an "educational dispute." But when contacted by a local reporter to discuss the standards, Messall read them through and was horrified at their anti-religious bias and emphasis on overpopulation and "controlling" reproduction. She urged the reporter to investigate them further, but the reporter "rebuffed" her. "The newspaper's political commitments were set in concrete," Messall concluded.

"I implore this board," she testified, "to stop the ambitions of this destructive, even murderous view of science. . . ."

Some religious conservatives complained of the misrepresentation of the dispute by the national media. D. Russell Humphreys, president of New Mexico's Creation Science Fellowship, said that creationists were being portrayed as "zealots trying to cram religion down the throats of others."

The other side, primarily academics from the University of Kansas, were just as zealous, demonstrating once again the cultural basis of the dispute over evolution, the class divide between Darwinists and creationists that had been evident all the way back to the Scopes trial. "The Kansas Board of Education will have an opportunity to make history, this month," wrote Leonard Krishtalka, director of the Natural History Museum at the University of Kansas in Lawrence in a piece entitled "Yokels' Approach to Science." "Kansas will instantly make yokel history," the long-haired, bearded Krishtalka predicted, "much as Tennessee did during the Scopes trial."

Others in the academic camp shrewdly pushed the economic panic button, a ploy that would often be used in disputes by the medical research community when confronted with religious opposition. Jobs would be lost, students wouldn't get into college, companies would flee the state—all because students didn't learn about evolution. It was as though the overall quality of education—English, grammar, history, math—was irrelevant to the state and the country. Everything hinged on what students learned during two weeks of tenth-grade biology.

"We emphasi[zed] economic effects, effects on education in Kansas, effects on whether or not corporations would want to relocate in Kansas" wrote Adrian Melott, a cosmologist from the University of

Kansas who went on to gain national prominence for his role in the Kansas dispute.

"We appealed to the prospect that children from Kansas might have trouble getting into good universities, even the ones in their own state.

"We think these pragmatic appeals to self-interest worked better than abstract appeals to some kind of truth."

EVENTUALLY, THE CHRISTIANS did an about-face—almost. They shelved the explicit anti-Darwin language that had been driven by creationists. Now they worked with the same NAS standards as did the original board-appointed committee, later claiming they'd retained at least as much as 80 percent of its language. But the 20 percent they removed was of far more of importance than the 80 percent they retained. Students would be required to learn about natural selection but only as it causes variations *within* a species, not as the engine that transforms one species into another. They would not be required to learn about the Big Bang theory of the universe's origins or that Earth is billions of years old. Individual school districts could decide to teach evolution. But they were not *required* to do so.

As the entire world watched, this version was passed by the board, in a 6-4 vote, on August 11, 1999.

PHILLIP E. JOHNSON, a law professor at Berkeley, knew from the e-mails and piles of letters he received that "the Kansas story was going to be a big one."

Himself an evangelical Christian, Johnson was one of the leaders of a movement known as "intelligent design," a challenge not to evolution itself but to Darwin's theory of evolution by natural selection.

Unlike creationists, advocates of intelligent design believed that Earth was billions of years old. Although they proposed that some form of intelligence drove evolution, this intelligence was not necessarily the God of the Bible.

Using the lawyer's techniques of cross-examination, Johnson, in his 1993 book *Darwin on Trial*, exposed what he saw as the logical fallacies of Darwinism. Its logic and simplicity made the book attractive to many non-scientists and presented a more optimistic worldview than the dismal purveyors of randomness. But, because of its reliance on a deity, intelligent design created a furor within the scientific establishment, whose methods, by definition, did not allow for any supernatural explanation. Johnson, a brilliant law professor and evangelist, was dismissed as a Christian—hardly a flattering label in the culture wars—and was dismissed as "merely a lawyer" and "not a scientist."

Unlike the earlier creationist movements, there were some well-credentialed individuals supporting intelligent design. And though the movement was often accused of being "Christian," in fact only a few of them were Protestant evangelicals. A few were Catholic. At least one was a secular Jew. All were highly educated; many held advanced degrees from the very best universities. These were hardly the "yokels" of Scopes-trial fame.

"There are a few people in intelligent design who have biological training," one critic said about the intelligent-design proponents. "These are all smart guys. But they're a cult. No one in the scientific community takes them seriously."

Michael Behe, a tenured professor of biological sciences in microbiology at Lehigh University in Pennsylvania was, with Phillip Johnson, a major player in the intelligent-design movement. In his 1996 *Darwin's Black Box*, Behe argued that some features of a cell could not have been developed independently of each other, that there must have been a force that pulled them all together.

David Berlinski, a mathematician and philosopher, wrote a series in *Commentary*, a publication of the American Jewish Committee, called "The Deniable Darwin," arguing that the eye was an example of an organ whose component parts could not have evolved independently of each other, but only could have come about together.

William Dembski, also a philosopher and mathematician, renewed the mathematical challenges to Darwin's theory of evolution by natural selection that had been the basis of the 1965 Wistar conference. In 2002, he was appointed to head the Michael Polanyi Center at Baylor University, a Christian university in Waco, Texas. Accusing Dembski of being a "stealth creationist," the Baylor faculty voted 27-2 to dismantle the center, and Dembski was promptly demoted. Intelligent-design proponents argued that they were subject to "intellectual McCarthyism," which punished them for challenging entrenched science.

During the Kansas debates, Jonathan Wells, then a post-doctoral biology student at Berkeley—and a disciple of Reverend Sun Myung Moon—wrote an opinion piece in the *Kansas City Star*, arguing that teaching evolution "indoctrinates students in an anti-religious worldview that ignores scientific evidence." He went on to argue that students should be taught about Darwinian evolution but should also be given the resources to "evaluate the theory critically." It was not quite the "balanced treatment" laws that had been stricken down by the Supreme Court, but it was an invitation for students to raise scientific questions about Darwin.

THE ONSLAUGHT BEGAN within hours of the board's vote.

Columnist James Carroll of the *Boston Globe* accused the board of "racism." British columnist A.N. Wilson used the Kansas vote to express his wrath towards all things American, the "millions of roly-poly, Coca-Cola swigging cretins." "[T]he Land of the Free is making itself as obscuran-tist [sic] and as backward looking as any of the European tyrannies from which the poor and huddled masses and the brave Pilgrim Fathers fled in the first instance to create the land, and the idea of America," he wrote in London's *Evening Standard.*

Referring to Kansans and Americans who live outside of Boston and New York, Wilson wrote: "These are the people who believe that Elvis Presley has risen from the dead. . . . The Land of the Free, telly and burger-fed, has become the Land of the Credulous Moron."

Governor Bill Graves called the vote "a terrible, tragic, embarrassing solution to a problem that doesn't exist." University of Kansas Chancellor Robert E. Hemenway said the vote was "deeply humiliating to proud Kansas." The National Academy of Sciences accused the Kansas board of attempting to "politicize the teaching and learning of science." The American Civil Liberties Union of Kansas and Western Missouri fired off letters to the superintendents of all 304 school districts in Kansas.

"We write you today to ask that you reject tailoring the science curricula in your district to conform, promote, or advance theories of evolution based on religious doctrine," the letter read. "Adopting such religiously based standards would place the district at risk of facing legal action by district residents who are opposed to a religiously based science curricula."

Within the state, celebrity-scientist wannabes basked in their fifteen minutes of fame. John Staver, a professor of science education at Kansas State University, told the media that the document passed by the board "censors science, demeans teachers, and cheats students." He went on to boldly offer himself up as a "resource" to the National Academy of the Sciences, the American Association for the Advancement of Science, and the National Science Teachers Association, as well as others.

It had been the strategy of the University of Kansas academics to frighten citizens into thinking that the failure to teach evolution would bring economic ruin to the state and jeopardize their children's futures. It worked. An editorial in the *Atlanta Journal-Constitution* said the board's vote "could well plunge science education in the state into the pre-Darwin past" and predicted that "high-tech firms will bypass Kansas for states where prospective workers are likely to be better."

Science, the magazine of the American Association for the Advancement of Science, proposed that colleges and universities refuse to recognize high school biology courses from applicants in Kansas. The editor of *Scientific American* agreed. "The qualifications of any students applying from that state in the future will have to be considered very carefully," he wrote.

Maxine Singer, president of the Carnegie Institution and herself a highly respected scientist, urged biology professors not to take positions in Kansas universities.

"The students who come to Kansas State University will not have had appropriate preparation in biology in high school to undertake serious study," she said.

In a similar vein, the heads of the biology departments of nineteen colleges and community colleges in Kansas jointly signed a statement. "We expect Kansas high school students to graduate and enter our institutions with a basic, minimal understanding of elementary chemistry and physics. . . . To remove evolution from the K-12 science curriculum will deny a full and legitimate biology education to Kansas school students.

"[The science standards] will necessitate remediation in college, and negatively impact future Kansas biological research that serves the people of Kansas and the United States."

The *Topeka Capital Journal* reported that a software company, expected to employ a well-paid staff of twelve, had decided not to relocate in Kansas because of the board's vote. "The president of a small Oregon software company was reviewing a list of potential midwestern expansion sites Wednesday when news came of the Kansas State Board of Education's decision to remove evolution from the state's science teaching standards.

"He quickly scratched Topeka off the list of possible locations for Broadcast Software International's new regional technical center."

"It's an image thing," the company's president reportedly said.

Only at the end of the article did the reporter note that the company had never really considered moving to Kansas, that, in fact, the state's relocation officials had never even heard of the company. The threat of losing jobs and businesses was a unifying theme in all contemporary disputes between religion and science; it was a powerful way of rallying the public to the side of science.

The hysteria aside, the whole dispute actually enlivened science education in Kansas.

Several weeks after the board's vote, a group of high school science teachers told the *Topeka Capital-Journal* that they and their students were becoming more, not less, interested in evolution and the questions it raised made students more interested in science overall. This had been the goal all along, to make science more interesting to students, not dry and rote. Students were inspired to learn more about evolution because—not in spite of—its relevance to the existence of God.

"I think there is more interest in evolution now that this has happened," said one high school biology teacher.

"Kids have more questions," said another.

HOLLYWOOD, TOO, A bastion of liberalism in designer clothes, soon reinforced the ranks of scientists.

Its war against conservative Christians had started in 1980, just about the time when Christian groups began to politicize their concerns about a lapsed America. Norman Lear, a secular Jew who had produced the wildly successful television series *All in the Family*, planned on doing a film critical of the Christian right. But after watching Jerry Falwell's *Old Time Gospel Hour* and Pat Robertson's *700 Club*, Lear was so alarmed that he dropped the project and made a sixty-second commercial on religious intolerance.

Falwell fought back. "Norman Lear is clearly anti-Christian," he said, igniting the television mogul to accuse Falwell of anti-Semitism. "To an anti-Semite," Lear retorted, "a wealthy Jew is different from someone else who is wealthy."

Lear raised $5 million from his Hollywood pals and formed People for the American Way, a tax-exempt organization that soon became a leftist liberal assault missile that launched attacks on conservative judicial nominees, charter schools, and dozens of other objects of their ideological wrath. PFAW speakers plied the lecture circuits, accusing one secretary of education of being the "Secretary of Evangelism" and raising funds by "painting the opposition in fearsome colors."

Unlike many other political organizations which focus on lobbying, PFAW aggressively worked the media. Its approach was "to get an editorial in the *Philadelphia Inquirer* or the *Baltimore Sun*," said CEO Anthony Podesta. "We raise hell in the *Chicago Tribune*. We send material to 300 radio stations."

While much of PFAW's funding came from its 300,000 members, Hollywood celebrities liberally enriched the organization's coffers. PFAW's contributors included such luminaries as Alec Baldwin, Kim Basinger, and Kathleen Turner. They were soon joined by motion picture studios, television cable networks, and Internet companies.

"People for the American Way is an alliance of actors, artists, and activists banded together to oppose and resist the many attempts at repression and bigotry that come from the right wing and the churches," Noemie Emery wrote in the *Weekly Standard*, a conservative weekly.

"Their critics see them quite differently. They see a group of extremely rich people and corporations who make a great deal of money selling sex and violence, often to children, and who want to make sure that their business is protected, that there is always a ready audience at hand.

"These are the people and companies that drive parents crazy, who make them feel the culture itself is their enemy. These are the people who want the loosest possible limits on what can be seen, sung, and sold."

In 2000, PFAW raised $12.6 million. Scandalously, some contributions came from the news media itself—the very target of the organization's work—creating the appearance of collusion and casting doubt on the media's ability to report on the organization and its causes with appropriate neutrality. The *New York Times* contributed to PFAW, as did Time Inc., NBC, Disney, and America Online. At a 1998 dinner honoring Arthur Sulzberger Sr., retired publisher of the *New York Times*, the newspaper of record purchased tables for $600 a seat.

The *New York Times* never would apologize for helping subsidize an organization it was supposed to cover without fear or favor. But others proved more ethical. Time Inc. said the company had changed its policy about participating in events sponsored by PFAW. "We determined that for a news organization such as ours, it would not be appropriate for us to do that, so we stopped doing it," said *Time* spokesman Peter Costiglio.

In the name of tolerance, PFAW descended upon Kansas in the summer after the board's vote, just weeks before the Republican primaries that could oust Linda Holloway and her supporters.

The group recruited several Kansas natives-turned-celebrities. Ever since *Inherit the Wind,* Hollywood emerged as a "spokes-person" for science and, even more so, a crusader against religion. Among the PFAW stars was Ed Asner, best known for his role as the cranky but lovable newsman Lou Grant in the 1970s hit series *The Mary Tyler Moore Show.* Then nearing seventy, Asner, an admitted socialist, had a long history of leftwing radicalism. Indeed, he was perceived as so radical that CBS canceled *The Mary Tyler Moore Show* after two large advertisers withdrew their sponsorship. Reaganites despised him because he raised money to aid rebels in El Salvador who were fighting the U.S.-backed regime.

A graduate of the University of Chicago, Asner at least had been respectably educated. But how likely was it that Alec Baldwin or Kim Basinger or any of the many other glitzy Hollywood stars had ever seriously studied biology or understood Darwin's theory of evolution by natural selection or ever read anything on the subject other than PFAW press releases? Their reaction against religion was reflexive— and highly political. They were protecting their own turf.

During "Scopes Week" in Kansas—July 9 through July 14—Asner played William Jennings Bryan in a reading of *Inherit the Wind* at the Lied Center at the University of Kansas. An audience of 1,300 cheered and applauded throughout the performance, spurred on by cue cards that instructed: "laughter," "hiss," and "hubbub."

"This act by the board sorely hurts the education and potentialities of the children of this state," Asner said. "We must fight anything which limits freedom."

Following the cue cards, the audience duly cheered him on.

AFTER THE KANSAS board's historic vote, Bill Wagnon, a moderate board member from Topeka, warned that "an awakened public will vent its wrath on the Board of Education in November 2000." Linda Holloway was one of the three board members up for reelection. In the year since the notorious science standards had been passed, she'd received threatening letters and e-mails and had ridicule heaped upon her.

"SHAME!" said one letter, written in an erratic handwritten scrawl. "You're obviously not qualified to hold public office."

Still, Holloway never doubted that she would win the August 2000 Republican primary and serve out another four years on the state board of education. Though confident about the outcome, she knew the race would not be pretty. The academic community, galvanized since the board's vote, was urging Democrats to re-register as Republicans so they could vote in the Republican primary and defeat the conservative Christians. "Democracy got us into this," one liberal activist remarked. "Democracy will get us out."

In July 2000, just weeks before the vote, NBC's *Nightline* devoted an entire broadcast to the Kansas vote. The state's three major newspapers had all endorsed Holloway's opponent, Sue Gamble.

"The vote was embarrassing to many Kansans who felt it resulted in their being unfairly portrayed by national media as a bunch of backwater rubes who do not value science education," said the editorial board of the *Kansas City Star*.

Three of the board's conservative members were up for reelection in the 2000 Republican primary: Linda Holloway, Steve Abrams, and Mary Douglass Brown. (A fourth conservative, Scott Hill, had moved out of the state, leaving one seat vacant.)

Now, as primaries approached, signs cropped up like weeds on suburban lawns. In years past, wrote *Kansas City Star* reporter Kate Beem, school board elections "were about as exciting as watching corn grow." "I didn't even know there was a school board," said one Johnson County resident and public school parent.

Candidates from both sides campaigned on the evolution issue, a subject that had never been a campaign issue before. Holloway managed to raise $90,000 from friends and conservative organizations such as the Republican's Woman's Club and Kansans for Life. Money came from out of state as well, including a donation from the religious conservative icon Phyllis Schafly.

Holloway's opponent, Sue Gamble, raised $30,000—a third of what Holloway had but still a hefty amount for a school board election. During the campaign, Gamble claimed the standards had "put students at a disadvantage on a national level."

Mary Douglass Brown, another conservative board member, was challenged by Carol Rupe, former president of the Wichita school board, who raised $18,300, much of it from the teachers' union. Brown's supporters came from the less affluent parts of the district, while Rupe's support came from parts of Wichita that the *Wichita Eagle* characterized as "affluent and educated." Once again, social class was as relevant as religion in the debate between creationists and evolutionists. Rupe said she was "embarrassed when suddenly, after the vote last summer, we were called by our friends and relatives in other states wondering what kind of state we lived in." The claim took advantage of what appeared to be the state's inferiority complex, its overall fear that as the home of Dorothy and Toto it was the object of ridicule by the intellectual East.

"Image-conscious Kansans cringed every time they turned on the television and heard the state's name used in the punch line of a Jay Leno or Bill Maher joke," the *Topeka Capital-Journal* wrote.

Holloway spent election night at the home of a friend, planning to join other Republicans at the Overland Park Marriott later that evening in what was supposed to be a victory celebration. Then came the calls from precincts reporting the election results: she had lost to Gamble by a margin of 60 to 40. Urged on by the science community,

Democrats had switched parties so they could vote against her in the Republican primary. But it wasn't just Democrats and moderates who had voted against her. So had many conservatives, some from her own base, who Holloway believed had succumbed to propaganda and the economic fear. Holloway was stunned—and deeply hurt—by their defection.

As a Chinese paleontologist later remarked, "In China, we can criticize Darwin, but not the government. In America, you can criticize the government, but not Darwin."

PART III

RAISING THE DEAD

11

THE MIRACLE CURE

On August 22, 1989, at 8:00 AM, George Carillo, forty-nine, slept under anesthesia in the operating room of Lund Hospital in Sweden. Nurses wheeled him into radiology for a "computerized axial tomo-graphy" (CAT) scan, in which high density x-rays produce a three-dimensional image of the brain on a screen. Soon George would be among the first patients in the world to receive an implant of fetal-neural cells which—it was hoped—would replace the dopamine-producing cells in his brain destroyed by Parkinson's disease.

Parkinson's disease is typically idiopathic, meaning that its cause is generally unknown, its symptoms gradual in onset. George was an exception. He had acquired the disease after injecting himself with tainted synthetic heroin. Minutes after his blood stream sent the drug to his body, George began to hallucinate, walking through doors that weren't there. By the fourth day, he could hardly move his arms. By the sixth, he wouldn't talk or move his head, and when he blinked, his eyelids wouldn't open again. Then in prison for a parole violation, George was rushed off to Santa Clara Valley Medical Center in Santa Clara, California. He just lay there like a log, hearing everything the doctors and nurses were saying, unable to speak or gesture.

Parkinson's disease, which affects more than one million

Americans, generally occurs after the age of sixty when dopamine-producing cells at the base of the brain gradually die off. Without dopamine, the brain cannot transmit signals to the rest of the body, making movement progressively difficult. Symptoms include tremors, slow movements, rigidity, and the appearance of a masked face, in which there is no expression and little blinking of the eyes. While not fatal, the disease can lead to total disability and make a patient vulnerable to life-threatening infections.

In the late 1980s, the only treatment for Parkinson's was the drug L-dopa, a chemical precursor of dopamine which reverses some of the disabling symptoms. But the drug has its problems; it works best when concentrated in the blood, shortly after injection, gradually wearing off throughout the day. It tends to lose its effectiveness after about five years.

When George Carillo was given L-dopa, many of his symptoms were reversed, but the drug had a devastating side effect: hallucinations, in which spiders, beetles, and fires attacked his face. His doctor, Dr. J. William Langston of Stanford University Medical School, scoured the medical journals, determined to find a way to ease George's discomfort, or, better yet, to cure him.

Decades before, in 1961, two Harvard researchers had announced that Parkinson's was "on the way out" and in twenty years would "cease to be a medical problem." After examining 1,436 patients at Massachusetts General Hospital, they said that most cases of Parkinson's were the result of a separate disease: encephalitis. But they were wrong. More than twenty-five years later, the disease had not disappeared.

In the late 1980s, promising work on Parkinson's was developed in Mexico. Dr. Ignatio Madrazo transplanted a patient's own adrenal tissue into his brain, seemingly bringing recovery. On the heels of that report, American researchers traveled to Mexico only to discover that "recovery" was in the eyes of the beholder. Because the symptoms of Parkinson's vary from day to day, it is essential that a patient be monitored over a period of time and that improvement be measured using objective criteria. But the Mexican team had measured success based on the patient's subjective reports and videotapes taken on his better days. Science requires more.

When two researchers at Vanderbilt University attempted to replicate the Mexican procedure, they found that the "miracle cure" was neither a miracle nor a cure. Younger patients did show measurable improvement for up to eighteen months—but no longer—while older patients showed no improvement at all. Nonetheless, researchers around the world plunged ahead, performing the adrenal-graft on three hundred patients. The treatment had never been subjected to the rigors of clinical trials—with controls and safety criteria. The result was disastrous: In Mexico, a number of patients, including some Americans, died from complications. When word got out, patients refused to volunteer for trials of the treatment. By 1990, the adrenal-tissue graft was abandoned.

But by then, another ray beaconed: fetal-tissue implants. Dr. Curt Freed of the University of Colorado reported success after injecting fetal substatia nigra tissue—the fetus's dopamine-producing brain cells—into a patient's brain. In 1987, researchers at the Lund Hospital in Sweden tested the procedure on two women, aged forty-seven and fifty-four, who were followed at intervals over a period of two years. The forty-seven-year-old woman was able to walk again and felt less rigidity in her arms, but the fifty-four-year-old experienced only modest improvement: Though she could walk somewhat better, scans of her brain showed no increase in cell production.

In 1989, the Swedish team prevailed on their government to fund George Carillo's operation and travel expenses: all told, between

$30,000 and $50,000. George would be about the fifth patient to undergo the procedure but the very first to receive implants on *both* sides of the brain. A golden rule of neurosurgery holds that a patient should never be operated on both sides of his brain lest he lose all function. But George's symptoms were so severe that the Swedish doctors decided to treat both sides of his brain over the course of several weeks. As a Hispanic, a prisoner, and a drug addict, perhaps George was the perfect research subject, someone totally expendable. Or perhaps it was just the severity of his suffering.

A single fetus has a million dopamine-producing cells, but even that wasn't enough: It took a number of fetuses to produce enough cells for a single implantation. Six elective abortions were carefully scheduled to coordinate with George's surgery, the brain cells laboriously extracted from each fetus and delivered to the operating room. Doctors drilled a hole in George's skull, then deposited the fetal material in eight different sites in his brain.

As Dr. Langston watched the operation, he hoped for a cure, not only for George but also for all his other Parkinson's patients.

Langston also hoped that a successful operation would persuade Republicans to lift their funding ban on fetal research.

BIOETHICS, THE STUDY and implementation of what is right and wrong in medical research, was highly political, especially when a fetus was involved. Fetal research had been sanctioned in the late 1970s, but the election of Ronald Reagan in 1980 changed all that.

Beholden to the pro-life community, and himself pro-life, Reagan vowed to preserve life wherever possible. In 1983, Richard Schweiker, head of the Department of Health and Human Services, issued an order making it unlawful for a hospital receiving federal funds to withhold care and feeding from handicapped infants. Hospitals would now be required to post a notice to this effect along with the toll-free "Handicapped Infant Hotline."

The American Academy of Pediatrics immediately challenged the restriction all the way up to the U.S. Supreme Court. Eventually, anti-abortion advocates in Congress collaborated with physician groups. On April 15, 1985, after pro-lifers met with some members of Congress, HHS issued new guidelines that distinguished between treatment that helps an infant remain alive versus treatment that merely prolongs its life.

Upon assuming office, Reagan banned federal funding for any type of research on the fetus, whether dead or alive. In 1985, Congress passed the Health Research Extension Act, imposing a three-year funding moratorium on fetal research. When the ban came up for renewal in 1988, a new group spoke out in favor of the ban. On October 10, 1988, more than 650 prominent physicians, nurses, and academics joined the religious community in urging Reagan to renew the ban, charging that fetal research is a "crass pragmatism which would reduce the human fetus to a research object for the convenience of other human beings and medical experimentation."

The signatories, who included liberal columnist Nat Hentoff of the *Village Voice*, Dr. Joseph D. Murray, the first physician to success-fully transplant a kidney, and Rabbi Samuel J. Fox, president of the Massachusetts Council of Rabbis, went on to quote the cautionary words of the great philosopher Hans Jonas:

> Progress is an optional goal, not an unconditional commitment. Let us remember that slower progress in the conquest of dis-ease would not threaten society, grievous as it is to those who have a particular disease.
>
> But society would indeed be threatened by the erosion of those moral values whose loss, possibly caused by too ruthless a

pursuit of scientific progress, would make its most dazzling triumph not worth having.

The ban was renewed. Nonetheless, in 1988, the National Institutes of
Health continued to fund more than $10 million a year for fetal-tissue
research. How these millions had escaped the funding ban remains
unclear.

But that changed in the fall of 1987 when Ed Oldfield, of the
National Institute of Neurological and Communicative Disorders,
asked his boss, Dr. Irwin Kopin, for permission to transplant fetal tissues into the brains of Parkinson's patients. Because of the volatility of
anything involving the fetus, Kopin bounced the request up to his
own boss, James Wyngaarden, head of NIH, who, in turn, sent it on to
Robert E. Windom, assistant undersecretary of the Department of
HHS. On March 22, 1988, Windom told Wyngaarden that the proposal raised a number of questions—primarily ethical and legal—that
have not been satisfactorily addressed.

"[B]efore making a decision on your proposal," he wrote, "I would
like you to convene one or more special outside advisory committees."

EVER SINCE THE revelations of research abuses in the 1970s, panels,
commissions, councils, and the like became absolutely *de rigeur*—a
shrewd political move to satisfy the public that their concerns were
being carefully addressed—and almost always a way to rubber stamp
the wishes of the party in power. But the 1988 Human Fetal Tissue
Transplantation Panel was most decidedly *not* Republican. Appointed
by the NIH, the twenty-five-member panel was stacked from the start
with members known to favor fetal research. Heading the panel was
the Honorable Arlin Adams, recently retired from the Philadelphia-
based U.S. Court of Appeals in the Third Circuit, a highly respected

jurist who opposed abortion. Adams ultimately proved flexible enough to separate his views on abortion from the use of dead fetuses for research and treatment, bringing respectability to the research.

But, going in, nearly all the panel members were pro-choice and had a track record for approving fetal research. One prominent member was Dr. Kenneth Ryan, chair of the now-defunct National Commission for the Protection of Human Subjects, which in 1975 had given the greenlight to research on living fetuses up to twenty weeks of gestation. Such panels would always include token members who would disagree with the majority but otherwise have no effect. Accordingly, this panel included three religious members, hardly a majority, who were decidedly against any form of fetal research.

Indeed, according to the assistant secretary of Health and Human Services, most of the panelists had indicated that "moral and ethical considerations were *not* central to their view." In other words, most didn't care about ethics. It was unclear why such individuals were called upon to decide key ethical issues.

"The NIH knew what they wanted the committee to say and picked people that agreed with them, and the vote went the way they wanted," a dissenting member complained to the *New York Times*. "It was a sham, not a serious look at the ethical issues."

Whatever the biases of the panel, it soon appeared that their role was merely ceremonial: the White House had already drafted an order banning federally-funded fetal-tissue research. The panel went ahead nonetheless, perhaps believing that its recommendations would influence the administration.

At first, the panel had decided to close its meetings to the public but, after an outcry, opened them up to the public. The first meeting was held on September 14, 1988.

One concern from the religious quarter was that fetal-tissue therapies might encourage abortions, that physicians might subtly influence women to abort their fetuses in the interest of science, or, worse, that some women might intentionally become pregnant in order to create fetal tissue for an ailing family member. Professor Lars Olson, who had traveled from the Karolinska Institute in Sweden, told the panel that fetal transplants did not increase the abortion rate in his country, where one in four pregnancies ended in abortion.

Other experts explained that fetuses of different ages would be needed depending upon the disease being treated. The best age for fetal-neural tissue was between six and eight weeks after fertilization; for fetal thymus tissue, eleven to fourteen weeks; for fetal pancreas implants, ten to twenty weeks. No one on the panel expressed concern about the possible use of a twenty-week-old fetus. Would women be encouraged to delay their abortions well into the second trimester in order to produce thymal tissue?

Most fetal tissue remains alive for only a week or so after the abortion, but it still can take hours for doctors to dissect the necessary cells. If fetal-tissue therapies were approved, would doctors eventually decide to keep a fetus alive while its parts were dissected in order to produce fresh tissue? Abortion was a *fait accompli*—like it or not, *Roe v. Wade* was not going to be overruled any time soon. But abortion was one thing; tailoring it to meet a specific therapeutic end was quite another matter.

"A decisive majority of the panel," the panel observed, "found that it was acceptable public policy to support transplant research with fetal tissue either because the source of the tissue posed no moral dilemma or because the immorality of its source could be ethically isolated from the morality of its use in research."

In other words, most of the panel believed either that there was no problem with abortion or that, regardless of the morality of abortion, the use of fetal tissue was justified. As was nearly always the case with issues relating to the fetuses, it was black or white: nuances, such as the age of the fetus, were not addressed.

To three dissenting panel members, the issue was clear-cut: Any product of abortion, even a dead fetus, was *ipso facto* immoral, no matter what its therapeutic possibilities. James Burtchall, a theologian at Notre Dame, posed an interesting analogy: Suppose a banker accepts deposits from drug dealers because the money would benefit the community. Burtchall believed that the banker would be complicit in the drug sales because his acceptance of the deposits could encourage the illegal behavior. But the other side argued that fetal-tissue implants were like taking organs from a murder victim: Salvaging something from an immoral act did not encourage or excuse it.

According to the Bishops' Committee for Pro-life Activities of the National Conference of Catholic Bishops, "it may not be wrong in principle for someone unconnected with an abortion to make use of a fetal organ from an unborn child who dies as the result of an abortion; but it is difficult to see how this practice can be institutionalized . . . without threatening a morally unacceptable collaboration with the abortion industry."

This was not a new argument. Thirty years before, theologian Paul Ramsey of Princeton University said much the same thing in connection with fetal research in general.

"Today one hears statements like, 'fetal research must be done' or 'it would be immoral not to do this research,'" he wrote.

"[But] there are other moral imperatives beside the 'research imperative.' . . . Suffice it to say that an immediate . . . untroubled, and uncomplicated justification of fetal research is thoughtless— because it assumes something that is questionable in ethics."

The "research imperative," the blind race to find a cure, picked up momentum in the late 1980s, encouraged by patient-advocacy groups. Often heavily funded, these groups were becoming politically sophisticated, hiring lobbyists in Washington D.C. and forging ties to Congress, particularly those members who had been personally affected with the lobbied-for disease. During public hearings before the Fetal Tissue Transplantation Panel, a plethora of such groups made themselves heard, including the Juvenile Diabetes Foundation, a power-house then headed by Carole Lurie, whose thirty-one-year-old son was afflicted with the disease. Not to be outdone, others likewise joined in: the American Paralysis Association, the American Diabetes Association, the Huntington's Disease Society of America, the United Parkinson Foundation, and the National Spinal Cord Injury Association. Though tame by today's standards, these organizations made clear that any vote in favor of the religious views was a vote against "the cure."

More subtly, these groups advanced what had long been a pri-mary goal of many of the medical research community: to be free of regulation. Historically, the consequences of such latitude were disas-trous: Without regulation, researchers had repeatedly abused human subjects, not only in well-publicized cases like the Tuskegee tragedy, but also more quietly on live fetuses, prisoners, people in the devel-oping world, the mentally ill, and a host of other "helpless" or dis-abled subjects. But memory was short; once again it was laissez faire for science.

"[I]t is terribly important," said a spokesperson for the spinal cord group, "that we . . . look at the entire issue of scientific and intellectual freedom. . . . There are researchers . . . I know of in my work with spinal-cord injury around the country who are doing science that I flat out don't understand. . . .

"But it is important work that they are doing, and it is controlled by ethical guidelines that are established by *scientists themselves*. I think that that is the appropriate forum, not a political forum" (emphasis added).

Beginning with the Mondale hearings in the late 1960s, researchers had made clear that they wanted freedom from the political process and from a scientifically illiterate public and Congress. In one respect, these scientists were correct: A scientifically illiterate public is in no position to pass judgment on medical procedures beyond the understanding of a layperson. But this argument forgets that Congress routinely regulates equally complicated sectors of the economy that most of the public doesn't understand, that Congressional committees and subcommittees hold hearings on the most intricate issues affecting the public and go on to pass restrictions and rules. The advantage of public hearings is that the media and interested members of the public can attend the hearings and bring their knowledge to the general public. There is no reason why the research sector should claim exemption from public scrutiny; yet, they would continue to do so.

Whatever the outcries from the patient advocacy groups, the research community was hardly starved from funds. No matter who sat in the White House, the NIH budget grew far more than the economy. In the 1940s, the federal government gave a mere $700,000; by 1955, it was $98 million; in the 1960s, it was $1.4 billion; by 2005, it was nearly $30 billion. Even adjusting for inflation, the growth was staggering—and not subject to political whim.

In theory, the allocation of research money should be fair, based on objective, non-political criteria, including the number of deaths from a particular disease, the severity of the disease, the number of Americans afflicted with the disease, and other criteria. There is no reason why one disease should receive funding priority at the expense of others that are equally lethal. But by the 1980s, NIH funding was fast becoming an *entitlement,* something the government owed the afflicted, especially the well-heeled and politically favored who increasingly demanded instant results. While basic medical research often yields the best results for all concerned, its fruits may not appear for decades and, hence, can be politically irrelevant. Each advocacy group demanded an increasingly larger slice of the research pie for their own disease—no matter what the needs of Americans. Congress, too, had its own agenda. As James Fallows wrote in the *New Yorker,* "[F]unding patterns for the NIH over the decades show that politicians frequently support additional investments on a particular disease after a grandchild or spouse has contracted it."

In 1970, President Richard Nixon declared "war" on cancer, one of the leading causes of death in the country, then and now. As though a mere declaration of war ensures victory, some researchers promised that the disease would be cured "by 1976," in time for the country's bicentennial. Although a cure for cancer has yet to materialize thirty years later, the concept of declaring "war" on disease gained currency in the ensuing decades, reflecting the apparent, but erroneous, belief that any disease could be cured with enough money and resolve. NIH funding became highly politicized as each disease gained its own political base. In the 1980s, breast cancer was all the rage; in the 1990s, it was AIDS, which went on to become the best-funded disease in history. HIV research received $1,069 per afflicted individual, compared to $93 per patient for heart research and $26 per patient for Parkinson's research. Perhaps the stepped-up funding was appropriate to attack what appeared to be an epidemic; certainly, a great deal of progress was made in the treatment of the disease. Still, other fatal diseases affecting larger numbers of Americans were neglected in favor of "celebrity" diseases, generally whatever disease affected the most visible and wealthy Americans, particularly Hollywood stars.

With NIH funding no longer discretionary, the funding ban on fetal-tissue research was characterized as a "death sentence" for millions of Americans afflicted with a range of diseases. Because funding was now seen as a right, not a privilege, the government was obligated to fund research on each and every celebrity disease—no matter what the moral objections of some and no matter how remote the cure. The ban was, like other "restrictions" on science, also characterized as placing the country at a competitive disadvantage in the world, a variation on the Sputnik paranoia of the late 1950s.

"European and, to a lesser extent, Japanese scientists have begun to surpass their American counterparts," wrote Leon Jaroff in a *Time* cover story in 1991.

Though there was never any evidence of this claim, the fib became larger with each telling. Writing about a conference held in Pittsburgh in the summer of 1992, *Scientific American* reported that "workers" (a rather strange, communistic description of highly educated medical researchers) from China, Japan, Russia, Hungary, Singapore, Sweden, and Yugoslavia "put Americans to shame."

"The paucity of reports by U.S. scientists was mute testimony to the effects of a 1988 federal moratorium on funding for studies on fetal cell transplantation," the writer proclaimed.

Increasingly, religion was blamed as blocking medical progress, literally "killing" millions of Americans.

"Spinal-cord injury, Parkinson's disease, and diabetes cripple and kill millions of Americans," said Democratic congressman Henry Waxman.

"Breakthroughs are now being found. But the [George H.W.] Bush administration has ordered the National Institutes of Health to ignore them—not because of concern about their scientific merit but because of misplaced allegiances to the most extreme elements of the anti-abortion movement."

During hearings convened by Waxman, Harvard Medical School's Dr. Kenneth J. Ryan, a member of the Fetal Tissue Transplanation Panel and long-time advocate of fetal research, testified that the "ban" (actually a funding ban) "impedes progress toward ameliorating and perhaps curing chronic debilitating diseases such as Parkinsonism and Diabetes and thwarts hope of the progress for Alzheimer's and even Acquired Immune Deficiency [AIDS]." The policy, he charged, "creates a 'siege state of mind' and a sense of 'government repression.'"

Another tactic soon became popular: to claim the cost-effectiveness of a cure. With little supporting data, it was claimed that the disease in question—be it diabetes, spinal cord injury, Parkinson's—costs the country $10 billion a year, $20 billion a year, $30 billion a year, or some other number plucked out of thin air. Thus, a "mere" expenditure of $10 million a year for diabetes research would save the American economy "$20 billion each year," said J. Richard Munro, then-CEO and co-chairman of Time Warner Inc. and president of the Juvenile Diabetes Foundation. He went on to attack the religious:

> JDF and the nation's diabetic population look to transplantation research as an important step towards discovering a cure for diabetes. Such a therapy could ameliorate not only the most severe form of diabetes, but would reduce the incidence of the numerous acute and chronic end-stage renal disease, heart disease, and amputations.
>
> JDF pleads that Congress resist falling prey to the cries of the anti-abortion movement. . . .

Patient groups learned to invoke public sympathy, often exploiting parents and children as a ploy for increased funds. Representatives of the Epilepsy Foundation of America spoke of small children who endured as many as 150 seizures a day—as though these seizures would immediately stop if the funding ban were lifted.

"What keeps us going is hope," said the mother of an epileptic child, "the hope that one day a new drug or a new surgical procedure will be developed which will stop the seizures. The hope that one day Jeremy, and all the other children like him, will be able to go out to play without their parents having to worry that he will be seriously injured when a seizure occurs or that one day he will have a seizure which cannot be stopped."

No matter how unlikely it was that fetal-tissue research could produce the "cure," the government and the religious were characterized as evil forces directly responsible for the death of millions, if not the disease itself.

Bioethicist John Fletcher accused the federal government of "moral recklessness."

The *Washington Post* charged that the ban on fetal-tissue research had turned Parkinson's disease into "a political hostage."

The American Medical Association and thirty-two other research organizations charged that the ban ignores the "suffering of millions of Americans."

The Juvenile Diabetes Foundation said the country has a "responsibility to use tissue which embodies the promise of a cure for some of the most dreaded diseases of our times."

The American Paralysis Association asserted that "the ban in essence abrogates the rights of the living."

With hope for a cure for Alzheimer's and Huntington's diseases, Dr. Stanley Fahn of Columbia University Physicians and Surgeons in New York City charged that "the administration's position is greatly hindering progress toward treatments that could relieve enormous suffering."

Some years before, Nobel Laureate Joshua Lederberg had chillingly summed up the "research imperative" as an inviolable obligation that, if broken, was morally on par with murder. He told Hastings Center cofounder Daniel Callahan that "[t]he blood of those who

215

will die if biomedical research is not pursued will be upon those who don't do it."

WHEN BILL CLINTON assumed office in 1993, he immediately lifted the ban, announcing that science would no longer be "shackled" by politics.

Fetal-tissue transplantation was still the rage. George Carillo was the walking—literally—testament to the therapy's success, his once-frozen body released from its prison. In 1992, a front-page story in the *New York Times* hailed Carillo's recovery as the "first unequivocal evidence that fetal cells can do the work of brain cells that have died."

The *New York Times* went on to report that Carillo, now fifty-two, was moving "independently" and "almost normally." "Mr. Carillo even rode a bicycle," the *Times* reported. "Brain scans showed that the fetal cells were producing chemicals that the patients' brains had lacked."

Dr. Eugene Redmond Jr. of Yale and Dr. Curt R. Freed of the University of Colorado had achieved similar success after they implanted fetal tissue into the brains of ten Parkinson's patients. "Patients did better in tests like touching a thumb and forefinger together and tapping their feet," the *New York Times* reported. "They were less likely to freeze, unable to move, and had smoother movements in general." The article and others predicted similar results for an ever-growing litany of diseases, including diabetes, Alzheimer's, and spinal cord injury.

"It's spectacular," one neurologist remarked.

According to the *New York Times*, fetal-tissue implants might even cure spinal cord injury. "The most exciting developments are still highly experimental, involving the transplantation of fetal nerve tissue to fill in the gap in the spinal cord or bypass the injury site."

A 1992 article in the journal *Geriatrics* reported the views of three prominent researchers. Nobel Laureate Dr. Paul Berg of Stanford University spoke of transplanting fetal-beta islet cells into the pancreas of adult patients to treat diabetes. Dr. Luc Mantagnier, a professor at the Pasteur Institute in Paris, said the cells could be of "therapeutic use for older people." Dr. Georgiana Jagiello of Columbia University said fetal-tissue research could advance an understanding of cancer.

But in order to cure all these diseases, and save all those lives, something would have to budge. That something was religion which then was literally killing many Americans. In 1992, *Time* reported that Elliot Osserman, a cancer researcher, would have been cured of his Parkinson's disease but for religious conservatives. Fetal-tissue implantation was Osserman's "last hope;" but by the time he was accepted into a program at Yale, "all federally supported research involving the transplant of tissue from aborted fetuses into humans was halted." Osserman died a few months later.

"He may have been the first victim of the moratorium," declared Dr. Eugene Redmond, who headed the Yale team.

"He might not be the last," warned *Time* reporter Dick Thompson Washington.

WITH ALL THE hype, all the promise, all the raised expectations, there was an insurmountable problem with fetal-tissue implants: They didn't work.

The "miracle cure" was heralded on the front pages of the *New York Times* and other major media outlets, but the peer-reviewed studies themselves told quite a different story. Remarkably, reporters who hailed the cure read the press releases, but never the underlying data. The public got whatever spin the research community cared to put on a study and nothing more, not even a single dose of skepticism.

In fact, according to a series of papers published in the *New England Journal of Medicine* on November 26, 1992, fetal-tissue implants did not produce the "unequivocal" *success* touted by the media, but unequivocal *failure*. Parkinson's patients over the age of sixty—nearly all of the patient population—showed no improvement whatsoever from fetal-tissue implants. The only patients who benefited were the handful of patients who, like George Carillo, had acquired the disease from tainted heroin that had long since been taken off the streets.

One of the *New England Journal of Medicine* pieces, authored by Dr. Langston and the Swedish team who had performed Carillo's surgery, glowingly reported on Carillo (though not by name): "By 24 months after surgery, muscular rigidity had virtually disappeared. His gait was smooth. . . ." A second patient who had also acquired Parkinson's from tainted heroin was presented as yet another source of optimism. "Twenty-two months after surgery, the patient's gait pattern was nearly normal and she could readily manage tasks requiring fine motor skills."

Although the results seemed encouraging on the surface, they were limited to the few who had acquired the disease from the tainted heroin. These results alone, statistically inconsequential and never measured against a control group, did not belong on the front pages of America's newspapers.

In another *New England Journal of Medicine* article, Dr. Eugene Redmond Jr. and his team reported on their controlled study of four patients who had been injected with fetal-neural cells. Over a period of eighteen months, three patients (a fourth died from an unrelated cause) showed "bilateral improvement on motor tasks" and could resume some daily activities—even without L-dopa.

But the control group *also* improved in many categories, suggesting that the surgery itself, and not the fetal implantation, may have produced the encouraging results. Motor skills improved "more among the case patients after surgery than among the controls, *but the difference was not significantly different,*" the team reported (emphasis added).

In 1992, the same year the front pages sang of the cure that would save millions of Americans, Dr. Robert J. White, a professor of surgery at Case Western Reserve University, wrote an opinion piece in the *New York Times* warning that "results obtained so far on the nearly 1,000 patients who have received transplants throughout the world, [show that] *there are no cures* and minimal evidence of sustained improvements among those with Parkinsonism" (emphasis added).

Dr. Curt Freed, who performed sixty-one fetal-tissue implants, found that patients did no better from fetal-tissue implants than they did on L-dopa and that "older folks were not good responders." Dr. Langston, George Carillo's doctor, eventually found the therapy to be of no use at all.

In 2001, published studies proved what should have been evident from the outset. Reporting on a study of forty patients, the National Institute of Neurological Disorders and Stroke published its own findings in the *New England Journal of Medicine.* The institute was the first to use "double blind" controls in which neither patient nor researcher knew what was being injected into the brain. The study found *no* difference between the two groups. Even more troubling, in about 15 percent of patients, the cells grew *too* well, producing chemicals that made patients even *worse* than before.

"*Ad hoc* reports of spectacular results can always occur," said one of the researchers. "But if you do these studies systematically, this is the result you get."

"The bottom line for patients is that human fetal cell transplants are not currently the best way to go," Dr. Paul E. Greene, a neurologist at the Columbia University College of Physicians and Surgeons, said in 2001. "If you are willing to pay for them, you can still have them done. But my advice is you ought not to do this."

With expectations at a feverish pitch for so many years, why had it taken so long to produce a scientifically controlled study of fetal-tissue implants? Some researchers blame the Republicans: With more funding, the failure of fetal-tissue implantation would have been noticed earlier.

Be that as it may, the media, which should have scoured the medical journals, served as unwitting publicists for the medical research community, helping to pressure Congress to override the funding restriction. No one seemed to care about the false hopes they had instilled in desperate patients and their families who clung to every report of a miracle cure.

Much to its credit, the *New York Times* finally ran a front-page story announcing the failure of fetal implants. But the rest of the media—those who had trashed religion for "murdering" millions of Americans—didn't bother correcting the record. Perhaps it was oversight; perhaps it was more important to vilify people of faith, to perpetuate the stereotype of science at the mercy of religion.

In any event, it was clear that no one was holding medical researchers accountable for their extravagant claims that they could cure "dozens of diseases" if only the religious would go away. The medical-research community could promise whatever it wanted without consequence of any kind. Millions of Americans afflicted with Parkinson's, diabetes, spinal cord injury, and many other diseases had been promised a cure that never came about, but their dashed hopes never quite found their way into the evening news or the front pages of the *New York Times*.

But soon the failure of fetal-tissue therapy was forgotten, shortly after the research community announced the next "miracle cure."

12

FIRST DO NO HARM

Jesse Gelsinger, eighteen, was one of the very few who had made it this far in life. He had a rare genetic disease called ornithine transcarbamylase (OTC) deficiency, a disorder in which the liver lacks the enzymes that rid the body of ammonia. Because the chemical accumulates in the blood and travels to the brain, most of those born with the disease do not survive for long. Within seventy-two hours of birth, most newborns slip into a coma. Half die in the first month, half by age five. Jesse, whose disease was managed by medication—thirty-two pills a day—and a low-protein diet, was among the few who survived into their teens. In 1998, Jesse was in relatively good health.

He learned about promising research on gene therapy that soon would go into human trials at the University of Pennsylvania.

BY THE 1990s, genes were big business. Biotechnology firms held patents on genes, animal and human, and exclusive marketing rights on resulting therapies. Times had changed since the days of Dr. Jonas Salk, the great researcher who declined to patent the polio vaccine. Scientists had moved out of the labs and into the marketplace, setting up their own companies which enabled them to commercialize on their research successes. Pressured by the profit motive, these researchers understood that they had to move human trials along as quickly as possible in order to get the treatment into the marketplace where their work would finally bear financial fruit.

In 1980, the U.S. Supreme Court had handed the still-nascent biotechnology community a big bonanza. In a controversial five-four decision, the Court held that a researcher could patent a biologically altered bacterium designed to absorb oil spills. While life itself could not then be patented, the Court held that a patent was appropriate on an organism that had been altered by human intervention.

Big money was at stake. "Whether the University has the right to patent its own manufactured micro-organisms will depend directly on the disposition that is made on this case," the University of California wrote in an amicus friend-of-the court brief.

Other groups, such as the American Society of Biological Sciences and the Pharmaceutical Manufacturers Association, outright admitted that their private funding was at stake. "Some of the *Amici* receive contract funds from commercial corporations whose future funding . . . is certain to be influenced by this Court's decision. All of the individual *Amici* receive or plan to receive indirect funding from royalties. . . ."

The central question was whether life itself, however altered, is subject to "ownership," a question that, although not characterized as such, touched upon religion: If God is the creator of life, then how can it be owned?* In the Supreme Court, the "religious" view of life was represented not by any religious group but by leftwing environmental activist Jeremy Rifkin, founder of the Peoples Business Commission (later renamed the Foundation for Economic Trends), who later would form alliances with religious groups to battle the biotech forces.

---

*A patent holder does not technically "own" his product but can control its use for a designated period of years. During the period in which the patent is in force, the patent holder can license out the patent at whatever royalty rate the market allows.

Although the patenting of human life was outside the scope of that case, Rifkin made clear his objection to the scientific view of life that reduced mankind to no more than a repository of "selfish genes."

"Reproduction is analyzed in terms of the interaction of chemical units contained in the sperm and egg," the Peoples Business Commission argued. "[T]he brain is mapped and manipulated . . . to 'explain' how thought processes work; sociobiologists reduce human emotions like love and altruism to an ill-defined genetic base. . . ."

The emerging biotech community applauded the Court's decision in favor of patenting the organism. "The Court has assured this country's technology future," announced one of the first biotech firms, Genentech, whose stock went through the roof within hours of the Court's decision.

In the years that followed, the U.S. Patent and Trademark Office (PTO) gradually enlarged the scope of that ruling, gradually conferring patent protection on higher and higher forms of life that had been genetically engineered. There was little public notice of this trend until 1987 when Congressman Robert W. Kastenmeier held hearings on the patentability of life. In 1989, the House of Representatives passed a bill that would have prohibited the patenting of human beings. But the bill went nowhere. Through the 1990s and into the new millennium, the PTO has granted patents on life itself, not just life that had been altered, such as genetically engineered animals, but also naturally occurring components of human beings, such as genes and cells. "Living things are patent eligible," Karen Hauda of the PTO told the President's Council on Bioethics in 2002. "[A] cell culture of human skin cells . . . may be . . . eligible for patenting. . . . [L]aboratory process or methods of making human cells and culturing cells are eligible for patenting. . . . [C]loning is eligible for patenting. . . ."

Thus, a researcher who "discovered" a particular human gene was now able to patent that gene as though it were something he himself had invented. To some, this meant that human life had become completely objectified, that it could be bought and sold like so many nuggets of gold.

On May 18, 1995, two hundred religious leaders representing eighty different faiths—Jews, Buddhists, Hindus, and Muslims, as well as different Christian denominations—gathered in Washington D.C. to call for a moratorium on the patenting of human and animal genes. "We believe that humans and animals are creations of God, not humans, and as such should not be patented."

In a speech delivered at the Pontifical Academy of Sciences in 1994, Pope John Paul II hailed the progress of genetic research, while also cautioning against gene patenting. "We rejoice that numerous researchers have refused to allow discoveries made about the genome to be patented," he said. But he went on to state: "Since the human body is not an object that can be disposed of at will, the results should be made available to the whole scientific community and cannot be the property of a small group."

Some scientists likewise argued that genes should not be the property of any one researcher, but must, in the interest of science, be available to all researchers. Nobel Laureate James Watson, famous for the "double helix," quit the Human Genome Project to protest an NIH patent application on 315 DNA fragments. Patenting genetic material was "sheer lunacy" that would "entangle genetic research in legal issues and slow it to a crawl."

"I think it would be a total mess for industry," he told the *New York Times.*

Scientists around the world feared that the patenting of human life would create a land rush in which companies, universities, and governments competed to lay claim to human parts and take them out of the public domain. In January 2001, the European Patent Office issued Myriad Genetics, a U.S. biotech company, a patent on

BRCA1, one of the two genes responsible for hereditary breast cancer. In 2004, the company secured a European patent on the BRCA2, the other gene. Any European researcher who used Myriad's proprietary gene was suddenly presented with a $2,500 bill. Other gene patent holders were, according to the *British Medical Journal*, demanding up front payments as high as $25,000 per laboratory plus a fee of $20 per test.

"It's a quick and dirty land grab, and it's not very innovative," said Jan Witkowski, director of the Banbury Center at the Cold Spring Harbor in Long Island, home of James Watson and other Nobel laureates.

"The problem is that you don't know what these things do. It's like laying claim to the wheel and then claiming everything that has a wheel in it."

"This is not science," said George Annas, a bioethicist at Boston University. "This is like the Gold Rush."

In 1998, J. Craig Venter left his post as head of the NIH Genome Mapping Research Team to set up his own company, Celera Genomics, which had attracted $70 million in capital and would compete with the public Genome Mapping project. Almost immediately, Venter's company applied for six thousand patents on human genes. Already held in professional disdain for his blatant pursuit of wealth, Venter was rebuked by his colleagues in the research community. He later withdrew some of these applications, but Celera's revenues reportedly doubled every year since its formation. When in 2000 President Bill Clinton and Prime Minister Tony Blair called on researchers to make their work available free of charge, biotech stocks plunged.

In the following years, biotechnology companies raced to secure patent protection on still more human genes, always arguing that they were advancing the "cure" of one disease or another and that they could only do so if allowed to make a profit. Actually the reverse was more likely: if only one researcher held a patent on a gene, then research costs would be higher than if the gene remained in the public domain.

In its quest to own human life, researchers often exploited the poor, developing world, where oversight was lax and opportunity great. In 1993, an NIH researcher took a blood sample from a twenty-six-year-old Guaymi Indian woman in Panama and applied for U.S. patents on her genes. When the issue came to the attention of the public, the NIH researcher argued that the Guaymi Indians have a rare gene that stimulates the production of antibodies and could possibly lead to a cure for AIDS. After public outcry from the Indian tribe, the U.S. patent office declined to issue the patent.

Just two years after the Guaymi fiasco, the NIH sought patents on genes from the Hagahai tribe of Papua, New Guinea. "U.S. Slaps Patent on Tribesman's DNA," read a headline in Britain's *Independent*.

In 1996, a nonprofit group in India learned that the NIH had illegally secured DNA and blood samples from patients in an Indian eye hospital without proper authorization. Researchers justified the raid as a search for genes that cause night blindness. But Indian law forbade the export of biological material without permission.

Bad policies produce absurd results. Though a researcher could lay claim to a human gene, the individual carrying the genes did not own it and—*Roe v. Wade* notwithstanding—had no right to decide its fate. In 1984, John Moore, an Alaskan businessman diagnosed with a rare cancer, sued the University of California after discovering that his body parts had been patented and licensed to Sandoz Pharmaceutical Corporation. He had not consented to the patenting of his gene, valued at about $3 billion, and would receive no share of the profits. In 1990, the California Supreme Court ruled against Moore, finding he had no rights to his own body, though others did.

The patenting of human genes was condemned by a broad array

of groups, not just the religious. After learning of Myriad Genetics' patent on the breast cancer genes, biotech foe Jeremy Rifkin of the Foundation for Economic Trends organized a coalition of women's groups from more than forty countries. The breast cancer-causing genes are products of nature, they argued, not human invention and as such should not be patented. Such a patent would impede much-needed research into breast cancer. Eventually, the company dropped its claims.

Countries outside the United States continued to fight the patenting of life. In 2004, Harvard University sued Canada because that country denied its application for a patent on a genetically altered mouse. In a 5-4 decision, the Supreme Court of Canada held that higher life forms cannot be patented. U.S. patents on living organisms were often not honored in other countries.

Because of the gargantuan profits at stake, the profit motive overrode the integrity of science itself. Claims of the next "miracle cure," however tenuous, upped a company's visibility in the financial markets and increased pressure for NIH funding and private investment. Companies "gain obvious credibility in their attempts to raise money," remarked Dr. Harold Varmus, head of the NIH, in 1995. "It helps in raising capital to say they actually have something in progress."

Often it was irrelevant to investors whether a cure ever arrived; what mattered was the hype that inflated stock prices. "[F]rom a purely business standpoint, most are interested in selling out," said Dr. Stuart Orkin, a molecular biologist at Children's Hospital in Boston and a co-chairman of a panel appointed by Varmus.

"They want to be bought or taken over. Whether they deliver a product is not germane."

During the biotech boom of the 1990s, biotech companies were bought and sold in the blink of an eye producing millions of dollars for their founders. Genetic Therapy, a biotech firm, had been involved in clinical trials of a gene therapy for glioblastroma, a deadly brain cancer. Although the results had been discouraging, in 1995, Sandoz bought up the company for $295 million.

By trumpeting each promised "cure," the media helped pump up biotech stocks. In 1998, after a front-page story in the *New York Times* announced a technique for killing cancer tumors, a company's stock price shot up. "When announcements like this are made," said one reporter, "if you dig a little deeper you find a biotech company in need of capital."

Perception was more important than reality: the *promise* of a cure was all that mattered. "Printing 'cancer cure' on the front page of a major newspaper is like shouting 'fire' in a crowded theater," observed another reporter.

Entangled with commercial interests, their own or their investors', researchers found themselves under unrelenting pressure to produce results as quickly as possible: halting clinical trials could send a company's stock spiraling.

In 1999, Bristol-Meyers Squibb announced that its partner, Entremac, discovered that a cancer-fighting drug should not be used in human trials. Entremac's stock went down by 50 percent. But after the National Cancer Institute successfully replicated the company's work—and the *New York Times* reported it—stock prices shot up by 60 percent.

Lost again in all this frenzy were the suffering patients and their families, those who clung to each announcement of an imminent cure and begged their doctors for anything to help. The newly afflicted believed in these fairy tales, while the more experienced perceived a pattern.

"My father died of cancer in 1963. A cancer cure was 'just around the corner,'" one man wrote in a letter to *Time* in 1998. "My mother died of cancer in 1972. A cancer cure was 'just around the corner.'

"Today, after billions of dollars spent on cancer research, the cure is still 'just around the corner.'"

IN THE 1980S, gene-transfer therapy was hailed as the new "revolutionary treatment." On October 4, 1988, an NIH advisory committee recommended that gene transfer proceed in ten trials of human volunteers in the late stages of cancer. In 1990, the Food and Drug Administration received two proposals: one would treat children suffering from an immune-deficiency disorder by injecting the correct gene; the other would insert a gene in cancerous patients that would produce a tumor-fighting enzyme. Caught up in the frenzy, the media proclaimed that this new miracle cure—gene therapy— would wipe out multiple sclerosis, cystic fibrosis, cancer, AIDS, and a "broad array of human ailments." In 1989, Harvard geneticist Philip Leder added allergies, diabetes, heart disease, and "many forms of cancer" to the ever-expanding list.

"The results," *Time* predicted in 1990, "could be little short of miraculous."

In a piece published in the journal *Nature*, researchers reported that they had successfully inserted mice with the correct gene for muscular dystrophy. The head of the Muscular Dystrophy Association was delighted, evidently unaware of decade-old evidence that results in animals are not always replicated in humans.

"If you can do it in an animal model," he said, "there is every reason to believe that you can do it in humans because the technology transfers across species."

In 1991, NIH researchers reported successful results on two girls with immune-deficiency disease, often called their "bubble boy" syndrome because earlier victims had to live in a plastic bubble to protect them from germs. In the world's first approved gene-therapy trial, the girls, age seven and twelve, were injected with normal cells. In May 1991, their immune systems restored, they appeared at a press conference to assume their honorary posts as "research ambassadors" for the March of Dimes. (A little more than a decade later, other "bubble boy" afflicted children treated with gene therapy developed cancer, thus trading one disease for another.)

By 1995, six hundred Americans were involved in one hundred trials of gene therapy, but there were still no published peer-reviewed reports (as opposed to anecdotal reports) of a human who had actually been cured.

Some scientists viewed the whole undertaking with deep suspicion. A 1995 report commissioned by NIH head Harold Varmus chided investigators for creating "the mistaken and widespread perception of success." Varmus was wary of the therapy because he thought the science was too "shoddy" to go into human trials. He particularly detested the biotech firms who touted approvals in the business pages. But still the work forged ahead, most of it funded by biotech firms.

All along there were questions about the safety of "vectors" used to deliver the gene to the correct location. Some vectors used viruses, some bacteria, some synthetic substances. No one was certain that the microbes couldn't infect the patient. In 1993, a trial of a cystic fibrosis gene therapy had to be shut down when a patient was hospitalized with inflamed lungs caused by a viral vector.

But James Wilson, head of the University of Pennsylvania's Institute for Human Gene Therapy, was confident that the adenovirus—an attenuated cold virus—was a safe way of delivering the healthy gene. He was also grateful that his work was funded by the Cystic Fibrosis Foundation and the NIH so he wouldn't be hounded by greedy investors who wanted to rush the cure to market.

After Wilson claimed success on rhesus monkeys and baboons, he asked the NIH Recombinant DNA Advisory Board for permission to proceed into Phase I trials with humans, the first stage of testing which is limited to a small group of patients. Upon learning that three monkeys had died from Wilson's adenovirus, one member recommended that the proposal be rejected. But because that committee was being dismantled by Varmus, Wilson was able to push the proposal through.

Because the treatment was designed for babies, Wilson sought permission to conduct trials on babies themselves, who, without the treatment, would likely die anyway in a matter of months. But NIH-resident bioethicist Arthur Caplan decreed that parents cannot give consent for the experimental therapy on behalf of their children. Wilson could test the therapy only on "stable adults."

JESSE GELSINGER'S FATHER wouldn't give permission for his son to enter Wilson's clinical trials. So Jesse waited until his eighteenth birthday, on June 18, 1999, before volunteering himself. Jesse didn't expect any personal benefit from the research—Wilson's "cure," if any, would work only on infants. Jesse just wanted to "save the babies." He was assured he could do so without any risk to himself.

Before Jesse received his first injection, seventeen patients had already been given varying doses of the gene and vector. Jesse, who received his first injection on September 13, 1998, got the highest dose.

That night, Jesse had a fever of 104.5 degrees. Within twenty-four hours of treatment, he was in a coma. The doctors began dialysis. His ammonia levels were more than a hundred times greater than normal. The hospital looked for a liver donor, but Jesse wasn't eligible. Five days after treatment, the young man was brain dead. Life support was removed, and he died.

Wilson immediately reported the death to the NIH—privately, at first (he was later criticized for not holding a press conference). An examination of the clinical trials revealed no human error; no one had messed up. The problem, it was soon learned, was the trial itself. It should never have gone forward to begin with, not for Jesse, not for anyone.

The Food and Drug Administration found that Jesse should not have been accepted for the trial because he had an elevated level of ammonia in his blood, an indication of a distressed liver. And, the FDA found, Jesse had not given informed consent because he was never told about the risks.

The FDA also found that the researchers had failed to report that two other patients suffered liver damage from the therapy, a disclosure that would have brought the trials to a halt. They cut corners in other vital areas, as well: Wilson and his team had not monitored subjects' IL-6 levels, a measure of inflammation in the lungs. Wilson later admitted that had he been aware of the increased IL-6 levels, he would have stopped the trials immediately.

The "common rule," a collection of rules from the various agencies that oversee human trials, requires that a research subject be told of all the risks and benefits involved in a trial, an overarching principle of the 1979 Belmont Report, itself released on the heels of Tuskegee and other abuses of human subjects. Paul Gelsinger, Jesse's father, believed that gene therapy was actually a cure and said that his son had never been informed of the risks.

"Consent forms . . . over-promise," said LeRoy Walters, a famed bioethicist and professor at Georgetown University. "They make Phase One studies sound like the cure for your cancer."

More troubling still for medical research overall, Wilson later concluded that animal trials are not reliable in predicting adverse reactions and that scientists should spend more time in their labs before testing gene therapies on humans.

An FDA investigation of Wilson's clinical trials revealed that out of 691 "adverse" events—that is, complications requiring clinical trials to stop—652 had *not* been reported.

If Wilson and his team, the stars of medical research, had cut corners, what did this say about the current state of medical research, driven as it now was by money-hungry investors eager for their stock to triple a single day or sell their companies at twice their worth?

Wilson seemed purer than others—his funding came from NIH and the Cystic Fibrosis Foundation, not from money-grubbing investors. But, as the *Washington Post* reported, he did in fact have a financial stake in the outcome of the trials: his 30 percent ownership in Genovo, the biotechnology firm he founded. Because it takes years for a therapy to go to market, Wilson said he would have received no immediate financial benefit from the treatment. Still, armed with successful clinical trials, the value of his company would have immediately risen. With millions at stake, could he really be trusted to cover every base?

Ruth Macklin, a bioethicist at the NIH advisory committee, agreed that gene therapy was suspect because "large numbers of researchers themselves have a financial stake."

"More and more, clinical investigation in gene therapy is being done by those with equity interests, severely stressing their clinical judgment," said Alan Schechter of NIH. "Gene therapy has many of the worst examples of clinical research that exist."

Nobel Laureate David Baltimore, president of the California Institute of Technology, said researchers had "lost their innocence with the emergence of biotechnology."

The University of Pennsylvania was forced to pay $517,000 to the U.S. Justice Department for lying to the FDA, and another $1 million to settle a lawsuit. In 2000, the FDA permanently barred Wilson from conducting any research on humans; in 2002, he stepped down as head of the center.

But even as Wilson and his team were being punished, the university's own Center for Bioethics was receiving funding from Pfizer, DuPont, Celera, Monsanto, and other biotech firms. Without this funding, perhaps the Center, which allowed Wilson's trials to proceed, might have been more protective of human life, but now the advisors were fast becoming as commercialized as the researchers. Who was looking out for human subjects? After intensive study, the FDA passed stringent rules designed to lift "the cloak of secrecy" from gene therapy and other experimental procedures. The agency would now release to the public detailed information on the safety and progress of clinical trials along with copies of participants' consent forms.

Even in the aftermath of Gelsinger's death, biotech companies battled against further regulation. Their trade group, the Biotechnology Industry Organization, argued that the regulations were harmful to the "fledging field of genetic medicine" and went on—quite remarkably, in light of the Gelsinger tragedy—to say they were "unnecessary for patients." The organization's president, Carl Feldbaum, said that full disclosure would "unnecessarily frighten" prospective patients by giving them "too much information."

"We believe that the release of raw data to the public in real-time," read a statement issued by the Seattle-based company Targeted Genetics, which had just bought out Wilson's company, "will hinder rather than enhance public understanding of the potential benefits and risks of participating in gene transfer trials."

After Jesse's death, gene therapy came to an immediate halt. Who would want to invest in a therapy that had been publicly disgraced? In addition to the young man's death, there was another tragedy: Gene therapy, which cost the NIH $4 billion, might indeed have been as promising as it sounded at first; it might have cured many diseases and done so with the blessing of the religious community. But the rush and carelessness curtailed further study.

Despite the tragic outcome of gene therapy, Wilson landed on his feet—at least financially—earning a hefty $13.5 million when he sold his Genovo stock in 2000. The University of Pennsylvania, which also owned some shares, received more than a million dollars.

"He didn't have to die," Paul Gelsinger said. "My kid is dead so they could make billions more."

WILSON WAS HARDLY the only researcher conducting sloppy human trials. He was just the one who got caught.

In 1999, the NIH placed restrictions on Duke University for a series of infractions. Jane Henney, commissioner of the Food and Drug Administration, reported that "some researchers at prestigious institutions have failed to follow good clinical practices" and went on from there to list conflict-of-interest as one of the main causes of research sloppiness.

Inevitably, those human subjects who suffered the most from the rush to find a cure were those who had no voice or political power. According to an article in the *New England Journal of Medicine*, during the 1990s, pregnant women in Africa were used in trials for an experimental AIDS drug. It was not clear what the subjects were told, but it was evident they were involved in research that could not be done in the United States.

According to one study, private industry was spending $26 billion annually on medical research compared to $15 billion by NIH on clinical trials conducted between 1990 and 2000. Based on data obtained through the Freedom of Information Act, Adil E. Shamoo of the University of Maryland School of Medicine examined *reported* problems with clinical trials. Between 1990 and 1999, the number of reported problems had soared, rising 1,000 percent from 1990 to 1999—just as biotech was booming. For every adverse event actually reported, there were likely ten others that went undisclosed. If the best research centers weren't reporting problems, it's highly likely that there were legions of other unreported problems from lesser researchers.

WITH THE REVELATIONS that flowed from the Gelsinger death, the media was up in arms about the biotech industry, overlooking its own complicity in hyping the miracle cure and raising public expectations.

"The disclosure of worse-than-shoddy research practices . . . sends a cold shiver through the field," the *Washington Post* editorialized. "Critics have long expressed concern (which we share) that gene therapy research is vulnerable to abuse because it is mostly backed by venture capital. Researchers who are also investors . . . may be tempted to oversell the promise of experiments and keep 'adverse events' quiet lest they depress stock prices."

An investigation by *USA Today* revealed that 30 out of 171 federally-funded scientists had been issued patents for various gene therapies. The paper also found that out of 372 human gene-therapy trials registered with the NIH, 215 were funded exclusively by private industry.

"[T]he most obvious danger is that scientists could made decisions based on business interests rather than patient safety."

Still, there were lessons to be learned from Gelsinger's death. For one, members of the media should be wary of any claimed "miracle cure." They should investigate the financial holdings of any researcher who hails an imminent cure. They should read the medical journals and challenge the data. They should refrain from giving front-page treatment to every press release that hails the next miracle cure. And, of course, because human lives are at stake, the research community should have sobered up to its responsibilities, toned down the hype, and treated human subjects with the respect they deserved.

"Gone are the days of a lot of hype," said Amy Patterson, director of the Office of Biotechnology Activities at the NIH. "Now there's a focus on careful monitoring and careful science."

But the lessons of gene therapy, the cries for regulation and realistic assessment of risks and benefits, for full disclosure to research subjects, for careful reporting by the media—all this, like gene therapy itself, was almost immediately forgotten.

Now there was a new "miracle cure" on the horizon: human-embryonic stem cells.

13

TO WALK AGAIN

On January 30, 2000, a miracle occurred. It was Super Bowl Sunday, and millions of Americans watched actor Christopher Reeve, a quadriplegic, rise from his wheelchair and walk again.

Best known for his role in the 1978 movie *Superman* and its three sequels, Reeve had evaded the laws of physics on the silver screen: he could fly; he could stop time; he could halt the spin of the earth. If Superman had once soared above the heavens, he could certainly defy the limits of the human body, paralysis included.

Reeve's life had changed forever on the Saturday of Memorial Day weekend in 1995. He was just forty-two, in the prime of his career, due soon to film a television mini-series with Francis Ford Coppola.

In a matter of seconds, Superman was helpless.

The accident was a total fluke, a senseless, random blow that made life seem so purposeless and cruel. Reeve hadn't planned to compete in the Virginia race; he'd actually signed up for another in Vermont. But at the last minute, friends prevailed on him to ride in another equestrian competition in Culpepper, Virginia.

Even more unfairly, Reeve hadn't been reckless. He had scrupulously followed all the rules—and then some. On the day before the race, he painstakingly "walked the course," inspecting the jumps and grounds until he knew every inch of the course. He repeated this on the day of the race before suiting up.

He and his new thoroughbred easily flew over the first two jumps. The third should have been a piece of cake. But as Reeve roared towards it at five hundred yards per minute, his thoroughbred suddenly stopped in its tracks. Had his arms been free, he could have blocked the fall and emerged with no more than a couple of scratches. But as fate would have it, his hands got caught in the bridle; there was nothing to blunt the force of the fall.

"The next thing I remember," Reeve later told *Time*, "was Wednesday afternoon in the hospital at the University of Virginia."

The higher the break on the spinal cord, the more devastating the paralysis. Reeve was diagnosed a "C1-C2": his spinal cord was broken between the first and second cervical vertebrae, between the neck and the brain stem. Short of death, a break this high on the cervix is the worst possible blow to the spinal cord, the body's hub, where messages from the brain are transmitted to the body, telling the legs to walk, the lungs to breathe, the hands to move. The spinal cord is the one area in the body that cannot heal itself. Once dead, these nerve cells cannot regenerate. There was no hope that Reeve would ever lead a normal life again.

"You feel as though you're a creature from another planet," he said. "Because here on earth people walk around and breathe on their own. But where I come from, people are on a hose, and they're in chairs, and they don't stand up."

At first, he could only move his jaw. Gradually, he was able to move his head, though he still couldn't breathe on his own. He was a hostage to his wheelchair—a Quickie P300, the "Porsche" of wheelchairs—itself an array of tubes, dials, wheels, and wires. Black straps bound his hands to the arms of his wheelchair; a tracheotomy tube stayed in a slit below his Adam's apple, enabling him to talk between breaths.

"This can't be life," he thought to himself when he began to understand his diagnosis. "There's been a mistake."

Victims of spinal cord injury react in various ways to their condition. Some rage against their fate. Others sink into a stupor of hopelessness, depression, self-pity. Some commit suicide. Some drink. A very few eventually learn to accept their condition, even to grow from it, to go on to live life fully, connecting with other victims, fighting for respect in a society that kills the weak.

It is difficult for the newly injured to accept that they will never walk again, and, depending upon the site of the injury, never breathe on their own again, move their hands, or parent a child. Some convince themselves that they will soon be cured; they scour the websites and the medical journals, clinging to every announcement of progress, anything, anywhere, however anecdotal or exaggerated or untested.

Reeve was hardly representative of other "quads"—the name used by the disability community to describe quadriplegics—those who had no voice and little money and were invisible to the abled world. Nearly 70 percent of quadriplegics in America are unable to work, living off meager disability payments. But Reeve was a multimillionaire and cultural icon. His riches bought round-the-clock nurses and aides to feed him, to lift him out of his wheelchair, to take him to the bathroom—all at an annual cost of $400,000.

To the American public, Reeve soon emerged as a resurrected Superman. Nothing would prevent him from walking again, not the dead nerves in his spinal cord, not the limits of medical research, not the Republicans in Congress, and certainly not the religious community. With instant access to the media, he hit the circuits, working tirelessly to raise research money for spinal cord injury, an area long neglected by the medical community. Reeve told Congress, the media, and his many fans that a cure for spinal cord injury would save the country nearly $100 billion in treatments and expenses and bring hope to 400,000 wheelchair-bound Americans.

This new Superman set out to convince everybody that he would soon be cured. He told Barbara Walters on *20/20* that he would walk again before he turned fifty. He went on to appear with Katie Couric on the *Today Show*, then on Larry King, eventually traveling to Washington D.C. in his relentless quest for funding. Reeve used his own wealth to establish the Christopher Reeve Paralysis Foundation to fund research on spinal cord injury. President Bill Clinton promised him $10 million from the National Institutes of Health for the study of spinal cord injury. (Clinton later reneged, and Reeve silently seethed.)

Reeve pressed on with his life. In 1996, he appeared on the Academy Awards. He hosted the 1996 Paralympic Games and narrated a film about people with disabilities. In 1998, he starred in a remake of Albert Hitchcock's 1954 film, *Rear Window.* He wrote two memoirs: *Still Me* and *Nothing Is Impossible.* Letters from his many fans poured in, many from the very young.

"I'm twenty-two years old," wrote a paralyzed woman in Pennsylvania, "grew up watching you on the silver screen and always saw you as a childhood idol. I now see you as a real-life idol and I hope I can feed off your aggressiveness to defeat this."

Soon Superman was hailed as Christ-like himself, rising above the weakness of ordinary men.

"Superman," wrote spiritual guru Marianne Williamson, "is a Christ figure. He who is Fathered by one who is not of this world. . . . Superman is a powerful archetype, suggesting as it does to the unconscious mind that through connection to the Father, we rise above the limitations of this world."

Reeve's pleas were heard. In January of 1996, a California philanthropist donated $1 million to establish the Reeve-Irvine Research Center for Spinal Cord Injury at the University of California at Irvine.

The donor upped the ante: She would give $50,000 to the scientist who made the greatest stride in finding a cure.

So now, with all this money, the publicity, the political connections, the inspiring messages, was it any wonder that in the year 2000, even before he turned fifty, Christopher Reeve would walk again?

On the Monday after that Super Bowl Sunday, the National Spinal Cord Injury Association was besieged with phone calls from patients and their families.

"How did Christopher Reeve get cured?" they asked breathlessly, hopefully.

Callers spoke of young sons or daughters, children whose budding lives had been crushed because he or she had turned right instead of left, skied down the wrong hill, drove drunk, or dove into a near-empty swimming pool. Some of the callers were victims themselves, hooked up to tubes, unable to control their bowels and bladder, to eat without assistance, to walk, to work, to hold a baby. Now Reeve filled them all with hope.

But there was a problem with this miracle: it didn't really happen.

AS THESE DESPERATE callers soon would learn, the producers of the Super Bowl commercial had digitally altered Reeve's image to make it *appear* as though he could walk.

For those whose hopes had been so cruelly deflated, there was yet another blow: The commercial wasn't seeking to raise funds for medical research. It was a glitzy $2 million ad for Nuveen Investments, a Chicago-based company specializing in "wealth management." The commercial was aimed not at the disabled but at the wealthy, those who sought a place to park their millions and make millions more. The episode was a cruel reminder to the wheelchair-bound that disabled Hollywood stars live in very different wheelchairs.

"I agreed to do the ad because it is a motivating vision," Reeve later said in an online chat on ABCNews.com. "[I]t is only a question of money and time before people who have suffered from spinal cord injuries will be able to recover."

Dee, a quadriplegic for fifteen years, asked the actor how long it would be until there was a "light at the end of the tunnel."

"The light at the end of the tunnel is right now," Reeve replied.

But some of the wheelchair-bound had a very different reason for wanting to recover the use of their limbs; some wished they could have smashed their televisions during Reeve's phony walk. Invisible to the cure-happy media, they seethed as they watched Reeve with Barbara Walters, on the Academy Awards, at the Democratic convention. Many had been around for a long time, had heard too many promises from each new snake-oil salesman, had suffered through too many needless operations, too many Jerry Lewis-type telethons.

Rather than chasing the elusive cure, they had worked to improve life for the disabled, fought long and hard for access to public buildings, restaurants, schools, busses, for legislation banning discrimination against the disabled. They did their best to fight the "bioethicists" who viewed them as a drain on society, as "non-persons" best left to die.

In January of 2003, the Australian government invited Reeve to address a forum on spinal cord injury. They flew him over, at taxpayer expense, on a specially modified Boeing 747 and paid him a $75,000 fee.

"[W]e need to address human suffering with the kind of urgency you'd expect the fire department to see when the building's burning," Reeve told the cheering group.

Not everyone applauded. "Human suffering" meant something else to the disability-rights community.

"Reeve's fee hugely contrast[ed] with meager disability support pensions many Australians with disabilities live on," wrote two of his fiercest critics.

Reeve's obsession with a cure, they wrote, "ignores the unmet needs of people with disabilities for daily access to support services and for the ending of their brutal, dehumanizing, daily experience."

Christopher Newell, a bioethicist at the University of Tasmania in Australia and himself a quadriplegic, issued a sharp rebuke on behalf of others in the Australian disability community. "Social isolation, physical, social, and attitudinal barriers create much of the suffering that can arise from having a disability, including quadriplegia. It also comes from the devaluation of any human condition which is not reflective of the societal worship of youth, agility, and physical beauty.

"I can barely take an overseas holiday myself . . . yet my tax dollars are going to pay one for a celebrity."

To many, Reeve was the Uncle Tom of the disabled, assuaging society of its collective guilt for marginalizing the less-than-perfect. By showcasing an imminent cure, Reeve assured the public that the disabled would join the mainstream, that there really was no need for wheelchair accessibility or legal rights.

"The cure for this injustice [against the disabled] cannot be fixed by medical science. . . . We must . . . accept fragility as part of the human condition," wrote Mike Ervin, a disability activist in Chicago.

Most vocal in his outrage at Reeve's digitalized miracle was Dr. Charles Krauthammer. When the syndicated columnist was a twenty-two-year-old medical student, he dove into a near-empty swimming pool and broke his neck. Though wheelchair-bound, Krauthammer went on to win a Pulitzer Prize, to marry, to father a son, and to become one of the most respected pundits in the country.

"Reeve insists on parading his fantasies in public," he wrote in *Time*. "In his public pronouncements and now in his disgracefully misleading Super Bowl ad, he is evangelizing the imminent redemption. . . ."

IN 1998, AFTER the failure of fetal-tissue implants and gene-transfer therapy, there was a bright new hope for the many victims of spinal cord injury, Parkinson's disease, diabetes, and "many others." Dr. James Thompson of the University of Wisconsin isolated stem cells from a human embryo.

Stem cells are the most primitive type of cell; called "pluripotent," they have not yet turned into the specialized cells that govern a particular function, be it insulin or dopamine production. Embryonic stem cells (ES cells) were believed to be easier to harvest and more flexible than cells taken from non-embryonic sources, such as the bone marrow, blood from the umbilical cord, even fat cells. If the ES cells could be directed to the injured site and "coaxed" into becoming specialized, they could eventually regenerate what had long been dead. It was the biggest medical breakthrough in decades.

Thompson's stem cells and related technology were immediately patented by the Wisconsin Alumni Research Foundation (WARF). Among WARF's many patents was U.S. patent number 6,200,806, known as the "806" patent. The 806 patent covered all ES cell lines Thompson had created, plus the technology used to create and cultivate them. Because Geron, a biotech company based in Menlo Park, California, had provided $1 million in funding, WARF gave the company an exclusive license for the patent and exclusive rights to market ES cell therapies and diagnostic tools in six designated types of cells: pancreatic, heart muscle, nerve, blood, bone, and liver.

After Geron announced it had the exclusive rights to market therapies for additional cells, WARF soon realized it had given away the ranch and began to understand the scope—and financial value—of the 806 patent. The patent became particularly valuable after August 9, 2001, when President George W. Bush announced he would not permit funding for additional cell lines, a declaration that immediately upped the value of the 806 patent. On August 14, 2001, just five days after the Bush decision, WARF sued Geron in a federal court in Madison, Wisconsin, and on January 9, 2002, the two worked out a new agreement that took away some of Geron's rights: Researchers could use the patented cell lines and technology without charge, and Geron gave up the exclusive right to market certain therapies. Still, the biotech retained the exclusive right to market therapies and diagnostic products based on neural, cardiomyocyte (heart muscle), and pancreatic islet cells. And it retained non-exclusive rights to other liver, blood, and bone cells.

"[T]hese are large markets and our top priorities," said Thomas B. Okarma, Geron's president and chief executive officer.

Broad as the 806 patent was, Geron's patent portfolio essentially gave it exclusive commercial rights over most ES therapies, lines, and technologies.

By 2004, according to its annual report, Geron had amassed 135 U.S. patents and 175 foreign patents and had 400 patent applications pending worldwide. Geron, with its collection of patents, was required to share its patents with researchers but not with other companies, giving it the ability to squeeze out its competitors in key areas.

Okarma said that academic scientists would be free to convert stem cells into specialized cells. "We would only prevent them from trying to commercialize them," he said, as though that restriction were irrelevant.

But there was one thing Geron didn't own: non-embryonic stem cells. Other companies were grabbing up that market. On November 4,

2003, a Delaware jury awarded $7 million in damages to PharmaStem, another Menlo Park-based biotech, after a competitor used its patented methods of developing stem cells derived from umbilical cord and placenta blood. Other biotechs likewise acquired patent rights over various non-ES cells.

But in the world of ES cells, Geron virtually reigned as king. Its three hundred or more patents included "technologies it has developed to enable the scalable growth and differentiation of hESCs [human embryonic stem cells] . . . as well as various differentiated cell types that can be produced from hESCs."

This was a huge grant of power. Geron could assert patent rights on methods of helping ES cells differentiate into specialized cells, giving it rights not just over its own cells, but over much of the technology used to develop ES cells owned by other companies.

"[E]ven if American inventors are utilizing stem cell lines developed abroad," opined the law firm Baker Botts, "they may still be infringing the 806 patent."

In the past, ES cells had been grown in mouse cell cultures, a media that contaminated the human cells. Geron held a patent on all "feeder-free" cultures, non-animal media in which ES cells could grow without contamination, a technology that was needed by many of its competitors to develop their own stem cell lines.

Through agreements with other research institutions, including Dr. John Gearhart's work at Johns Hopkins University, Geron went on to capture even more of the ES cell market in the United States and abroad. Although the scope of its patents has yet to be tested in court, Geron appeared to be sitting pretty.

Dr. Douglas Melton, a Harvard professor and founder of Curis, a biotech company, was particularly enraged at his competitor's growing market share.

"Those conditions would mean that I am the ideal employee of

Geron," he quipped. "They don't pay my salary, they don't pay my benefits, but anything I discover they own."

BECAUSE ES CELLS are derived from "leftover" embryos from *in vitro*
clinics—embryos that couples do not implant—ES cell research
inevitably became embroiled in the abortion battles. The Christian
Right once again argued against any use of the human embryo, even
"leftovers," while the research community denounced the religious
as "backwards" and sentencing millions of Americans to death and
disability.

Not surprisingly, when researchers sought funding from the
National Institutes of Health, the other side attacked. In 1996, Clinton
had signed the "Dickey Amendment," extending the Republican ban
on embryonic research. But it all depended on what you meant by
"embryo." In 1999, NIH head Dr. Harold Varmus announced that
human ES cells were not "embryos" subject to the Dickey amendment.
Still, with Clinton's term soon to expire, the NIH did not fund any ES
cell research.

But the 2000 election of George W. Bush put researchers on
edge—and rightfully so, since Bush had made a campaign pledge not
to fund ES cell research. Before the September 11 attacks, many commentators believed that the ES cell funding decision would be the
president's "defining moment." Although various congressional subcommittees were already holding hearings on ES cell research funding, Bush announced that he would issue an executive order
"sometime during the summer of 2001." In the meantime, both sides
ratcheted up the rhetoric, reviving the earlier controversies over fetal
research and abortion.

Bush kept postponing the date of his decision—ironically, had he
postponed it another month, it would have been pre-empted by

September 11. His decision seemed foreordained when, on July 23, 2001, he traveled to the Vatican to meet with Pope John Paul II who urged him to "reject practices that devalue and violate human life at any stage from conception to natural death."

Bush delayed his announcement for another two weeks. Finally, on August 9, 2001, he held a press conference at his Crawford, Texas, ranch where he announced that the NIH would fund research on only those ES cell lines that had been created before that date, then believed to number about sixty-four. Researchers were free to create more ES cell lines but only with private money, and then only in "safe harbors," laboratories that did not conduct NIH-funded research. The NIH would, however, give $28 million for research on the approved ES cell lines.

"Research on embryonic stem cells raises profound ethical questions, because extracting the stem cell destroys the embryo, and thus destroys its potential for life," Bush said.

In the United States, the only existing ES cell lines were owned by Geron, WARF, and the University of California at San Francisco. The rest were either owned by overseas companies or had been contaminated by the mice feeders in which they had been cultured. Over time, it appeared that there were only about twelve usable lines, at least five of them owned by Geron.

"One of the ironic consequences of the Bush policy," said Arthur Caplan, chairman of the bioethics department at the University of Pennsylvania, "is that it says you can use the human embryonic cells that exist, but those that exist are all in private hands."

Bush's compromise left few happy. The National Right to Life Committee applauded the president for "a decision that prevents the government from becoming a party to any further killing of human embryos," but the Family Research Council complained that "by permitting research on existing stem cell lines obtained from past killings of embryos, Mr. Bush attempts to put redemptive gloss on previous bad acts and to distance himself from the immoral acts." The National Conference of Catholic Bishops joined in, calling the decision "morally unacceptable."

The American Life League went further. The pro-life organization took out a full-page ad in the *Washington Times,* likening the younger Bush's decision to his father's reneging of his "no more taxes" pledge. The ad went on to ominously evoke "the Bush family secret for one-term presidencies," a not-so-veiled threat that pro-lifers would oppose a second Bush presidency.

On the other side, there was much anger, too: religion was blocking scientific progress.

Netscape founder Jim Clark had a rather strange way of protesting the Bush policy: He withheld $60 million in funding he'd promised Stanford University's new biomedical research center, itself—ironically—the creation of Bush adviser (and later secretary of state) Condoleeza Rice during her tenure as provost.

"Our country risks being thrown into a dark age of medical research," Clark wrote. "Driven by ignorance, conservative thinking, and fear of the unknown, our political leaders have undertaken to make laws that suppress this type of research."

Other scientists complained about "America's standing in the world," fearing that scientists overseas would patent their stem cell lines and "charge plenty for licensing them."

The Bush decision was particularly hard on those parents whose children suffered from a disease that might be cured by ES cell therapy.

"I'm appalled to see science governed by religious beliefs," said one, whose son had Lou Gehrig's disease.

AT HIS AUGUST 9, 2001, press conference, George Bush made another announcement: He would create a council to "monitor stem cell research, to recommend appropriate guidelines and regulations, and to consider all of the medical and ethical ramifications of biomedical innovation." The council would be chaired by Dr. Leon Kass of the University of Chicago, who had been involved in bioethics since the early 1970s.

Bush's appointment of Kass was a shrewd political move. Defying the stereotype of the "backward Christian fundamentalist," Kass was an observant Jew with a string of gold-plated credentials: Addie Clark Harding Professor at the University of Chicago, Hertog Fellow in Social Thought at the American Enterprise Institute, and the author of many books on bioethics. On top of this, he held an M.D. from the University of Chicago and a Ph.D. in biochemistry from Harvard.

Still, Kass was discredited as an intellectual, his conservatism earning him the title "bio-Luddite," a new term that referred to anyone who challenged the new scientific technologies.

"Kass," wrote Brian Alexander, a biotech reporter for *Wired* magazine and other publications, "had come to be seen as something of an anachronistic zealot in the science and bioethics establishments."

Kass's views on the "post-human" future were already apparent from his many writings, often poetic, about the dignity of man. Involved in the Hastings Center since its creation, Kass opposed all interventions, however therapeutic, with the natural rhythms of life: *in vitro* fertilization, surrogate motherhood, the patenting of organisms, and euthanasia. Distinguished in appearance, a gentleman in manner, Kass seemed more like a rabbi than a scientist.

"[W]e must avoid runaway scientism and the utopian project to remake humankind in the image of our choosing," he warned in his 2002 book, *Life, Liberty, and the Defense of Dignity.*

Kass, in turn, appointed other stellar intellectuals to the President's Council on Bioethics (PCOB). Like Kass, Dr. Charles Krauthammer was Jewish, though secular, and politically conservative, and critical of the hype over stem cell research. Other intellectual luminaries, some appointed later, included Mary Ann Glendon, professor at Harvard Law School (and adviser to the Vatican); Gilbert Meilaender, Valparaiso University professor of Christian ethics; Francis Fukuyama (whose 1992 book, *The End of History*, topped international bestseller lists); and Dr. Paul McHugh, who, like Fukuyama, was on the faculty of Johns Hopkins.

The PCOB, already politicized, became ever more controversial when Kass fired two dissenting members. After they spoke out in favor of ES cell research, William May and Elizabeth Blackburn "resigned" and were replaced with others more in sympathy with Bush's views.

The events of September 11, 2001, took the ES cell issue off the table—but not for long.

ANY CONTROVERSY BETWEEN religion and science inevitably summons the Hollywood troops, who inevitably believe they are missionaries for science. Just as Hollywood stars and their representative organization, People for the American Way, invariably descended upon all of the creationist controversies, they now fixated on ES cells. Of particular service were those entertainers who themselves were afflicted with a disease that might be cured by ES cell therapy.

Mary Tyler Moore, a respected actress, honorary chair of the high-powered Juvenile Diabetes Research Foundation, and a longtime fundraiser for diabetes research, told Congress about her own bout with the disease, her regiment of insulin injections, fear of kidney failure, heart disease, and amputation. She respectfully acknowledged the religious objections to the use of embryos, but believed that a possible cure for the disease was worth the price.

"My thirty plus years of diabetes had led to visual impairment, painful neuropathy, the threat of limb loss from poorly healing foot wounds, and peripheral vascular disease which has just started to limit how far I walk."

On June 27, 2001, Moore led a parade of two hundred children, ages two to seventeen, into a U.S. Senate hearing to testify in favor of ES cell funding. If Tyler herself couldn't convince them, surely the children could.

"My life has already been shortened fifteen years just because I was diagnosed with diabetes," said an eleven-year-old girl from Texas, a member of the "Children's Congress."

Later, she and two hundred other diabetic children, strategically placed outside Congress, staged a Monday morning sing-along of "Promise to Remember Me."

The deployment of celebrities and the tear-jerking testimony of children were a gimmick that Hastings Center cofounder Daniel Callahan called "Laskerism," named after Mary Lasker, one of the leading fundraisers for medical research. Herself a wealthy benefactor, Lasker had perfected the art of raising funds for medical research by "rounding up support among the rich and powerful, cultivating presidents and congressmen, enlisting the help of prominent scientists and physicians, learning how to gain media attention, and using stories of desperately sick people to make the research point."

"It also became clear," wrote Callahan, "that success in advocacy required paid lobbyists, the ready testimony of doctors and important laypeople, [and] *the recruitment of celebrities with some personal connection to a lethal disease*" (emphasis added).

In the hands of Hollywood stars, the tenor of the *request* for funding soon morphed into a *demand.* In May of 2001, even before the Bush decision, Reeve and several medical researchers filed a lawsuit in the U.S. District Court to compel the government to fund stem cell research. However muddled with legalese, the implication of the lawsuit (later settled) was clear: Reeve himself was legally *entitled* to a cure—and researchers themselves were legally entitled to federal funding.

Other forms of political thought viewed government as omniscient, but not even communism placed the needs of a wealthy few above the common good. Hollywood liberalism was a curious philosophy indeed, sounding all the right notes, but at its core reactionary and elitist. American taxpayers, including the poor and the middle class, *owed* Reeve a cure, whatever the price tag, and whatever the healthcare needs of the less-privileged. In a creeping movement to circumvent democracy, researchers were beginning to claim constitutional protection to conduct medical research, a "protection" that included public funding. Nothing in the U.S. Constitution supported this, but some pressed on nonetheless.

"[N]o one and no activity has a constitutional right to federal funding," said Peter Berkowitz, a law professor at George Mason University. "There's no government obligation to fund most activities, not even the most worthy. . . .

"[N]o individual or cause has a right to sit at the government trough. Goods are many and varied. Resources are scarce. And scarce resources are insufficient to support all worthy goods, all worthy activities."

Whatever cures did emerge from stem cell research were likely to be beyond the grasp of many who needed them. On leaving his position as head of NIH, Harold Varmus warned his staff that their research would create products that most Americans could not afford. If ES cell research developed into a therapy, it would become like cosmetic surgery, a privilege of the wealthy. With more than forty million uninsured Americans, why should disease-specific research for the wealthy assume priority over pregnant women without access to prenatal care or uninsured cancer patients? Why should the taxpayers of

America provide Christopher Reeve with a high-priced "miracle cure" that the masses could never afford?

By implication, too, Reeve's demands meant that other forms of medical research—research on heart disease, cancer, AIDS, and less glamorous diseases—would have to shoved aside to accommodate Reeve's "I want it, and I want it now" approach to medical research. Who was speaking out on behalf of less glamorous diseases, those that had not yet afflicted a Hollywood celebrity?

The demand for ES cell research asked the NIH to place all its eggs in a single basket. What if it didn't pan out? There were other promising avenues for spinal cord injury, as well as for diabetes and Parkinson's. In the 1990s, researchers developed a steroid that if injected within forty-eight hours of injury appeared to reduce some of the spinal cord damage. In 2002, researchers found that electrical stimulation could help the injured regain bowel and bladder control. Some progress was observed from injections on non-ES cells. Were these areas of research to be suddenly cast aside because of still-theoretical ES cell therapies that had yet to even go into human trials? The demand for a cure included a demand that it be "miraculous," not incremental and science-based.

Hollywood fantasy, the happy storyline in which every dilemma is solved in the course of a two-hour made-for-television movie, led the public to believe that ES cell research would bring a miracle cure. As is always the case on the silver screen, there had to be a villain.

If only the religious would get out of the way, the paralyzed would walk again, just like the digitalized Christopher Reeve.

14

FOOLS RUSH IN

During the fourth quarter of a college football game, Roman Reed was closing in on his twelfth tackle when a 340-pound blocker plowed into him and broke his neck. Paralyzed from the neck down, Roman would never walk again, doctors told him, never close his fingers, never father a child, never lead a full life or a long one.

"You'll outlive your son," they told Roman's father, Donald Reed of Fremont, California.

Don Reed's love for his son had no bounds; he chased after each beacon of hope, anything that would restore his son to what he once had been before that tragic day, September 10, 1994. Don had expected to retire, but he soon tore through his savings, never giving up hope. With therapy and experimental medications brought in from abroad, Roman eventually regained some motion in his triceps, enabling him to lift himself out of his wheelchair.

"You feel so helpless," said Don, who later went on to raise nearly $20 million for spinal cord research.

Then came a letter from Christopher Reeve himself. "One day, Roman and I will stand up from our wheelchairs and walk again." Don treasured that letter, as he did each and every source of encouragement.

Roman eventually fathered two sons but couldn't coach their

soccer games or toss around footballs. It took him three hours just to go to the bathroom.

Then, eight years after Roman's tragic accident, hope arrived, real hope, something tangible he could—literally—hold in his hands: a rat. "The hair on the back of my neck stood up," Don said. "It was like holding the future in my hands."

What made this rodent so special was that, like Roman Reed and 400,000 other Americans, the rat had a spinal cord injury—albeit induced for research purposes. Injected with human embryonic stem cells, the rat could now move its hind legs. That was in 2002. Hans Keirstead, a young researcher at the University of California at Irvine, promised Don that his work would go into human trials "in the next couple of years." Keirstead was Don's hero, his shining light.

The Canadian-born wiz kid, a researcher at the Reed-Irvine Center and a professor at University of California at Irvine, was just in his thirties, with sun-streaked hair and a breezy California way about him. He was already wealthy, having made $8 million from the sale of one of three biotech companies he founded. On the walls of his small office was a huge poster of a rock star. The scientist was way cool. In his presence, young women giggled.

Patients loved him, too, because he gave them what more cautious scientists withheld. Keirstead believed that medical research progressed too slowly, that too much time was wasted on animal trials before bringing an experimental therapy to market.

"You've got a patient community out there that is in desperate need," he told the *New York Times*. "There will always be people who say slow down, slow down. I guarantee you none of them have relatives in wheelchairs."

Geron funded his work, and because its ES cell lines had been created before August 9, 2001, Keirstead received some funding from the National Institutes of Health. But, like most researchers, he needed more. Don and many others whose children were affected by incurable diseases seethed at the religious right for its worship of the embryo. On the scales of justice, certainly their children's lives were more valuable than those of near-invisible embryos that would be discarded in any event. Families mourning the disabilities of their sons and daughters hated George W. Bush—and who could really blame them? The Republican president had sentenced their children to lives of pain, disability, and premature death.

But this was California, home of Silicon Valley, Hollywood, Disneyland, the biotech capital of the world, and the world's seventh largest economy. In the hair-splitting 2000 presidential race, Californians had voted overwhelmingly for Al Gore, handing the Democratic candidate fifty-four electoral votes. If Bush wasn't reelected in 2004, future politicians would understand the power of science and the patient advocacy groups. If he was reelected, then an end-run around him and the pesky religious conservatives would still send a powerful message about who really was in charge of scientific research.

In September 2002, then Governor Gray Davis signed a law specifically permitting ES cell research and therapeutic cloning. But he sent only about $1 million a year, not very much. State Senator Deborah Ortiz, a longtime advocate of medical research, introduced a billion-dollar bond measure to fund the research only to find herself blocked by the religious conservatives in the California legislature.

It began to dawn on Ortiz and others that the only way to get funding for ES cell research was to appeal directly to voters, using the state's initiative process, a powerful way for voters to bypass the legislature. In the past, California voters had famously used the initiative process to stage a "tax revolt," blocking soaring property taxes and out-of-control state spending. This ES cell initiative would fall out of line with the spirit of those propositions because it would dramatically *increase* spending. Somehow the voters of California had to be convinced that the measure would bring in more money than it spent.

Ortiz and her allies found their most effective ally in Robert Klein II, a Palo Alto-based real estate developer, a heavy hitter whose own son suffered from juvenile diabetes. Klein took over the campaign—some say railroaded it—writing the proposition himself and gathering the sort of allies who really counted. A multimillionaire, Klein's Rolodex was packed with the unlisted numbers of high-powered Hollywood executives, including some whose children also suffered from juvenile diabetes.

Leading the charge were the many medical researchers in the state, the Nobel laureates, the University of California system, and the world-renowned Stanford University in Palo Alto. Another one of Klein's critical allies was the charming Hans Keirstead, whose promising work with rats could be sped up with public funds.

"You just may be benefiting from this bill," Klein told Keirstead.

"I could get at least ten million," Keirstead later told Connie Bruck of the *New Yorker.* "It would be huge."

Keirstead was referring to research funds, not personal profit, although there would likely be profits aplenty for his research center through its arrangement with Geron if the ES cell therapies went to market. Klein delivered a similar promise to Thomas Okarma, head of Geron, which claimed to have a number of therapies soon to be headed for human trials and, with its patent portfolio, also stood to make a fortune.

Private money could have been a solution, but there was never enough. Not even risk-happy venture capitalists were willing to fund a risk of this magnitude, one in which there was no more than a slim chance of economic return in the next decade or two. The perils were overwhelming: If only one patient died during human trials, a thinly capitalized biotech company could go bankrupt overnight. Though initially drawn to ES cell research, by 2003, venture capitalists had sunk a mere $3 million in ES cells, compared to $20 billion in other technologies. Many researchers blamed investor reluctance on the Bush administration, but in the United Kingdom, which publicly supported the work, investors were equally wary.

Some commentators warned that Californians were being asked to sink taxpayer money—money that might better be spent on schools and freeways—into a venture so risky that even venture capitalists wouldn't touch it with a ten-foot pole. Why then should tax-wary Californians be asked to assume this risk?

"[C]ash-strapped California taxpayers will be spending their money on a handful of second-rate biotech companies that the smart venture capital money . . . already passed on," a medical doctor wrote in *Forbes.com.*

"To the smart money, these companies had poor prospects and, in many cases, shoddy or highly speculative science. . . . [A]fter years of delays, disappointments, and dead ends, most of the venture capital that once flowed into these ventures is slowing down and awaiting better science to come out of institutions and academic research."

"Think about it," wrote Wesley J. Smith, a vocal critic of Prop 71 as well as ES cell research overall. "If this were really likely to bring about cures any time soon, you would have to beat venture capitalists away with a stick."

"Little note will be taken of the reluctance of venture capitalists to secure money for the research," wrote bioethicist Daniel Callahan in the *San Diego Union Tribune*. "California taxpayers are being asked to place an expensive bet on a gamble whose scientific difficulty and chances of success are too unknown and low to attract private capital."

Because they stood to benefit financially from public investment in their research, biotech firms in California understood they would have to lay low. If voters agreed to fund ES cell work, the resulting therapies, if any, would be patented by companies like Geron, with no economic benefit to Californians themselves. What would tax-revolting Californians, sick and tired of being taxed to death, think if they understood that the funds raised by Prop 71 would be for "corporate welfare," not research? If the ES cell work didn't pan out, private investors wouldn't lose a penny; Californians would.

Fearing exactly this, Okarma understood he'd have to take a back seat.

"Geron can't be waving the Prop 71 flag," he said. In addition to Keirstead's work, Geron was "just a few years away" from clinical trials of ES cell therapies for heart failure and diabetes, therapies protected by its "806" patent. In 2005, the Reeve-Irvine website, evidently not updated, promised that it "still hopes to go into human trials in 2003."

All Geron could do, though, was "to let people in California know that this is not crappy science, that it is within reach, that we are a year and a half from putting these [Keirstead's] cells into people with spinal cord injuries."

Biotech luminaries sought out special effects, shifting focus away from the bad business deal Californians were being asked to make and onto the magic of ES cells with their unlimited ability not only to regenerate dead cells but also to rescue the state from near financial ruin.

Jerry Zucker, producer of *Ghost* and other blockbusters and the father of a diabetic child, and his wife joined in the cause, recruiting other celebrities. They would not be derailed by the backward U.S. president and his religious constituents. They *would* bring on a cure, not just for diabetes, Parkinson's disease, Alzheimer's, and spinal cord injury, but for a potpourri of some "seventy other diseases."

The Zuckers and other Hollywood power couples held fundraising dinners, hobnobbing with Nobel laureates and watching videotapes of Keirstead's now-famous rats. In one clip, the famed rat is shown dragging his feet, unable to lift his tail, but in the next, the little rodent holds its tail high, bearing its own weight and moving about. (Keirstead also boasted that his rats had regained their bladder and bowel functions!)

Then came the big enchilada: Nancy Reagan, a onetime B-movie Hollywood actress and former first lady, whose husband Ronald Reagan was rapidly deteriorating from Alzheimer's disease. During her tenure as first lady, Nancy was often criticized for her designer clothes, Hollywood friends, and general disinterest in ordinary Americans. But now she was charged up by her Ronnie's illness, telling Republican pals in Congress about the importance of embryonic stem cell research and the parade of diseases it would cure. Eventually, notable Republicans such as Orrin Hatch and Arlen Specter joined the majority—still not large enough to overcome a veto—favoring ES cell research.

From the start, Republican governor Arnold Schwarzenegger, himself a Hollywood star, was a wild card: a fiscal conservative but social libertarian. On October 18, 2004, likely convinced by his Hollywood cohorts, he finally came out and endorsed the measure, reneging on his many campaign promises to fix California's finances.

Still, the glitterati didn't stop. They held more power dinners, more galas, more appeals to politicians. "If you're a parent of a sick child, you're never going away," said one Hollywood activist. Certainly they had the financial wherewithal to be seen and heard.

Science and Hollywood mingled famously, as they always had. There was Christopher Reeve, already in gear; Michael J. Fox, himself afflicted with Parkinson's disease; then Dustin Hoffman and Brad Pitt. Pitt toured children's hospitals in L.A. Famous scientists joined Hoffman and other Hollywood stars for a "Countdown to Cures" event in Los Angeles. Promoters sent out press releases boasting unequivocally that ES cell therapies "could save the lives of millions of California children and adults."

Deborah Ortiz believed the initiative would raise $1 billion. Klein shoved her aside, tripling that amount. Proposition 71 would take the issue to California voters, packaged with a plethora of economic benefits and heart-wrenching tales of children in wheelchairs. All told, the group raised more than $25 million—*not* for medical research but for the *campaign* to pass Prop 71. Three million came from Klein himself (who later repaid himself out of taxpayer funds), one million from the Juvenile Diabetes Foundation, millions more from the well-heeled Hollywood crowd. Biotech and investment firms also wrote checks: U.S. Venture Partners gave $664,000; Gund Investment Corp., $1 million; Asset Management Company, $519,000; Meritech Capital, $250,000. For them, it wasn't charity; this was business, the only infusion of capital they were likely to get.

Twenty-five million can buy a lot of television ads. Still, the Prop 71 backers faced a seemingly impossible barrier: the state's dismal finances.

THE CALIFORNIA ECONOMY was a train wreck.

The state was living off borrowed money—and borrowed time, fending off the bill collectors by borrowing still more money. It was as though the state took out a cash advance from Visa in order to pay its electric bill, then took out another cash advance to pay the mortgage. The day of reckoning would one day arrive, the bill collector would knock, and the tab would come due. Where the money would come from was anyone's guess.

California was in the hole so deeply that in 2003 all three of the major bond rating companies—Standard & Poor's, Moody's Investors, and Fitch—lowered its bond rating and placed the state on some version of a "watch list." The state's bond rating did inch up the next year, but it was still among the worst of the fifty states, making borrowing ever more expensive. Although borrowing had become the norm for many states, it was generally geared towards specific capital projects, such as schools, hospitals, highways, and the like—some initiative that would bring a solid benefit to taxpayers. Not so for California, which had to borrow just to make its pension fund contributions for state employees.

Californians were so sick of fiscal irresponsibility that on October 7, 2003, they recalled Governor Gray Davis—the first California governor ever to be recalled—and in the next election, replaced him with Hollywood superstar Arnold Schwarzenegger. Schwarzenegger had promised California taxpayers that he would cut spending—and taxes. "We spent ourselves into the largest budget deficit in the nation," he told voters.

Budgets are slippery things, hard to pin down, but conservative estimates put the state's budget deficit at $8 billion, at least. When Schwarzenegger took office in 2004, the legislature authorized a $15 billion bond to shuffle the state's debt. Based on the new governor's "recovery plan," all three bond rating services raised the state's rating to "A," an improvement, but hardly the "AAA" rating the state had once enjoyed.

In November 2004, other propositions would likewise be making demands on the state's budget: Proposition 61 to raise $750 million for children's schools; Proposition 1001 to raise $1 million for mental health services; Proposition 67 to increase funding for emergency health services. How would the Prop 71 backers convince voters that a still-speculative therapy should trump the needs of children, schools, and medical services?

Wesley J. Smith wrote:

The budget crisis is causing a world of hurt throughout the state. Essential government functions are crumbling. People injured in auto accidents or suffering gunshot wounds are in greater danger of dying because hospital trauma centers are closing for lack of funds. State health care for poor children is being cut to the bone. Services for senior citizens and the developmentally disabled are being slashed.

Now would seem to be exactly the wrong time for California to borrow a total of $3 billion ($6 billion including interest) to pay biotechnology companies and rich university research institutes to conduct research into human cloning and embryonic stem cells. And yet, this is precisely the snake oil being peddled by supporters of Proposition 71.

These competing propositions aside, what about the still-unanswered needs of the poor?

"Consider an alternative use of $3 billion," wrote Daniel Callahan,

an effort to radically reduce the estimated illiteracy of 3.8 million Southern California adults, which has enormous deleterious individual, economic and social consequences. Or spend that kind of money on the hundreds of schools in California that need new buildings, more teachers and better programs. Or on the thousands of medically uninsured.

Any one of those needs can be quickly and surely diminished, even if not eliminated, by large sums of money. Speculative medical research is just one of many public spending options, but one of the least needed and least promising.

"At UC [University of California] alone," wrote Daniel Weintraub of the *Sacramento Bee*,

$200 million could waive fees for 36,000 students, or about one-fifth of the student body, allowing the children of the working poor to attend the nation's most respected public university for free.

In kindergarten though 12th-grade schools, that's enough money to buy computers for 200,000 students . . . or to hire 3,000 full-time reading specialists. . . .

With $200 million, the state could enroll another 100,000 people in the Medi-Cal program, providing basic health care to low-income workers. . . .

DISGUISING WHAT AMOUNTED to no more than a multibillion-dollar ponzi scheme, the Prop 71 campaign set about persuading taxpayers that the initiative would benefit *all* Californians, including those who would never be able to afford whatever therapies Prop 71 produced.

Fortunately, the group had the imprimatur of science—the best scientists from the state's many fine universities—wrapped in the glitter of Hollywood stars, giving a Good Housekeeping seal of approval to their scheme. Still, with the state's sinking finances, Prop 71 backers would have to convince Californians to push aside the state's more pressing social needs in favor of their high-powered demands. So they set about constructing two different appeals: one to the pocketbook, the other to the heart.

"Prop 71 won't increase or create any taxes," said California Stem Cell Research and Cure, a broad coalition that backed Prop 71.

The empty promise was repeated so many times that it sounded true. But, with other priorities pushed aside, the state would eventually have to increase taxes to fund education, healthcare, highways, and the like. Unless the measure brought about the promised pot of gold to taxpayers themselves—not just biotechs and researchers—taxpayers would be writing the check when the $6 billion debt finally came due. If Prop 71 didn't pay off, taxes would have to shoot up or the state would go bankrupt.

So the Prop 71 backers set about persuading the public that the measure would bring in so much revenue that it would cover all obligations—with plenty left over. In other words, borrow the money today, win the lottery tomorrow, only it wasn't a lottery, it was a "sure thing."

"[T]here would be state revenues from research," said a state legislative analyst. "The state would be authorized to receive payments from patents, royalties, and licenses resulting from research funded by the measure."

Prop 71 backers hired Laurence Baker, an associate professor of Health Research and Policy at Stanford University, and Bruce Deal, a managing principle of Analysis Group Inc., to analyze the economics. According to their study, the measure would generate between $2.2 and $4.4 billion, create new jobs, and encourage construction. Additional revenues would come from income and sales taxes of "at least" $240 million and another $537 million in "royalty payments."

On top of this were all the savings.

"Prop 71 is also expected to help reduce California's skyrocketing health care spending costs . . . [about] $11 billion a year," Baker claimed.

Exactly how these vast savings were calculated remains unclear; therapies, organ transplants, dialysis, and other new treatments have always *increased* healthcare costs. ES cell therapy, if it ever came to market, would hardly be cheap.

Up to $1 billion of additional revenue, the two experts said, would come from royalties on therapies developed from the taxpayer-funded research, quite a surprising prediction since Prop 71 provided for *no* royalty split between the state and the researchers, leaving that detail open for future consideration.

The experts also overlooked the economic and social costs of deferring other priorities. How much would ordinary Californians really gain if, as a result of Prop 71, tuition doubled at the state university system? Or cut back MediCal, the state's medicare program, payments? Or closed public schools? Someone had to pay the piper, and it certainly wasn't going to be the biotech firms and certainly not Nancy Reagan, Jerry Zucker, Brad Pitt, or Dustin Hoffman.

Still, calling their own financial projections "modest," the authors concluded that Prop 71 would give taxpayers a staggering return on their original "investment" of somewhere between 120 percent to 236 percent.

Stephen Schmanske, an economist at California State in Hayward, wrote that taxpayers were

> totally unaware that massive borrowing, especially given the state's current fiscal imbalance, could have many deleterious economic effects.
>
> This is remarkable given the recent past which included: the recall of the governor; unprecedented and oxymoronic "borrowing to balance the budget"; sharp increases in student fees and other user fees; delayed raises and forced renegotiation of labor contracts; state raids of local funds leading to library, police, and fire cutbacks; cutbacks in emergency room and hospital funding; and downgrading of the state's credit rating; all because the state has spent more than it can afford and has had to borrow to cover the difference.
>
> Given this fiscal setting, borrowing $3 billion more could hardly be prudent. Unfortunately, if Proposition 71 passes we

will never know what benefits we had to forego because the $3 billion was not spent differently.

Ironically, Prop 71 wasn't even such a great deal for ES cell research itself: Interest payments could eat up as much as half of the annual $295 million in research funds. "Interest payments will begin immediately, paid out of the bond money itself—meaning that tens to hundreds of millions of 'research' dollars must be used to pay debt service," wrote Bernadette Tansey of the *San Francisco Chronicle*. Instead of running costly television ads, Prop 71 campaigners might have used their $25 million campaign chest for research itself. While Prop 71 attracted the limousine liberals and the not-truly-liberal Hollywood crowd, genuine leftwingers, those who truly cared about the poor, should have been mortified by the initiative. Cuts in MediCal were already in progress. How long until the knife cut even deeper? The glitterati didn't care; they sent their kids to private schools and, if health insurance didn't pay the doctor's bill, dug into their private treasuries.

With all the financial deception, the ultimate harm to the poor, the prospect of eventual tax hikes, rising borrowing costs, and cuts to education, it was hard to imagine how any right-thinking person could have voted "yes" to Prop 71.

But then there was all that human suffering out there, all of it immediately fixable by stem cell therapies. The group's $25 million campaign could bring a lot of suffering into voters' living rooms.

THE ILL AND disabled were everywhere to be seen.

Michael J. Fox, through television and radio, appealed to voters, stating that Prop 71 would "save millions of lives."

Greg Wasson, fifty-two, head of the Parkinson's Action Network and himself debilitated by the disease, traveled around the state, calling ES cell research an "outstanding, breathtaking development."

Thirty-second commercials featured a demographic array of young and old, black, white, and Hispanic, all suffering from demographically appropriate diseases: spinal cord injury, Parkinson's disease, juvenile diabetes, multiple sclerosis. Children were, of course, the most heart-wrenching. The best public relations came from June Gutierrez and daughter Leilani who were twice hit—June had recently been diagnosed with multiple sclerosis and Leilani was paralyzed from the neck down from an automobile accident.

The death of Christopher Reeve on October 10, 2004, gave the ES cell crowd even more ammunition. Though the actor actually died of an injury-related infection, somehow it appeared as though his death had been caused by Bush and his backward religious constituency. At a rally in Newton, Idaho, on October 12, 2004—a mere day after the announcement of Reeve's death—vice-presidential candidate John Edwards said: "If we do the work that we can do in this country, the work that we will do when John Kerry is president, people like Christopher Reeve are going to . . . get up out of that wheelchair and walk again."

EVER SINCE STEM cells captured the scientific imagination in 1998, it had been an article of faith among research advocates that embryonic stem cells were superior to those from non-embryonic sources: fat, bone marrow, umbilical cord blood, and many other sources, all known, inaccurately, as "adult" stem cells. The original preference for ES cells was justified at first: logically, they would be easier to mold into the specialized cells needed for regeneration. ES cells were also believed at first to be easier to isolate, reproduce, and preserve than non-ES cells.

In 1999, President Clinton's National Bioethics Advisory Board concluded—with virtually no discussion—that ES cells were superior, calling other sources "scientifically and technically limited."

Nearly all stem cell researchers agreed.

"[S]ince 1998, we have been able to grow embryonic stem cells in the laboratory. In addition, embryonic stem cells are known to have the ability to differentiate into virtually all cell types," Dr. Bert Vogelstein of Johns Hopkins told a U.S. Senate subcommittee on 2001.

"[T]here are important biological differences between adult and embryonic stem cells and among adult stem cells found in different types of tissue. . . . [E]mbryonic stem cells . . . clearly are capable of developing into multiple tissue types and are capable of long term self-renewal in culture."

At times it seemed as though ES cell research was being pushed for its own sake, either to bash the religious community or perhaps perpetuate science's ownership of procreation. Though few will speak for attribution, many non-ES cell researchers feared it was politically incorrect to criticize ES cell research. According to *National Journal* reporter Neil Munroe (the only journalist who has investigated financial ties between scientists and biotech companies), one prominent diabetes researcher, Dr. Ammon Peck of the University of Florida, was excluded from NIH and National Academy of Sciences conferences on diabetes. Unlike the attendees and speakers at these conferences, Peck achieved success with mice using stem cells from adult mice, not embryos.

"There is more politics in science," he told Munroe, "than there is in business or politics."

With its near-monopolistic grasp on ES cells and related technologies, Geron had every reason to reinforce this bias. In congressional testimony, in speeches, at conferences, in interviews, Geron chief Thomas Okarma repeatedly reinforced the superiority of ES cells—without ever disclosing his company's patents.

"[W]hen it comes to scalability—the ability to derive unlimited cells from the source," he told *Business Week* in 2003, "embryonic stem cells win hands down."

Geron's stock plunged 50 percent after Bush began reviewing Bill Clinton's policy towards NIH funding of ES cell research.

But few spoke of the most daunting problems with ES cells: their potential to develop into teratomas (tumors.) "Undifferentiated embryonic stem cells are not considered as suitable for transplantation due to the risk of unregulated growth," said the NIH on its website. "The question that remains is, at what point during differentiation does this risk become insignificant, if ever? Identifying the stage at which the risk for tumor formation is minimized will depend on whether the process of stem cell differentiation occurs only in a forward direction or is reversible."

And yet funding in California would go exclusively to ES cell research. Money raised by Prop 71 would fund "pluripotent stem cell and progenitor cell research that cannot, or is unlikely to, receive timely or sufficient federal funding, unencumbered by limitations that would impede the research. In this regard, other research categories funded by the National Institutes of Health shall not be funded by the Institute." Nationwide, this provision insured that more public funding would go to ES cells—nearly $300,000 a year from California and another $28 million a year from NIH—than the $190,000 the NIH was funding for non-ES cell research.

Prior to Proposition 71, some researchers were already arguing that non-ES cells were actually superior, an argument that, however valuable, was nearly always marginalized as "religious."

"[A]dult stem cells are already fulfilling the promises only dreamed of for ES cells," said David Prentice, a researcher from

273

Indiana State University, who soon fell out of favor with the university because of his religious leanings.

According to a paper Prentice submitted to the President's Council on Bioethics in 2003, non-ES cells were already producing results in human trials—not just in rats. The results were not anecdotal, but reported in peer-reviewed medical journals such as the *Lancet*.

Favorable reports of non-ES treatments also came from abroad. Although they were not yet published in peer-reviewed journals, they certainly bore further investigation. In Portugal, Dr. Carlos Lima reported considerable success in treating spinal cord injuries using stem cells from olfactory tissue. Two young Texan women with spinal cord injuries later told Congress of their remarkable progress from Lima's therapy. One said she had recovered some sensation in her legs, regained some bladder control, and could walk with the aid of braces. Another, paralyzed from the neck down, was regaining some motion and sensation in her legs. On November 28, 2004, South Korean researchers announced that a thirty-seven-year-old woman paralyzed from spinal cord injury was able to walk again with assistance. She had been treated with stem cells from umbilical cord blood, not ES cells.

Critics of ES cell therapy wondered why only ES cell "successes" received front-page gala. If the press was going to irresponsibly herald every new "miracle cure," then why not give some attention to all promising reports?

"It never fails," wrote Wesley J. Smith. "If an embryonic stem cell researcher issues a press release touting a purported research advance, the media trip over each other to give the story full dramatic fanfare. But if an even better adult or umbilical cord blood stem cell advance comes to light—even when the experiments involve humans—you can usually hear the crickets chirping."

ES cell research, however promising, was offensive to many in the religious community, hardly a majority of Americans, but still a portion of the country. If other possibilities were available for equal or better results, then why not proceed with therapies that no one objected to? Why was the medical research community so obsessed with the human embryo as the source of a cure?

"If a line of research morally offends many, why is not the alternative of adult cell research given priority?" wrote Hastings Center cofounder Daniel Callahan. "[I]n the name of deference to those offended by ES cells, could they not wait a bit to see what the possibilities of adult stem cell research are?"

Even as the Prop 71 merry-go-round was twirling around the Golden State, it was unclear what ES cells could actually accomplish. With all his rat miracles, Hans Keirstead had still not published his much-touted work in any peer-reviewed journals. When, on May, 11, 2005—five months after passage of Prop 71—Keirstead's work was finally published, it was clear that no one—not rodents, not men— would "get up out of that wheelchair and walk again."

In their piece in the *Journal of Neuroscience*, Keirstead and his coauthors admitted that there was "a limited therapeutic window for this treatment." The rats who recovered mobility were those that received the human oligodendrocyte cells derived from ES cells *within seven days of the injury*. Those who were treated ten months after injury received no benefit whatsoever, leading the authors to conclude that "treatment is limited to the early postinjury period." But even with Keirstead's success with newly injured rats, the results were not what he had led Californians to believe. Their injuries were only "moderate in severity" to begin with, and the rats "still had some hind limb motor function" before treatment. A layperson reading reports of Keirstead's work would also not understand that his success was not necessarily transferable to humans: rodents can spontaneously recover some mobility after a spinal cord injury; humans cannot. Although the handsome, young researcher had used controls in his study, the Prop 71 supporters didn't make this distinction clear. At best, Keirstead's Geron-funded work could optimistically be seen as hope for the newly injured—a major advance, but hardly good news for Roman Reed and hundreds of thousands of other Americans who were led to believe they would soon walk again.

Following treatment, Keirstead's rats did improve, but he kept them alive for only eight weeks (the life span of a rat is about two to three years) because, he said, at that point they reached a "plateau." The treated rats were not studied long enough to determine whether their recovery was permanent or whether the injected cells would lead to tumor growth.

In July of 2004, Ron Reagan, son of the late president, broke party lines to speak at the Democratic convention on the importance of ES cell research for Alzheimer's disease. Perhaps the young Reagan didn't understand. Just as he was proclaiming the cure, Ronald D.G. McKay, a stem cell researcher at the National Institute of Neurological Disorders and Stroke, made clear that there was no prospect of an ES cell-based cure for Alzheimer's—ever.

"To start with, people need a fairy tale," McKay told Rick Weiss of the *Washington Post.* "Maybe that's unfair, but they need a story line that's relatively simple to understand."

Since 2002, Keirstead repeatedly told his fans that he would take his work into human trials "in a year or two," a date that most recently moved to 2006. But there are many problems. The first is the safety of the human subjects. In another published study of ES cell-treated rats—those with induced Parkinson's—25 percent developed teratomas and died. Would human subjects be told of this risk? And if so, would they volunteer? And, on the other side, wouldn't even the most selfish researchers want to slow down human trials of ES cell therapy for fear that a single human death—like that of Jesse Gelsinger—would stop ES work forever?

Should Keirstead's limited "success" with rats really be the basis for human trials? Geron, his funder, announced at an April 11, 2005, conference that spinal cord injury would be the first clinical application of Geron's ES cells and technology. This rapid progression from rat to human, without long-term studies on other animals, either for safety or efficacy, should raise red flags.

"A lot of things make rats better," said Jerry Silver, a neuroscientist at Case Western Reserve University, one of many who argued that Keirstead should move on to primates before venturing into human trials. "You can't announce you are going into humans because you've gotten good results in rats."

Because Keirstead's success in rats was limited to the recently injured, clinical trials likewise would be limited to newly injured humans. Fresh from the calamities that produce spinal cord injury, is a human subject really capable of giving informed consent?

The "miracle cure" couldn't be decades away; it couldn't be the product of prolonged and careful study; it couldn't protect the safety of human subjects or the many who would receive the therapies when they went to market.

The "miracle cure" had to happen now.

15

THE ROAD TO HELL

Just as the rest of America voted by the slimmest majority to re-elect George W. Bush, Californians overwhelmingly voted "yes" to Proposition 71 in the 2004 election. Democracy had spoken; a firm majority of Californians agreed that embryonic stem cell research would proceed despite the state's sinking finances and despite the promise of non-ES cells.

Given all the campaign bluster, it is hardly surprising that Prop 71 was a disaster from day one. As of August 2005, nine months after the initiative's passage, bonds could not be sold because of lawsuits filed by religious and fiscally conservative groups, hardly a surprising development given the magnitude of opposition to ES cell research. Millions were spent, though not to deliver the much-heralded cure for diabetes, Parkinson's disease, Alzheimer's, and "at least seventy other diseases," but on high-priced lawyers and public relations firms to fend off interference from taxpayers and their elected officials. It slowly dawned on many in the state, including Prop 71's sponsor, California State Senator Deborah Ortiz, that taxpayers had been duped.

"When voters approved Proposition 71," the *San Francisco Chronicle* wrote, "it's likely that only a few of them actually read the fine print. Many were no doubt enticed to support the initiative by the promise of huge economic benefits to the state, such as revenues totaling some $14 billion from royalties and reduced health costs."

Prop 71 established the California Institute for Regenerative Medicine (CIRM), and a twenty-nine-member Independent Citizens Oversight Committee (ICOC) to oversee funding decisions, "regulatory standards," conflict-of-interest rules, salaries, ethical standards, protection of human subjects, and other vital decisions that could not be touched by the legislature.

Throughout the campaign, economists told voters that they would receive billions in royalties from technologies developed by the recipients of their largesse. But the law's fine print said something entirely different.

"[R]emarkably, the initiative makes no provision for the state to share directly in the wealth that might be generated by the project," wrote the editors of the *San Francisco Chronicle.*

"The initiative only states that the Independent Citizens Oversight Committee, the twenty-nine-member board appointed to oversee implementation of the initiative, must balance the state's financial interest against 'the need to assure that essential medical research is not unreasonably hindered by intellectual property agreements.'"

A glaring loophole, one among many. Despite campaign promises, ICOC was free to give full patent rights to researchers and their related companies (such as Geron) so as not to "hinder" medical research. In other words, it was highly unlikely that Californians would ever see a penny of the promised bounty.

The ICOC—the "Citizens Oversight Committee"—didn't include any "citizens" in the ordinary meaning of the word. Nor could it be counted on to render any meaningful "oversight." At best, the committee served as a buffer between the public and CIRM, creating the illusion of a representative body.

Under California law, an individual serving on a state agency cannot have any financial interest in the industry being regulated. The ICOC was exactly the opposite: Almost every member had a financial stake in the Prop 71 billions. ICOC's "citizens" included more than a dozen representatives of the University of California, the institution first in line for funding. By law, the ICOC would also include ten patient advocates for designated diseases, including diabetes (type one and two), Parkinson's, AIDS, spinal cord injury, and Alzheimer's—in other words, the diseases of Jerry Zucker's child, Michael J. Fox, Christopher Reeve, and Nancy Reagan's husband. No one represented the "seventy other diseases" that apparently had not yet afflicted the Hollywood crowd.

An investigation by the *Sacramento Bee* revealed that ten of the other ICOC "citizens" had direct ties to the biotech industry. The committee's vice chairman, Edward Penhoet, owned at least $3.36 million in stocks and stock options in biotech firms, served as board chairman of one, and was on the boards of two others. Michael D. Goldberg, another member, was managing director of a venture capital firm, and a partner in ten venture-capital and private equity funds with a value of at least $1.9 million that invest in biotech and high-tech firms. Goldberg, who had donated $58,256 to the Prop 71 campaign, also owned more than $1 million in stock in the pharmaceutical firm Bristol-Myers Squibb, another possible beneficiary of Prop 71 largesse.

The list went on: "citizen" David Baltimore served on the boards of Amgen and MedImmune Inc.; Ted Love was president, CEO, and director of Nuvelo Inc., and owned more than $1 million in the stock of two other biotechs; John C. Reed, CEO of the Burnham Institute—another Prop 71 beneficiary—served on the boards of one life sciences company and two pharmaceutical companies.

These were the "citizens" called upon to "oversee" the distribution of billions of dollars in borrowed money that taxpayers would eventually have to repay.

In most corporations, directors abstain from voting on a decision that might personally enrich them. But government agencies are quite different. Because they serve not just shareholders but the public at large, members must divest themselves of all stock holdings or at least place them in a blind trust. But the ICOC "citizens" refused to even disclose their holdings (the *Sacramento Bee* discovered them from outside sources), making it impossible for anyone to judge their impartiality. Chairman Robert Klein, the leader of the Prop 71 campaign and reputed author of the fine-print document, argued that this was the only way to attract top-notch "volunteers." (Actually the "volunteers" made $300 a day and received generous travel allowances.)

California law requires that all state agencies award contracts on a competitive basis. But not the ICOC. California law requires that meetings of state agencies be open to the public. Not the ICOC.

In its closed-door meetings, the ICOC hired President Zach W. Hall at a whopping $389,004 a year—more than twice the salary of the head of the National Institutes of Health. The "oversight" committee hired at least eight employees at salaries of more than $100,000 a year, along with an array of high-priced consultants.

Klein, who had spearheaded Prop 71, treated taxpayer money as though it were his own. By July of 2005, he had already spent $2 million, *none* of it on medical research. Among his expenditures were a high-powered law firm ($300,000), a public relations firm ($500,000), and a lobbyist ($10,000). And he went on to arrange reimbursements for the $3 million he'd "donated" to the Prop 71 campaign.

After Klein appointed his own high-priced pals to serve on CIRM's staff, ICOC members attempted a quiet uprising against him, but ultimately failed because the committee was packed with his allies. Enron executives had been sent to prison for using shareholder money as their own. Klein couldn't be touched.

As she attempted to dismantle some of the ICOC's astonishing power, Senator Deborah Ortiz asked CIRM's interim president, Zach Hall, to promise that therapies created with taxpayer money be affordable and available to *all* Californians. He waffled. After being told about all the "cures" that Prop 71 would deliver, taxpayers soon learned that if the "cure" ever came about, only the Hollywood celebrities could afford them.

Ortiz attempted other reforms. She wrote legislation to make ICOC decisions transparent to the public, to change its conflict-of-interest policies, and to protect human research subjects, including egg donors. But using its own taxpayer-funded public relations firm, the ICOC launched a campaign to cripple her efforts, once again tugging at the heartstrings.

"How dare she [Ortiz] steal hope from patients of California?" an AIDS advocate asked.

"In speaking out against the amendment, the leaders of the institution are engaging in inexcusable rhetoric," wrote the *Los Angeles Times*. "If enacted, said the institute's acting chief, the amendment would 'cripple our efforts.' A board member said it would lead to 'extra suffering and death.'"

But legislators couldn't touch the ICOC. The fine print in Prop 71 had erected a fortress around the research community. Funding was *guaranteed*. The fine print said the law couldn't be changed for another three years. Even if the state faced bankruptcy, even if it defaulted on its bonds, researchers would still get their $300 million a year.

THERE WAS ANOTHER little detail Prop 71 supporters sidestepped.

"Proposition 71 does not facilitate human cloning," the Los

Angeles Chamber of Commerce promised during the $25 million campaign. That promise was repeated again and again.

There is an important difference between ES cell research and cloning. ES cell research uses leftover embryos from *in vitro* clinics. Cloning, by contrast, actually *creates* an embryo. No one in the United States had yet successfully cloned a human embryo, but it was only a matter of time. South Koreans had already succeeded, implanting a donor's DNA into an "enucleated" egg—an egg stripped of its nucleus—and allowing it to grow for five days.

This was not the clone of Aldous Huxley's *Brave New World*. This clone was "just an embryo" kept alive for a mere five days in order to extract its cells, either for research or therapy. Still, even with this limitation, cloning was a frightening concept for most Americans. So Prop 71 supporters dropped the word and adopted a sanitized substitute: somatic cell nuclear transfer (SCNT).

Like ES cell research, SCNT was big money. And as with ES cell research, one biotech company stood above the rest: Geron. Having lain low during the Prop 71 campaign, Geron was now positioned to reap millions from cloning as well as ES cell research.

The U.S. Patent and Trademark Office (PTO), awaiting congressional guidance, had not yet issued a human-cloning patent. But Geron already held a patent on "primate" cloning, potentially enabling it to attack any competitor that ventured into human cloning. Some argued that a patent on human cloning would violate the Thirteenth Amendment's ban on slavery, but that prohibition had long before been breached by patents on human parts.

Whatever the PTO's final determination, Geron was muscling in on its competitors in the human-cloning race. In 1999, it acquired a patent on animal cloning when it bought the commercial arm of the Roslin Institute, creators of "Dolly," the cloned sheep. In 2001, Geron-competitor Advanced Cell Technology (ACT) claimed to have cloned a human embryo, but its work was questioned on scientific grounds. Nonetheless, the Massachusetts-based company sought patents on animal cloning, only to find itself blocked by Geron.

When ACT applied for a patent on its own method of cloning animals, Geron immediately filed a charge of "interference," arguing that its own patent already covered it. Geron won that dispute on February 24, 2005, shoving ACT out of the potentially lucrative and patentable market on human embryonic clones. Although ACT announced that it was opening an office in California, Geron was way ahead of the game.

When Geron partners pushed cloning, they rarely disclosed their connection with the company. In his September 2004 testimony before Ortiz's committee, Hans Keirstead argued in favor of human cloning without mentioning his Geron affiliation. Keirstead testified that "leftover embryos" would not provide useful ES cells after all because they came from couples who were "wealthy, white, and infertile," the young researcher said. He did not explain the scientific significance of race or net worth.

What Keirstead really meant was that he and others wanted to create their own clones of individuals afflicted with certain diseases—Parkinson's, cancer, diabetes—in order to study, not treat, these diseases.

"The value of nuclear transfer is not for cell therapy, it's to do molecular research to figure out how genetic disease is manifest," Tom Okarma, Geron's head, told *Wired* magazine several weeks after the Prop 71 vote.

If clones were put to therapeutic use, each person would need his own clone. Because they're not mass produced, each clone would have to be tested for safety.

"The amount of testing you can do for an individual patient is significantly less than if you're doing a drug for a million people," Dr. Michael J. Ross, chief executive of San Diego-based CyThera Inc., told the *New York Times*.

If clones were ever put to therapeutic use, experts said, the treatment would cost at least $200,000 and, as an experimental procedure, would never be covered by health insurance. Keirstead may have complained about embryos from "wealthy whites," but it appeared that this was only group who could ever afford cloning therapy.

CLONING HAD LONG been a concern of the American public.

On July 31, 2001, by a vote of 265-162, the U.S. House of Representatives passed a bipartisan measure that would ban all human cloning, reproductive or otherwise. (Another such measure passed the House in 2003.)

The ban was not a concession to religious conservatives. Countries far more secular than the United States recognized the dangers posed by any form of human cloning, however great its potential benefit. Although the European Union did not pass an anti-cloning ban, nine of its members, including France and Germany, banned cloning. In February of 2005, the legal committee of the United Nations voted 71-35 in favor of a ban on *all* human cloning.

The bipartisan momentum for a congressional ban was broken by the events of September 11, 2001. By the time the U.S. Senate took it up in January 2002, the bill, introduced by Senators Dianne Feinstein of California and Ted Kennedy of Massachusetts, had a new name: "Human Cloning: Must We Sacrifice Medical Research in the Name of a Total Ban?"

Hearings held by the Senate Judiciary Committee were filled with the high-minded wailings of those who believed in the "miracle cure," the panacea just around the corner for millions of Americans suffering from an assortment of debilitating diseases. The word "cloning" rarely passed their lips.

"I believe it would be a disaster to ban this kind of research," Dianne Feinstein said. "*[N]uclear transplantation* offers enormous potential for providing cures to diseases such as cancer, diabetes, cystic fibrosis, and heart disease, as well as conditions such as spinal cord injuries, liver damage, arthritis, and burns. . . .

"This technique could allow the creation of bone marrow for transplants to leukemia victims, islet cells for the . . . diabetic, healthy skin for . . . burn victims, and many other potential cures and treatments for a variety of diseases and ailments" (emphasis added).

Even though cloning was intended primarily for research, the diseased themselves spoke out. Kris Gulden of the Coalition for the Advancement of Medical Research, an umbrella group of patient-advocacy groups and researchers, said she was "the voice of millions of Americans living at [sic] ALS, MS, Parkinson's disease, spinal cord injuries, and other illnesses that may benefit from therapeutic cloning."

Gulden told her own story. While riding her bicycle on May 26, 1998, she was struck by a car, sustaining a spinal cord injury at T4, a less serious location than Christopher Reeve's but still disabling. Gulden testified that "nuclear transplantation" would lead to "breakthroughs in medicine, diagnostics, and potentially vaccines used to treat diseases like Parkinson's, Alzheimer's, cancers, heart disease, diabetes, and even paralysis from spinal cord injuries."

SOME OBJECTIONS TO cloning came not from the religious but from the secular left, making strange bedfellows out of two communities with vastly different political agendas. In June 2001, the women's health organization, "Our Bodies, Ourselves," announced its pro-choice, anti-cloning position:

> There is no way that human cloning could be developed without unethical mass experimentation on women and children. . . . [C]loning advocates are seeking to appropriate the language of reproductive rights and freedom of choice to support their case. This is a travesty and needs to be challenged. There is an immense difference between ending an unwanted pregnancy and creating a duplicate human. Most people readily under-stand this, and can support abortion rights while opposing human cloning.

During testimony before the U.S. Senate Health, Education, Labor, and Pensions Committee on March 5, 2002, Judy Norsigian, the orga-nization's executive director, complained that ES cell research and cloning were increasingly lumped together.

"It has been disheartening to see so little differentiation between embryonic stem cell research and embryo cloning, so that many people I meet tell me that they thought the two were the same," she testified.

While pro-abortion groups such as NARAL favored cloning in order to protect abortion rights, others feared exploitation. Would women understand that the hormones used to encourage egg produc-tion could lead to strokes, cancer, cardiac problems, even death? Would they be fully told of these risks?

"Women want to do the best they can for research and want to be part of it, so they say, 'Sure, I will donate my eggs.' But they have no idea what kind of risks they are putting themselves in line for," said the president of the California Nurses Association.

"For the progressive community," public-interest lawyer Andrew Kimbrell told the Senate committee, "this is not a right-to-life issue."

[There] are going to need to be 5 and 8 million eggs harvested from women in order to make therapeutic cloning possible. . . . Surely we are not going to let this happen without some regulation, some legislation to make sure there is not an open industry where poor women sell their eggs to researchers. . . .

Many of us have experienced the tragedy of disease or disability either personally or through family and friends. Facing the crucible of disease, we search for some hope when bodies and minds are cruelly decimated by illness. . . .

Unfortunately, in the past we have seen a continuous pattern of research and [biotech] companies peddling hype instead of healing. These false promises about healing are not merely harmless self-promotion by research companies eager for venture capital, or benign wishful thinking by naïve legislators. Researchers' hype cruelly misleads those who are suffering into thinking that cures are imminent.

Perhaps even more disturbing is that this hype is often successful in "blackmailing" legislatures and regulators into taking a "hand's off" approach to regulation. . . . The resulting public policy towards medical technologies has been misguided, inadequate, and even dangerous. It has resulted in the trampling of some [of] our most important ethical norms and in some cases to increased suffering and mortality among the very people we seek to cure.

I think it is important to note that for the very first time in human history, we will have produced a human life form solely for its destruction, solely for its use as spare parts.

After passage of Prop 71, Ortiz sought to impose a three-year moratorium on egg collection in order to study its health effects on women, only to find her efforts caught up in abortion politics. Invoking the "right to choose," male researchers argued that the ban "interferes with a woman's right to choose whether she wishes to donate her eggs or not," a curious reading of *Roe v. Wade.*

And, once again, there was the "cure."

"Three more years . . . could be a matter of whether I make it out of this chair or not," said a woman who had suffered a spinal cord injury. "I don't understand this push to delay this for three more years when we have all fought so hard, and people are dying."

In any event, at least in California, the ICOC would be the sole arbiter of what was good or bad for a woman's health.

"The Legislature doesn't know anything about scientific research or the practice of medicine," said David Magnus, director of Stanford University's Center for Biomedical Ethics. "That is why they should not be the ones to be passing laws like this."

ALL THE WHILE, the distinction between "reproductive cloning" and "therapeutic cloning"—bad cloning and good cloning—had created a convenient straw man: By trumpeting the evil of the first, cloning proponents bought themselves wiggle room for the second. Even as spokesmen for the research community expressed outrage at anyone who cloned an embryo to create a full-grown human, they were subtly giving the research community latitude to do as they pleased.

A report issued by a committee of the National Academy of Sciences on January 18, 2002, condemned "reproductive cloning." Heading the NAS committee was Dr. Irving Weissman, one of the driving forces of Prop 71 and himself a cofounder of two biotech firms, Systemics Inc. and Stem Cell Inc. When he did disclose his biotech connections—which wasn't very often—Weissman said that his companies dealt only with adult stem cells. But, having already established his entrepreneurial bent, who was to say he wouldn't eventually partner with a company like Geron? Weissman, like so many entrepreneurial researchers, was in no position to speak impartially on human cloning and certainly shouldn't have headed the committee on "reproductive cloning."

Although Weissman often parroted the "good cloning" and "bad cloning" distinction, the NAS committee didn't exactly condemn "reproductive cloning." In reality, the committee subtly wrote a loophole. Any ban on reproductive cloning, Weissman and his committee said, should be reviewed within five years and lifted if there is a "broad national dialogue" and "new scientific and medical review indicates that the procedures are likely to be safe and effective."

In other words, the only barrier to the full-scale replication of human beings was technology. Once the safety problems were resolved, all systems would go.

But even "safety" proved elusive. "Safe," it seemed, didn't actually mean "safe." Henry T. Greely, a law professor at Stanford University, director of the Center for Law and Biosciences and member of the California Advisory Committee on Human Cloning, proved to be even more of a wordsmith than Weissman.

"[B]efore we should consider seriously allowing human reproductive cloning," Greely testified, "the procedure should have been demonstrated in non-human mammals (and preferably primates) that it is safe *or nearly as safe* as normal reproduction or *in vitro* fertilization technologies" (emphasis added).

When South Korean researchers created a human clone, the embryo was kept alive for only five days. Prop 71 inched the limit up, stating that the period "shall *initially* be 8-12 days after cell division begins" (emphasis added). The NAS didn't address the embryo's age at all.

In reality, the distinction between reproductive and therapeutic cloning was a false one, designed to assure fearful Americans that no actual cloned human beings would be produced. More troubling—and far more likely—was the possibility that cloned embryos would be kept alive far beyond twelve days, not to produce an actual infant but a fetus of sufficient development to provide missing body parts for its donor. In order to remain alive past the twelve-day limit, the embryo would have to be implanted in a woman's womb, unless some other technology was created. Many women in America, and more likely in the developing world, would happily lend their wombs if offered enough money or told they were helping to find a "cure."

The deliberate creation and destruction of an embryo for medical purposes was beyond anything envisioned by the early bioethicists. But their utilitarian, stealth-eugenic philosophies had already established the moral framework. If lives of full-born human beings could be served by creating clones, why not? Annexed to the Senate hearings was a detailed list of organ shortages in the United States. More than 80,000 Americans—at least 800 of them below the age of five—were desperately in need of organs. Why not clone an embryo, let it grow in a woman's womb for five or six months, then declare open season on its organs?

The reasons for doing so would be compelling. Those in need of organs would no longer have to be placed on long waiting lists, sustained by dialysis and medication as they awaited the death of a donor. Because an organ from a clone would be "custom-made," it would not be rejected as foreign by the recipient. What a perfect solution to the organ shortage. Succumbing to the "religious fanatics" would be far more of a crime than creating the clone to begin with, the reasoning would go.

In addition to those in need of organs, there would be millions of others—those with diabetes, Parkinson's disease, spinal cord injuries—who might also benefit from custom-made body parts plumbed from a near-viable embryonic clone. How long until patient-advocacy groups demanded this new cure? How long until researchers in California invoked their newfound rights and, behind closed doors, gradually lengthened the initial twelve-day limitation?

When pressed by the President's Council on Bioethics at its February 2, 2002, meeting, the squirmy Weissman all but admitted this possibility. It may have been easy to fool the scientifically illiterate American public, but it was not so easy to fool the scientists on the PCOB, whose prominent members, including Dr. Leon Kass and Dr. Charles Krauthammer, had long voiced their opposition to all forms of cloning.

"[T]he logic of defense that has been given for the nuclear transplantation to produce stem cells," asked Dr. Leon Kass, "wouldn't it actually countenance the taking of the blastocyst further if it were possible? Not with reproductive intent but with the intent of . . . perhaps getting organs and tissues."

"It was not covered in our report," Weissman said.

It was not clear exactly why the lengthy report produced by the NAS committee had not addressed this possibility. But by vilifying "reproductive cloning," the committee happily skipped over the most likely therapeutic use of human clones.

"Today a blastocyst is created for harvesting," Dr. Charles Krauthammer wrote in *Time*. "Tomorrow, researchers may find that a five-month-old fetus with a discernible human appearance, suspended in an artificial placenta, may be the source of even more promising body parts.

"Stem-cell research will one day be a boon to humanity. We owe it to posterity to pursue it. But we also owe posterity a moral universe not trampled and corrupt by arrogant, brilliant science."

THE CLONING ISSUE embraced yet another vital issue: To what extent, if at all, should science be regulated?

The same question popped up again and again each time a new miracle cure came around the bend. Anti-cloning measures had never passed in Congress, and, except for a handful of states, the practice was perfectly legal as long as it was privately funded. This was the Wild West. Should the scientific community be granted freedom from regulation not granted stockbrokers, mutual funds, or public companies? Scientists were increasingly claiming that their work was too complex to be regulated by the legislature, that they should operate outside of regulation, as though Congress didn't already regulate highly complex sectors of the economy.

In an essay in *U.S. News and World Report*, former NIH head Bernadine Healy addressed the need for federal regulation of ES cell research and human cloning.

A human embryo in its earliest ball-of-cells stage is still not the same as a lab rat. Creating such embryos to be research tools of commercial value tugs at the moral fiber of society and raises numerous ethical and social issues that are simply not being addressed by the silence of the law. . . .

A national effort to develop legally enforceable guidelines to oversee human-embryo research is urgently needed. And the rules must be clear, transparent to the public, and apply to all. . . . Doing nothing will keep stem-cell biology wealthy for a while, *but science unregulated and mired in controversy will be damaging in the long run.* (emphasis added)

Pushing the moral envelope, trading one life for another, risking the safety of human subjects—science was, if anything, the sector most in need of regulation. But the research community routinely attacked attempted regulation as "religiously inspired," poisoning the debate. This stereotype invited a reflexive response from the secular community: If the religious are driving regulation, there must be something wrong. Lost in the stereotype were the human rights implications of unhindered science: the use of human subjects, the exploitation of women, and the commercialization of human parts.

"Scientists don't like the fact that the ugly democratic process has stopped them from doing certain kinds of research," a science policy expert wrote in the *Los Angeles Times*.

Ever since the 1960s, when Senator Walter Mondale held hearings on organ transplants, he was met with firm resistance by a community that believed itself above democracy. It took the Tuskegee tragedy and other abuses of human subjects to awaken the public and Congress about the need to oversee medical research. Nearly thirty years later, researchers continued abusing human subjects, rushing therapies into clinical trials in order to cash in on the "cure." Women in the developing world and in American ghettos served as guinea pigs for AIDS medication trials; Jesse Gelsinger was not told of the risks of gene therapy; and researchers increasingly failed to abide by the regulations of the FDA and the NIH. Was a hands-off policy toward science really desirable?

Prop 71 took scientific protectionism to a new height. Now scientists had the constitutional "right" to conduct ES cell and cloning research, using standards that they, and not the legislature, would establish. Some cloning advocates have even argued that human cloning is not subject to regulation by the Food and Drug Administration. In California, this would leave oversight to the ICOC.

At least a half-dozen other states have proposed or enacted their own versions of Prop 71, all equally protective of science and muddied with conflicts of interest. In some states, this was accomplished by executive order, bypassing the public altogether. A central theme of the battles between religion and science is the extent to which medical research should be governed by democracy. Democracy is troubling to scientists because it inevitably, as with the Bush funding ban, encourages opposition from the religious. California's Prop 71 was written to protect controversial research from virtually any intervention.

Perhaps most troubling of all, Prop 71 created an unprecedented state constitutional "right" to conduct ES cell research and cloning. Many medical researchers began seeking the same protection under the U.S. Constitution.

"Given the federal government's threat to prohibit certain lines of research," wrote Nobel Laureate Paul Berg, professor emeritus of cancer research at Stanford University, "it seems relevant to ask if the freedom to conduct scientific research . . . is legitimately different from the rights afforded to the press for their freedom of inquiry and publication. . . . *I believe the case can be made that the freedom to conduct scientific inquiry is inherent in the right to free speech granted in the Constitution's Bill of Rights*" (emphasis added).

Freedom to conduct certain types of medical research would, according to Berg, be on par with the right of free speech, freedom of religion, and freedom from unreasonable searches and seizures. If medical research is exalted to this level, does this mean the government should be required to fund every type of medical research without further review? And why should medical research alone be protected; why not also create a right to practice law or market securities or sell real estate?

If granted constitutional protection, the medical research community could challenge virtually any government-imposed restriction, be it open-meeting laws or regulations designed to protect human subjects. A constitutional right protects certain activities from legislative interference; speech can be regulated only if there is a "compelling state interest," a very high bar. Armed with this right, scientists could bring a legal challenge to President Bush's decision to restrict ES cell funding, while demanding billions in taxpayer money. The medical research community would be able to resist most forms of regulation, leaving the government powerless to ban reproductive cloning and other activities that most Americans find morally reprehensible.

In its challenge to science, religion won many skirmishes, most notably President Bush's ill-considered August 9, 2001, funding ban. Still, the medical research community was quietly winning the war by positioning itself to exist above the law.

"Most scientific research is conducted with high attention to ethical standards," wrote Daniel Sarewitz, professor of science and society at Arizona State University. "But when abuses have occurred—such as the infamous Tuskegee experiments . . . the death of gene therapy patient Jesse Gelsinger . . . mechanisms of democracy have been available to ensure open investigation, appropriate censure and the imposition of necessary new protections.

"Without this active oversight capability, such abuses would assuredly increase, and public trust in science would be eroded."

Those who fear encroaching scientism often invoke visions of a brave new world of eugenics and made-to-order designer babies. But there are more realistic fears, fears that no longer are "merely" religious. Science undoubtedly will make new breakthroughs, perhaps developing a cure or better treatment for at least some forms of cancer, perhaps diabetes, Parkinson's disease, and spinal cord injury.

But it will also grow in political and economic stature, gaining its own set of constitutional "rights" to both research and funding, arrogating to itself alone the power to make morally troublesome decisions. Increased funding on speculative research will inevitably harm the poor, pushing aside spending on healthcare and education and eventually creating therapies that only the wealthy can afford. Human subjects, many desperate for a cure, will find themselves imperiled in clinical trials that have not been adequately researched in animals. The human body will be a commodity in which women sell their eggs and a handful of companies owns human genes, stem cells, and body parts. The unborn, including some near viability, will exist to serve those who already are born and indeed will be created for that purpose alone.

The Galileo prototype of the scientist martyred by religion is now purely a myth. Science long ago won its war against religion, not just traditional religion, but any faith in a power outside the human mind. Now it wants more.

NOTES

CHAPTER 1—Science on Trial

"Boston Rounds," *Medical World News*, vol. 15, no. 19 (10 May 1974).

Barbara Culliton, "Edelin Jury Not Persuaded by Scientists for the Defense," *Science*, vol. 187, no. 4179 (7 March 1975).

Judith Cummings, "U.S. Aide Denies Ban on Embryo Testing," *New York Times*, 20 July 1978.

Judith Cummings, "Test-Tube Case Hears Evidence on Dr. Shettles," *New York Times*, 1 August 1978.

Judith Cummings, "Clash of Physicians Described at Trial," *New York Times*, 29 July 1978.

"The Edelin Trial," a project of Legal-Medical Studies, Inc., 1975.

"The Edelin Trial Fiasco," *New England Journal of Medicine*, vol. 292, no. 13 (27 March 1995).

"The Edelin Trial: Jury Not Persuaded," *Science*, vol. 187, no. 4179 (7 March 1975).

Newman Flanagan, author interview.

Prinia Gupte, "Woman Testifies to Her Anguish over Destruction of Lab Embryo," *New York Times*, 19 July 1978.

Robin Marantz Henig, *Pandora's Baby* (Houghton-Mifflin, 2004).

Seth Mydans, "When Is an Abortion Not an Abortion," *Atlantic Magazine*, TheAtlantic.com, May 1975.

William A. Nolen, *The Baby in the Bottle* (Coward, McCann & Geoghegan, 1978).

"A Rampage of 'Know-Nothingism,'" *Hospital Practice*, June 1974.

CHAPTER 2—Redefining Life

"Abortion Debated by Senate Panel," *New York Times*, 7 March 1974.

"Abortion: The New Ruling," *Hastings Center Report*, vol. 3, no. 1 (February 1973).

Lawrence K. Altman, "Curbs on Fetal Research Impede Fight on Disease," *New York Times*, 20 April 1974.

Sissela Bok, "Ethical Problems of Abortion," *Hastings Center Studies: Institute of Society Ethics and the Life Sciences*, vol. 2, no. 1 (January 1974).

Jane E. Brody, "All in the Name of Science," *New York Times*, 30 July 1972.

Robert M. Byrn, "Wade and Bolton, Fundamental Legal Errors and Dangerous Implications," *Catholic Lawyer*, vol. 19 (Autumn 1973). Reprinted from *Fordham Law Review*.

G. Chamberlin, "An Artificial Placenta," *American Journal of Obstetrics and Gynecology*, vol. 100, no. 615 (1968).

Linda Charlton, "Start of Life Debated at Abortion Hearing," *New York Times*, 2 May 1974.

Victor Cohn, "Fetal Research Said to Save Many Lives," *Washington Post*, 15 May 1975.

Victor Cohn, "Live Fetus Research Debated," *Washington Post*, 10 April 1973.

Victor Cohn, "Scientists and Fetus Research," *Washington Post*, 15 April 1973.

Congressional Record-House, 22 June 1973, 5182.

Congressional Record-House, 24 April 1974, 120.

Robert A. Destro, "Abortion and the Constitution: The Need for a Life-Protective Amendment," *California Law Review*, vol. 63, no. 1250 (1975).

Ann Taylor Fleming, "New Frontiers in Conception," *New York Times Magazine*, 20 July 1980.

Joseph Fletcher, *The Ethics of Genetic Control* (Anchor Press, 1974).

Willard Gaylin M.D. and Marc Lappé, "Fetal Politics: The Debate on Experimenting With the Unborn," *Atlantic Monthly*, vol. 235 (5 May 1975).

Hastings Center Report, vol. 5, no. 2 (April 1975).

André Hellegers, "Wade and Bolton: A Medical Critique." *Catholic Lawyer*, vol. 19 (Autumn 1973).

Jean Heller, "Syphilis Victims in U.S. Study Went Untreated for 40 Years," *New York Times*, 26 July 1972.

Human Life Review, vol. 1, no. 1 (Winter 1975).

Albert R. Jonsen, *The Birth of Bioethics* (Oxford University Press, 1998).

Journal of Medical Education, vol. 50, no. 5 (May 1975).

Leon Kass, author interview.

"Kennedy Says 45 Babies Died in a Test," *New York Times*, 12 October 1972.

Robert J. Lifton, *The Nazi Doctors* (Basic Books 1986).

Medical World News, vol. 14, no. 365 (October 1973).

Steven Maynard-Moody, *The Dilemma of the Fetus* (St. Martin's Press, 1995).

National Commission for the Protection of Human Subjects, Reports and Recommendations, "Research on the Fetus," 1975, dissenting opinion.

"NIH Guide for Grants and Research," vol. 3, no. 3 (27 December 1974), National Archives, College Park Maryland, Record Group 443.

William A. Nolen, *The Baby in the Bottle* (Coward, McCann & Geoghegan, 1978).

James W. Prescott, "Ethical Issues in Fetal Research," *The Humanist*, vol. 35, no. 3 (May/June 1975).

Paul Ramsey, *The Ethics of Fetal Research* (Yale University Press, 1975).

Roe v. Wade, 410 U.S. 113 (1973).

Harold M. Schmeck Jr., "Playing God: Necessary and Fearful," *New York Times*, 15 July 1973.

Seymour Siegel, "A Bias for Life," *Hastings Center Report*, June 1975.

Peter Singer, "Bioethics: The Case of the Fetus," *Hastings Institute Reports*, 5 August 1976.

Peter Singer, *Rethinking Life and Death: The Collapse of Our Traditional Ethics* (St. Martin's Press 1994).

Peter Steinfels, "Dr. Joseph F. Fletcher, 86, Dies; Pioneer in Field of Medical Ethics," *New York Times*, 30 October 1991.

CHAPTER 3—For the Good of Mankind

Aristotle, *Politics*.

Judith Blake, "Population Policy for Americans: Is the Government Being Mislead," reprinted in *The American Population Debate* (Doubleday, 1971), edited by Daniel Callahan.

Malcolm W. Brown, "Ongania Disputes McNamara's Views," *New York Times*, 19 October 1968.

Larry Bumpass and Charles F. Westoff, "Unwanted Births and U.S. Population Growth," reprinted in *The American Population Debate* (Doubleday, 1971), edited by Daniel Callahan.

Edward C. Burks, "Blacks and Puerto Ricans Up Million Here in Decade," *New York Times*, 6 March 1972.

Edward C. Burks, "White Population in City Fell by 617,127," *New York Times*, 30 December 1971.

"Census Table of Racial Trends," *New York Times*, 20 October 1971.

Allan Chase, *The Legacy of Malthus: The Social Costs of the New Scientific Racism* (University of Illinois Press, 1975).

Donald T. Critchlow, *Intended Consequences: Birth Control, Abortion, and the Federal Government in Modern America* (Oxford University Press, 1999).

Kingsley Davis, "Population Policies: Will Current Plans Succeed?" reprinted in *The American Population Debate* (Doubleday, 1971), edited by Daniel Callahan.

Paul R. Ehrlich, *The Population Bomb: Population Control or Race to Oblivion* (Sierra Club-Ballantine Book, 1968).

"Episcopal Group Backs Birth Control", *New York Times,* 10 Jan 1960.

"The Food Glut," *New York Times,* 14 April 1969.

"Food Production Up in '67, FAO Says," *New York Times,* 13 September 1968.

Henry Ginger, "Birth Curb Gains in Mexican Study," *New York Times,* 30 April 1967.

Garrett Hardin, "The Right to Breed," *New York Times,* 5 May 1971.

Garrett Hardin, "Multiple Paths to Population Control," reprinted in *The American Population Debate* (Doubleday, 1971), edited by Daniel Callahan.

Betsy Hartmann, *Reproductive Rights and Wrongs: The Global Politics of Population Control* (South End Press, 1995).

Gladwill Hill, "A Sterility Drug in Food Is Hinted," *New York Times,* 25 November 1969.

"Humanity's Slowing Growth," *New York Times,* 17 March 2003.

Melvin M. Ketchel, "Fertility Control Agents as a Possible Solution," reprinted in *The American Population Debate* (Doubleday, 1971), edited by Daniel Callahan.

"Papal Birth Edict Scored," *New York Times,* 30 December 1968.

Franklin E. Payne Jr., *Making Biblical Decisions* (Hosanna House Book Publishing, 1989).

"The Population Bomb Reconsidered," *New York Times,* 30 November 1978.

Robert Reinhold, "Foe of Population Sees Lack of Time," *New York Times,* 10 August 1969.

Jack Rosenthal, "Declining Birth Rate May Spell Widening Prosperity," *New York Times,* 7 January 1973.

Jack Rosenthal, "Fertility Study Made by Census," *New York Times,* 26 November 1971.

Jack Rosenthal, "U.S. Population Growth Rate Declined," *New York Times,* 5 November 1971.

James V. Schall, "The Bomb That Will Never Go Off," *Natural Family Planning,* vol. 1, no. 3 (Fall 1977).

James P. Sterba, "Every Birth in Asia Limits Hope," *New York Times,* 19 March 1973.

"Sterilization Persists as Political Issue in Latin America," *Hastings Center Report* vol. 5, no. 1 (February 1975).

U.S. Census Bureau, "Population," Statistical Abstract of the United States, 1997.

U.S. Census Bureau, "Total Midyear Population for the World," 1950-2050, U.S. Census Bureau, census.gov/ipc/www/worldpopulation.html.

Donald P. Warwick, "Foreign Aid for Abortion," *Hastings Center Report*, vol. 10, no. 2 (April 1980).

Ben Wattenberg, "The Nonsense Explosion," reprinted in *The American Population Debate* (Doubleday, 1971), edited by Daniel Callahan.

World Population and U.S. Government Policy and Programs, edited by Franklin T. Brayer M.D. (Georgetown University Press, 1968).

CHAPTER 4—Breeding a Better Race Horse

"Archbishop Hayes on Birth Control," *New York Times*, 18 December 1921.

"Mrs. Sanger Replies to Archbishop Hayes," *New York Times*, 20 December 1921.

Edwin Black, *War Against the Weak: Eugenics and America's Attempt to Create a Master Race* (Four Corners Press, 2003).

Grant Bogue, "How to Get Along without Race," *Social Biology*, vol. 18, no. 4 (December 1971).

Daniel Callahan, "Doing Well by Doing Good, Garrett Hardin's 'Lifeboat Ethic,'" *Hastings Center Report*, vol. 4, no. 6 (December 1974).

Allan Chase, *The Legacy of Malthus: The Social Costs of the New Scientific Racism* (Illini Books Edition, 1980).

David Dempsey, "Dr. Guttmacher Is the Evangelist of Birth Control," *New York Times Magazine*, 9 February 1969.

Eugenics Quarterly, vol. 3, no. 4 (December 1956).

"Fewer American Babies Born Here," *New York Times*, 22 January 1922.

H. Bentley Glass, "Science: Endless Horizons or Golden Age?" *Science*, vol. 17 (AAAS 1971).

Irving J. Gottesman and L. Erlenmeyer-Kimbling, "Prologue: A Foundation for Informed Eugenics," *Journal of Social Biology*, vol. 18 (Supplement 1971).

Heredity Counseling, A Symposium Sponsored by the American Eugenics Society, edited by Helen G. Hammons (Hoeber-Harper, 1958).

"Immigration Bill Opposed in House," *New York Times*, 8 December 1920.

"Japan Still Stirred by Our Exclusion Act," *New York Times*, 30 November 1924.

Journal of the American Eugenics Society, vol. 17, no. 1 (March 1970).

Journal of Social Biology, vol. 20, no. 1 (March 1973).

Daniel J. Kevles, *In the Name of Eugenics* (Harvard, 1995).

Robert Jay Lifton, *The Nazi Doctors* (Basic Books, 1986).

Chaplain Kenneth C. MacArthur, "Eugenics and the Church," a publication of the Eugenics Society of Northern Califrornia, circa 1922.

"Marshall Depicts Suffering of Jews," *New York Times*, 19 November 1924.

"Proceedings of the Annual Meeting and Round Table Conferences of the American Eugenics Society," Robley Press Service, 7 May 1936.

David Rorik, "The Embryo Sweepstakes," *New York Times*, 15 September 1974.

Christine Rosen, *Preaching Eugenics: Religious Leaders and the American Eugenics Movement* (Oxford, 2004).

Margaret Sanger, *An Autobiography* (Dover Publications, 1938).

Margaret Sanger, *Women and the New Race* (Brentanos, 1920).

Harold M. Schmeck, "Nobel Prize Winner Urges Research on Racial Heredity," *New York Times*, 18 October 1966.

Sixth International Neo-Malthusian and Birth Control Conference (Marstin Press, 1926).

"Sterilization Condemned by Pope: Nazi's Plan Is Held UnChristian," *New York Times*, 24 December 1933.

U.S. Census Bureau, "Immigrants by Continent 1820-1978," Statistical Abstract of the United States, 1980.

Van Buren Thorne M.D., "The Control of Life," *New York Times*, 25 September 1921.

"Wood Sees Peril in Japanese Ban," *New York Times*, 6 December 1924.

CHAPTER 5—The Boat Is Full

ABC News Nightline, with Ted Koppel, 16 November 1984.

Lawrence Altman, "Baby Fae Dies, But Doctor Sees Gain for Science," *New York Times*, 17 November 1984.

Tom L. Beauchamp and James F. Childress, *Principles of Biomedical Ethics*, third edition (Oxford University Press, 1989).

C. Keith Boone, "Splicing Life, with Scalpel and Scythe," *Hastings Center Report* (April 1983).

Daniel Callahan, "Why America Accepted Bioethics," *Hastings Center Report*, supplement (November-December 1993).

Daniel and Sidney Callahan, author interview.

Conference Report on the National Research Act, no. 93-960, 93rd Congress, 2nd Session, 24 June 1974.

Congressional Record-Senate, 27 June 1974, 11776.

David Dempsey, "Transplants Are Common: Now It's the Organs That Have Become Rare," *New York Times Magazine*, 13 October 1974.

Joseph P. Fletcher, *Humanhood: Essays in Biomedical Ethics* (Prometheus Books, 1979).

Ellen Goodman, "No More Baby Faes," *Washington Post*, 24 November 1984.

Hastings Center Records, Yale University Library Manuscript Collections, Box 1.

Hastings Center Records, Yale University Library Manuscript Collections, Box 5.

H.R., 7850, 93rd Congress, 1st Session, 15 May 1973.

Albert R. Jonsen, *The Birth of Bioethics* (Oxford University Press, 1998).

Charles Krauthammer, "The Using of Baby Fae," *Time*, 3 December 1984.

Dr. Maurice Mahoney, author interview.

Gregory E. Pence, *Classic Cases in Medical Ethics*, third edition (McGraw Hill, 2000).

James W. Prescott, "Ethical Issues in Fetal Research," *The Humanist*, vol. 35, no. 3 (May-June 1975).

Paul Ramsey, *The Patient as Person: Explorations in Medical Ethics* (Yale University Press, 2002).

Report and Recommendations, "Research on the Fetus," National Commission for the Protection of Human Subjects, 1975.

Nicholas Rescher, "The Allocation of Exotic Medical Lifesaving Therapy," *Ethics*, vol. 79 (1969).

"The Roman Catholic Tradition: Religious Beliefs and Health Care Decisions," Park Ridge Center for the Study of Health, Faith, and Ethics, 1996.

Senate Committee on Government Research, hearings on S. J. Resolution 145, U.S. Government Printing Office, 8 March 1968.

Seymour Siegel, "Experimentation on Fetuses which Are Judged to be Nonviable," appendix, "Research on the Fetus," National Commission for the Protection of Human Subjects, 1974.

Peter Singer, *Practical Ethics* (Cambridge University Press, 1993).

Peter Singer, *Rethinking Life and Death: The Collapse of Our Traditional Ethics* (St. Martin's Press, 1994).

David H. Smith, "On Letting Some Babies Die," *Hastings Center Studies*, vol. 2, no. 2 (May 1974).

Wesley J. Smith, *Culture of Death* (Encounter Books, 2000).

Peter Steinfels, "Dr. Joseph F. Fletcher, 86, Dies; Pioneer in Field of Medical Ethics," *New York Times*, 30 October 1991.

Lidia Wasowicz, "Fae's Legacy to the Medical World: Lessons from Baboon Heart Transplant," United Press International, 4 December 1984.

Dr. Jon Watchko, University of Pittsburgh School of Medicine, and Douglas Kniss, Ph.D, Ohio State University, author interviews.

CHAPTER 6—That Old Time Religion

Thomas F. Brady, "Red Probe in Hollywood," *New York Times*, 18 May 1947.

Bosley Crowther, "Screen: Triumphant Version of Inherit the Wind," *New York Times*, 12 October 1960.

Charles Darwin, *The Origin of Species*.

Adrian Desmond and James Moore, *Darwin: The Life of a Tormented Evolutionist* (W.W. Norton, 1992).

Lewis Funke, "Theatre: Drama of the 'Monkey Trial,'" *New York Times*, 17 April 1955.

Stephen Jay Gould, *Ever Since Darwin, Reflections in Natural History* (W.W. Norton, 1977).

Gladwin Hill, "Coast Red Hearing Closes in Battle," *New York Times*, 8 April 1953.

Gertrude Himmelfarb, *Darwin and the Darwinian Revolution* (Elephant Paperbacks, 1959).

H.L. Mencken on Religion, edited by S.T. Joshi (Prometheus Books, 2002).

Patricia Horn, Foreword to Charles Darwin, *The Origin of Species* (Gramercy Books, 1979).

Carol Iannone, "The Truth about Inherit the Wind," *First Things*, February 1997.

Edward J. Larson, *Summer of the Gods : The Scopes Trial and America's Continuing Debate Over Science and Religion,* (Harvard University Press, 1998).

Jerome Lawrence and Robert E. Lee, *Inherit the Wind* (1955), Act I, Scene I, *Best American Plays, Fourth Series 1951-1957* (Crown Publishers, 1958, 1987).

"Mathematical Challenges to the Neo-Darwinian Interpretation of Evolution, Held at the Wistar Institute of Anatomy and Biology, April 25 and 26, 1966," (Wistar Institute Press, 1967).

"Mountaineers Won't Hear Arguments on Evolution," *New York Times*, 12 July 1925.

David Ray Papke, "Law, Cinema, and Ideology: Hollywood Legal Films of the 1950s," *UCLA Law Review*, vol. 48, no. 6 (2001).

Michael Ruse, *Mystery of Mysteries* (Harvard University Press, 2001).

Alexander Sandow, "Social Factors in the Origin of Darwinism," *Quarterly Review of Biology*, September 1938.

Murray Schumach, "12 in Hollywood Sue on Blacklist," *New York Times*, 30 December 1960.

Murray Schumach, "'Monkey Trial' Staged," *New York Times*, 17 April 1955.

Murray Schumach, "Muni's Second Fling with Fame," *New York Times*, 22 May 1955.

Terry Teachout, *The Skeptic: A Life of H.L. Mencken* (HarperCollins, 2002).

Chapter 7—The Federalization of Science

AAAS Project 2061, "Big Biology Books Fail to Convey Big Ideas," June 2000, ActionBioscience.org.

Biology Teacher's Handbook (New York Wiley, 1963).

John R. Dunning, "If We Are to Catch Up in Science," *New York Times*, 10 November 1957.

John W. Finney, "Science Program Halved in Budget," *New York Times*, 16 January 1958.

John W. Finney, "U.S. Research Gains But Is Short of Goal," *New York Times*, 20 October 1957.

Bess Furman, "President Sends Congress Billion Education-Aid Plan," *New York Times*, 28 January 1958.

Bess Furman, "Science Aid Bill Clears Congress," *New York Times*, 24 August 1958.

Bentley Glass, in a briefing session for teachers in the BSCS 1960. Reprinted in a BSCS publication entitled "Revolution in Biology."

Arnold B. Grogman, *The Changing Classroom: The Role of the Biological Curriculum Study* (Doubleday, 1969).

"High School Biology," Yellow Version-Text II: For experimental use during the school year 1961-1962 (BSCS, 1961).

Gertrude Himmelfarb, *Darwin and the Darwinian Revolution* (Elephant Paperback Edition, 1996).

Fred Hoyle, "We Can Take the Lead in Science If—," *New York Times*, 12 January 1958.

John Hubisz, author interview. The report is available online at PSRC-online.org.

George William Hunter, *A Civic Biology* (American Book Company, 1914).

Donald Janson, "Science 'Failure' Laid to President," *New York Times*, 19 October 1957.

Edward J. Larson, *Summer for the Gods : The Scopes Trial and America's Continuing Debate Over Science and Religion*, (Harvard University Press, 1997).

Warren E. Leery, "Biology Teaching in U.S. Gets Stinging Criticism." *New York Times*, 20 September 1990.

Joseph A. Loftus, "New Eisenhower Education Program Draws Criticism," *New York Times*, 5 January 1958.

"Mathematical Challenges to the Neo-Darwinian Interpretation of Evolution, Held at the Wistar Institute of Anatomy and Biology, April 25 and 26, 1966," (Wistar Institute Press, 1967).

John A. Moore, *Science as a Way of Knowing: The Foundations of Modern Biology* (Harvard University Press, 1993).

National Center for Education Statistics, "The Nation's Report Card, Science 2000," NCES.ed.gov.

National Science Education Standards (National Academy Press, 1995).

Dorothy Nelkin, *The Creation Controversy: Science or Scripture in the Schools* (toExcelPress, 1982, 2000).

National Science Teachers Association, 2004 Report, NSTA.org.

James Reston, "The U.S. and Science," *New York Times*, 6 November 1957.

Michael Ruse, *Mystery of Mysteries* (Harvard University Press, 1999).

"Science and Our Society," *New York Times*, 11 November 1957.

Social Biology, vol. 17, no. 1 (March 1970).

"Strengthening American Science," Report of the President's Science Advisory Committee, 27 December 1958.

Walter Sullivan, "Scientists Found Rising in Esteem," *New York Times*, 9 November 1957.

"Teacher's Manual: Biological Science an Inquiry into Life" (Regents of the University of Colorado, 1969).

"U.S. Satellite Lag Tied to Education," *New York Times*, 9 November 1957.

W.C. VanDeventer, "BSCS Biology," 1961, reprinted in *School Science and Mathematics*, February 1963.

Bruce Wallace, "Population Genetics," American Institute of Biological Sciences (BSCS, 1964).

Pamela R. Winnick, "A Textbook Case of Junk Science," *Weekly Standard*, 9 May 2005.

CHAPTER 8—Monkey Business

"3 Rabbis Explore Darwin's Theory," *New York Times*, 29 November 1959.

Amicus Brief of Americans United for Separation of Church and State before the U.S. Supreme Court in *Edwards v. Aguillard*.

Amicus Brief of the National Academy of the Sciences before the U.S. Supreme Court in *Edwards v. Aguillard*.

Amicus Brief of the New York Committee for Public Education and Religious Liberty before the U.S. Supreme Court in *Edwards v. Aguillard*.

Henry Steele Commager, *Documents of American History*, seventh edition (Appleton-Century-Crofts, 1963).

Edwards v. Aguillard, 482 U.S. 578 (1987).

"Ellington Signs Bill Ending 'Monkey Law,'" *New York Times*, 19 May 1967.

Encyclopedia Judaica (Macmillan, 1971).

Epperson v. Arkansas, 393 U.S. 97 (1968).

Norman L. Geisler, *The Creator in the Courtroom* (Mott Media, 1982).

Stephen Jay Gould, "Dorothy, It's Really Oz," *Time*, 23 August 1999.

Stephen Jay Gould, *Rock of the Ages : Science and Religion in the Fullness of Life* (Ballantine, 1999).

Ken Ham, *The Lie: Evolution* (Master Books, 1987, 2000).

John F. Haught, *Responses to 101 Questions on God and Evolution* (Paulist Press, 2001).

Philip J. Hilts, "Religion Influenced Arkansas Legislator Who Wrote Creationism Law," *Washington Post*, 14 December 1981.

Institute for Creation Research, ICR.org.

Dena Kleiman, "Foes of Evolution Theory Ask School Time," *New York Times*, April 7, 1980.

McClean v. Arkansas Board of Education, 529 F. Supp. 1255 (E.D. Arkansas 1982).

Alex Mindlin, "Religion and Natural History among the Ultra Orthodox," *New York Times*, 22 March 2005.

Henry Morris, *Scientific Creationism* (Creation Life Publishers, 1974).

Dorothy Nelkin, *The Creation Controversy* (toExcel Press, 1982, 2000).

NewsHour with Jim Lehrer, 24 July 1997.

"Public Beliefs about Evolution," ReligiousTolerance.org.

Robert Reinhold, "U.S. Science Agency's New Chief Pushes for Change," *New York Times*, 29 September 1981.

Peter Slevin, "Battle Over Teaching Evolution Sharpens," *Washington Post*, 14 March 2005.

Anston Stokes, "Church and State in the United States," (Harper & Brothers, 1950).

Reginald Stuart, "Judge's Conduct of Creation Trial Is Praised," *New York Times*, 17 December 1981.

Reginald Stuart, "One Battle Lost, Creationists Regroup for Second Round," *New York Times*, 7 March 1982.

Alexis de Tocqueville, *Democracy in America* (Regnery, 2002).

Jay Topkis, author interview.

CHAPTER 9—Celebrity Science

Cosmos, Episode One (DVD Collector's Edition 2000).

Francis Crick, *The Astonishing Hypothesis: The Scientific Search for the Soul* (Scribner, 1994).

A.C. Crombie, *The History of Science from Augustine to Galileo* (Dover Publications, 1995).

Richard Dawkins, *The Blind Watchmaker* (Norton, 1996 edition).

Richard Dawkins, "Put Your Money on Evolution," *New York Times*, 9 April 1989.

Richard Dawkins, *The Selfish Gene* (Oxford, 1989 edition).

Richard Dawkins, "Snake Oil and Holy Water," Forbes.com, 4 October 1999.

Daniel C. Dennett, *Darwin's Dangerous Idea* (Touchstone, 1996).

Michael Denton, *Evolution: A Theory in Crisis* (Adler & Adler, 1986).

Stephen Jay Gould, "Bright Star among Billions," reprinted in *The Lying Stones of Marrakech* (Harmony Books, 2000).

Stephen Jay Gould, "Darwinian Fundamentalism," *New York Review of Books*, vol. 44, no. 10 (12 June 1997).

Stephen Jay Gould, "More Things in Heaven and Earth," reprinted in Hilary and Steven Rose, *Alas, Poor Darwin* (Harmony Books, 2000).

Stephen Jay Gould, *Rocks of Ages: Science and Religion in the Fullness of Life* (Ballantine 1999).

John Horgan, *The End of Science* (Helix Books, 1996).

John Horgan, "In the Beginning," *Scientific American*, February 1991.

Robert Jastrow, *God and the Astronomers* (Reader's Library, 1978).

Michael Kelly, "Arguing for Infanticide," *Washington Post*, 21 November 1997.

Richard Lewontin, "Billions and Billions of Demons," *New York Review of Books*, vol. 9 (January 1997).

Edwin McDowell, "Books on Science Riding Wave of Popularity," *New York Times*, 28 November 1981.

Dorothy Nelkin, "Less Selfish than Sacred?" reprinted in Hilary and Steven Rose, *Alas, Poor Darwin* (Harmony Books, 2000).

John J. O'Conner, "'Cosmos'—A Trip Into Outer Space," *New York Times*, 28 September 1980.

John J. O'Conner, "Putting 'Cosmos' Into Perspective," *New York Times*, 14 December 1980.

Fred Reed, "The Metaphysics of Evolution," *Men's Daily News*, 8 March 2005.

Carl Sagan, *Intelligent Life in the Universe* (Pan Books, 1977).

Michael Schrage, "Revolutionary Evolutionist," Wired.com, 3 March 1995.

Robert Wright, "The Accidental Creationist," available online at Nonzero.com.

CHAPTER 10—Over the Rainbow

Author interviews. The narrative of the events in Kansas from August 1999 through August 2000 is compiled from author interviews with: Linda Holloway, Mary Douglass Brown, Celtie Johnson, Rebecca Massell, Janet Waugh, Professor Steve Case at the University of Kansas, Leonard Kristhtalka at the University of Kansas Natural History Museum, and Professor John Staver at Kansas State University.

Kate Beem, "At Odds Over Education: Kansas Reflects Nation's Struggle Over School Control," *Kansas City Star*, 9 May 1999.

Kate Beem, "New Plan Softens Evolution Standards," *Kansas City Star*, 9 August 1999.

Pam Belluck, "Board Decision on Evolution Roils an Election in Kansas," *New York Times*, 29 July 2000.

Diane Carroll, "Board Gets Earful on Evolution," *Kansas City Star*, 11 August 1999.

James Carroll, "A Victory for Shallowness," *Boston Globe*, 7 September 1999.

Fritz Detwiler, *Standing on the Premises of God* (New York University Press, 1999).

Phillip Johnson, "The Church of Darwin," *Wall Street Journal*, 16 August 1999.

Phillip E. Johnson, *The Wedge of Truth* (Intervarsity Press 2000).

"Kansas Board Is Threatening the Evolution of Young Minds," *San Jose Mercury News*, 18 August 1999.

"Kansas Goes Backward in Science," *Atlanta Constitution*, 16 August 1999.

Leonard Krishtalka, "Yokels' Approach to Science," *Lawrence Journal-World*, 8 June 1999.

Mary Beth Marklien, "Evolution's Next Step in Kansas," *USA Today*, 19 July 2000.

Adrian Melott, "How We Threw the Bums Out," *Freethought Today*, November 2000.

"A Needless Casualty," *Kansas City Star*, 18 September 1998.

"Politics of Distrust," *Topeka Capital-Journal*, 13 August 1999.

Barbara Vancheri, "Screenwriters Guild Will Honor Activist," *Pittsburgh-Post Gazette*, 26 April 2002.

Jonathan Wells, "Give Students the Resources to Critique Darwin," *Kansas City Star*, 1 August 1999.

"Willful Ignorance on Evolution," *New York Times*, 13 August 1999.

A.N. Wilson, "Land of the Born-Again Boneheads," *Evening Standard (London)*, 13 August 1999.

Pamela R. Winnick, "Proposed Rules Boost the Teaching of Creationism," *Pittsburgh Post-Gazette*, 29 November 2000.

Byron York, "Media for the American Way," *National Review Online*, 26 April 2002.

CHAPTER 11—The Miracle Cure

Tim Beardsley, "Aborting Research," *Scientific American* (August 1992).

Jane E. Brody, "More Hope for Spinal Injuries," *New York Times*, 6 July 1994.

James F. Childress, *Deliberations of the Human Fetal Tissue Transplantation Research Panel* (National Academies Press, 1991).

"An End to Parkinson's," *Time*, 8 September 1961.

James Fallows, "The Political Scientist," *New Yorker*, 7 June 1999.

Dr. Curt Freed, University of Colorado, author interview.

"Group Asks Pregan to Ban Fetal Research," *American Medical News*, 21 October 1988.

Philip J. Hilts, "Abortion Debate Clouds Research on Fetal Tissue," *New York Times*, 16 October 1989.

Human Fetal Tissue Transplantation Research Panel, transcript of meeting, 14–16 September 1988.

Leon Jaroff, "Crisis in the Labs," *Time*, 26 August 1991.

Albert R. Jonsen, *The Birth of Bioethics* (Oxford University Press).

Gina Kolata, "Parkinson's Research Is Set Back by Failure of Fetal Cell Implants," *New York Times*, 8 March 2001.

Gina Kolata, "Success Reported Using Fetal Tissue to Repair a Brain," *New York Times*, 26 November 1992.

Dr. William Langston, author interview.

J. William Langston M.D. and Jon Palfreman, *The Case of the Frozen Addicts* (Pantheon Books, 1995).

Paul Ramsey, *The Ethics of Fetal Research* (Yale University Press, 1975).

David Reskik, "Setting Biomedical Research Priorities: Justice, Science, and Public Participation," *Kennedy Institute of Ethics Journal*, vol. 11, no. 2 (Johns Hopkins University Press, 2001).

Amy E. Schwartz, "Treasure the Ideology, Slight the Suffering," *Washington Post*, 31 May 1992.

Kevin Tanzillo, "Fetal Tissue Implants: Therapy for Parkinson's Disease?" *Geriatrics*, vol. 47, no. 7 (July 1992).

Christopher M. Tedeschi, "Foetal Tissue Transplantation Research: Scientific Progress and the Role of Special Interest Groups," *Minerva*, vol. 33 (Spring 1995).

"Unilateral Transplantation of Human Fetal Mesencephalic Tissue into the Caudate Nucleus of Patients with Parkinson's Disease," *New England Journal of Medicine*, vol. 327, no. 22 (26 November 1992).

Dick Thompson Washington, "When Abortions Save Lives," *Time*, 6 August 1992.

Henry A. Waxman, opening statement, Hearings of Fetal Tissue Transplantation Research, House Committee on Energy and Commerce, Subcommittee on Health and the Environment, 2 April 1990.

Robert J. White M.D., "The Myth of a Transplant Cure," *New York Times*, 15 August 1992.

CHAPTER 12—First Do No Harm

Amicus Brief on Behalf of the Peoples Business Commission, before the U.S. Supreme Court in *Diamond v. Chakrabarty*.

Amicus Brief Curiae of the Regents of California; Amicus Briefs of the American Society of Biological Chemists, the Association of American Medical Colleges, the California Institute of Technology, and others before the U.S. Supreme Court in *Diamond v. Chakrabarty*.

Edmund L. Andrews, "Religious Leaders Prepare to Fight Patents on Genes," *New York Times*, 12 May 1995.

Edmund L. Andrews, "U.S. Seeks Patent on Genetic Codes, Setting Off Furor," *New York Times*, 21 October 1991.

Natalie Angier, "Foreign Genes are Inserted in Humans, A Study Reports," *New York Times*, 30 August 1990.

Alex Berenson and Nicholas Wade, "A Call for Sharing of Research Causes Gene Stocks to Plunge," *New York Times*, 15 March 2000.

Neil Boyce, "And Now, Ethics for Sale?" *U.S. News & World Report*, 30 July 2001.

Daniel Callahan, *At Price Better Health?* (University of California Press, 2003).

Conference on Human Subject Protection and Financial Conflicts of Interest, 15 & 16 August 2000, National Institutes for Health. The transcript of the conference is available at HHS.gov.

Diamond v. Chakrabarty, 447 U.S. 303 (1980).

Donald C. Drake, "How a Worried Medical Team Pinpointed What Went Wrong," *Philadelphia Inquirer*, 22 December 1999.

Philip Elmer-Dewitt, "The Genetic Revolution," *Time*, 17 January 1994.

"FDA Proposes New Rules for Gene Therapy Trials," National Journal Group Inc., American Health Line, 18 January 2001.

Tim Friend, "It's in the Genes: Scientists Confront Money Issues," *USA Today*, 22 February 2000.

"Gene Therapy Run Amok?" editorial, *Washington Post*, 29 January 2000.

Linda Greenhouse, "Science May Patent New Forms of Life," *New York Times*, 17 June 1990.

Tim Hilchey, "Genetic Therapy Found for Dystrophy in Mice," *New York Times*, 31 August 1993.

Leon Jaroff, "The Gene Hunt," *Time*, 20 March 1989.

Leon Jaroff, "Giant Step for Gene Therapy," *Time*, 24 September 1990.

Tony Karon, "Cancer 'Cure' Means Big Bucks," *Time*, 4 May 1998.

Klaus Keuneck, Letter, *Time*, 8 June 1998.

Gina Kolata, "Biologist's Speedy Gene Method Scares Peers but Gains Backer," *New York Times*, 28 July 1992.

Gina Kolata, "In the Rush Toward Gene Therapy, Some See a High Risk of Failure," *New York Times*, 25 July 1995.

Michael D. Lemonick and Dick Thompson, "Racing to Map Our DNA," *Time*, 11 January 1999.

Peter Lurie and Sidney M. Wolfe, "Unethical Trials to Interventions to Reduce Parinatal Transmission of the Human Immunodeficiency Virus in Developing Countries," *New England Journal of Medicine*, vol. 337 (1997).

"Patentability of Human Organisms," Hearings of President's Council on Bioethics, 20 June 2002.

"Patenting Genes May Slow Down Innovation, and Delay Availability of Cheaper Genetic Tests," *British Medical Journal*, 11 December 2004.

Jeremy Rifkin, *The Biotech Century* (Jeremy Tarcher-Putnam, 1999).

Teresa Riordan, "Patents," *New York Times*, 27 November 1995.

Harold M. Schmeck Jr. "The Promises of Gene Therapy," *New York Times Magazine*, 10 November 1985.

Adil E. Shamoo, "Adverse Events Reporting—The Tip of an Iceberg," *Accountability in Research*, vol. 8 (2000).

Sheryl Gay Stolberg, "The Biotech Death of Jesse Gelsinger," *New York Times Magazine*, 28 November 1999.

Sheryl Gay Stolberg, "Teenager's Death Is Shaking Up Field of Human Gene-Therapy Experiments," *New York Times*, 27 January 2000.

"Teen Who Died in Gene Therapy Test Wasn't Eligible For Study, FDA Says," *Chicago Tribune*, 9 December 1999.

CHAPTER 13—To Walk Again

Brian Alexander, *Rapture: How Biotech Became the New Religion* (Basic Books, 2003).

Peter Berkowitz, testimony before the President's Council on Bioethics, 4 September 2003.

Baker Botts, "The Current State of Embryonic Stem Cell Patents," 26 September 2001.

Daniel Callahan, *What Price Better Health? Hazards of the Research Imperative* (University of California, 2003).

Daniel Callahan, testimony before the President's Council on Bioethics, 24 July 2003.

Christopher B. Caroll, "Selling the Stem Cell," University of Illinois, *Journal of Law, Technology, and Policy*, vol. 435 (2002).

"A Chat with Christopher Reeve," ABCNews.com, ChrisReeveHomepage.com, 1 February 2000.

Jim Clark, "Squandering Our Technological Future," *New York Times*, 31 August 2001.

Perkins Cole, "Litigation Victory Upholds PharmaStem's Pioneering Stem Cell Patents," press release, PerkinsCole.com, 4 November 2003. Perkins Cole is the law firm that represented PharmaStem.

Mike Ervin, author interview.

Mike Ervin, "Australian Activists Protest Visit by Christopher Reeve," *Disability World*, DisabilityWorld.org.

Gerard Goggin and Christopher Newell, "Fame and Disability," *M/C Journal*, vol. 7, no. 5 (November 2004).

Geron Annual Report 2004, Geron.com.

Claire E. Hulsebosch, "Recent Advances in Pathophysiology and Treatment of Spinal Cord Injury," *Advanced Physiology Education*, vol. 26, no. 238-255 (2002).

Leon R. Kass M.D., *Life, Liberty, and the Defense of Dignity: The Challenge of Bioethics* (Encounter Books, 2002).

Ronald Kotulak and Peter Gorner, "Stem Cell Limits Bring New Fears," *Chicago Tribune*, 9 September 2001.

Charles Krauthammer, "Restoration, Reality and Christopher Reeve," *Time*, 2 February 2000.

Michael D. Lemonick, "Stem Cells in Limbo," *Time*, 11 August 2003.

"Mary Tyler Moore Testifies before Congress in Support of Stem Cell Research," JDRF.org.

Dana Reeve, *Care Packages: Letters to Christopher Reeve from Strangers and Other Friends* (Random House, 1999).

"Reeve Ad Fools Viewers," BBC News, BBC.co.uk, 2 February 2000.

Roger Rosenblatt, "New Hopes, New Dreams," *Time*, 26 August 1996. The account of Reeve's accident is taken from this article.

Sheryl Gay Stolberg, "Patent Laws May Determine Shape of Stem Cell Research," *New York Times*, 16 August 2001.

Sheryl Gay Stolberg, "The President's Decision: The Research; U.S. Acts Quickly to Put Stem Cell Policy in Effect," *New York Times*, 11 August 2001.

Alessandra Tanley, "Bush Hears Pope Condemn Research in Human Embryos," *New York Times*, 24 July 2001.

"U.S. Patent Office Enters Final Judgment in Nuclear Transper Interference in Favor of Geron," Press Release, 6 January 2005, Geron.com

Arlene Weintraub, "Biotech Frontier: Repairing the Engines of Life," *BusinessWeek*, 24 March 2004.

CHAPTER 14—Fools Rush In

Alliance for Stem Cell Research, CuresforCalifornia.com.

L.M. Bjorklund, R. Sanchez-Pernaute, et al, "Embryonic Stem Cells Develop into Functional Dopaminergic Neurons after Transplantation in a Parkinson Rat Model," *Proceedings of the National Academy of Sciences*, vol. 99 (2002).

Connie Bruck, "Hollywood Science," *New Yorker*, 8 October 2004.

Daniel Callahan, "Combining Hope, Hype, and Hucksterism," *San Diego Union Tribune*, 22 October 2004.

"Credit Ratings California History," Treasurer.ca.gov.

Scott Gottlieb, M.D., "California's Stem Cell Follies" Forbes.com, 1 November 2004.

"Information on Stem Cell Research," NIH.gov.

Hans Keirstead, PhD., e-mail to author, 12 August 2005. Keirstead, a frequent lecturer, was a speaker on stem cell research at a conference the author attended in San Diego on 11 and 12 April 2005.

Hans Keirstead, et al, "Human Embryonic Stem Cell-Derived Oligodendrocyte Progenitor Cell Transplants Remyelinate and Restore Locomotion after Spinal Cord Injury," *Journal of Neuroscience*, 11 May 2005.

Nuala Moran, "Tough Cell to Investors," ScientificAmerican.com, 27 June 2005.

National Biotheics Advisory Committee, "Ethical Issues in Human Stem Cell Research," September 1999, available online at Bioethics.gov.

Thomas Okarma, "Don't Ban Stem-Cell Research," *Business Week Online*, 2 June 2003.

Andrew Pollack, "Moving Stem Cells Front and Center," *New York Times*, 23 February 2005.

David E. Prentice, Ph.D., "The Fountain of Youth," *Regeneration*, vol. 6 (2000).

David A. Prentice, Ph.D., Paper Commissioned for the President's Council on Bioethics, July 2003. The paper can be found online at Bioethics.gov.

Donald Reed, author interview.

Reeve Irvine Research Center, Reeve.UCI.edu.

Senate Committee on Health and Human Services, State of California, hearing of Proposition 71, 15 September 2004, transcript.

Wesley J. Smith, "Does California Really Need Embryonic Stem Cell Research Funding?" Lifenews.com, 11 October 2004.

Wesley J. Smith, "The Proposition 71 Stem Cell Scam," *Christianity Today*, 16 August 2004.

Wesley J. Smith, "A Stem Cell Tale: Why One Type of Stem-Cell Research Gets Fawning Media Coverage and Another Is All but Ignored," *Weekly Standard*, 22 December 2004.

Terri Somers, "Prop. 71 Opens Tap for Stem-Cell Studies," *San Diego Union Tribune*, 8 October 2004.

Bernadette Tansey, "Prop 71's Fine Print Contains Surprise: Tightly Written Law Leaves Little Room for Oversight or Changes," *San Francisco Chronicle*, 8 December 2004.

Bert Vogelstein, professor of Oncology and Pathology at Johns Hopkins University, testimony before the Senate Subcommittee on Labor, Health, and Human Services, 31 October 2001.

Daniel Weintraub, "Proposition 71 Is an Intriguing, but Flawed, Idea," *Sacramento Bee*, 28 October 2004.

Rick Weiss "Stem Cells an Unlikely Therapy for Alzheimer's," *Washington Post*, 10 June 2004.

CHAPTER 15—The Road to Hell

Paul Berg, "Right to Inquire, Freedom of Expression Go Hand in Hand," *San Jose Mercury News*, 2 January 2005.

"Critics Say Stem Cell Panel Skirting the Law; 'Board Didn't Give Proper Notice of Meeting,' They Say," *San Francisco Chronicle*, 16 December 2004.

Bernadine Healy M.D., "To Create, or Not to Create?" *US News & World Report*, 21 March 2005.

"Human Cloning: Must We Sacrifice Medical Research in the Name of a Total Ban?" hearings before the Committee on the Judiciary, United States Senate, 107th Congress, 2nd Session, 5 February 2002 (U.S. Government Printing Office, 2002).

Steve Johnson, "Stem-Cell Oversight Bill Is Criticized," *San Jose Mercury News*, 24 May 2005.

Jonathan Knight, "Critics Slate Ethical Leeway in California Stem-Cell Proposal," *Nature*, 16 September 2004.

Charles Krauthammer, "Mounting the Slippery Slope," *Time*, 23 July 2001.

Laura Mecoy, "Stem Cell Allies Divided over Egg Collection," *Sacramento Bee*, 27 March 2005.

Laura Mecoy, "Stem Cell Holdings Criticized," *Sacramento Bee*, 21 January 2005.

National Academy of Sciences, *Scientific and Medical Aspects of Human Reproductive Cloning* (National Academy Press, 2002).

"Our Bodies Our Selves Statement on Human Cloning," OurBodiesOurselves.org.

Kristen Philipkoski , "Costly Cloning Isn't a Cure-All," *Wired News*, 1 December 2004.

Andrew Pollack, "The Stem Cell Debate,Use of Cloning to Tailor Treatment Has Big Hurdles, Including Cost," *New York Times*, 18 December 2001.

President's Committee on Bioethics, transcript of 12 February 2002 meeting. The transcript is available at Bioethics.gov.

"Proposition 71 Stem Cell Research, Funding Bonds Initiative Constitutional Amendment and Statute," hearing, 14 September 2004.

Daniel Sarewitz, "Proposition 71 Is an Intriguing, but Flawed, Idea," *Los Angeles Times*, 25 October 2004.

"State Deserves a Share of Stem-Cell Benefits," editorial, *San Francisco Chronicle*, vol. 9 (December 2004).

"Stem Cell Follies: Crank Up the Spin Machine," editorial, *Sacramento Bee*, 17 July 2005.

"Stem Cell Follies: Crank Up the Spin Machine," editorial, *Sacramento Bee*, 17 July 2005.

"Stem Cell Research Accountability," editorial, *Los Angeles Times*, 26 May 2005.

BIBLIOGRAPHY

Alexander, Brian, *Rapture: How Biotech Became the New Religion* (Basic Books, 2003)

Andrews, Lori B., *The Clone Age* (Henry Holt, 1999)

Angus, John, and Stephen C. Meyer, editors, *Darwinism, Design, and Public Education* (Michigan State University, 2003)

Annas, George, Leonard Glantz, and Barbara Katz, *Informed Consent to Human Experiments: The Subject's Dilemma* (Ballinger, 1997)

Barsky, Arthur, *Worried Sick: Our Troubled Quest for Wellness* (Little Brown, 1998)

Beaumont, Tom L., and James F. Childress, *Principles of Bioethics* (Oxford University Press, 1979)

Behe, Michael, *Darwin's Black Box* (Free Press, 1996)

Bell, Robert, *Impure Science: Fraud, Compromise, and Political Influence in Scientific Research* (John Wiley & Sons, 1992)

Black, Edwin, *War against the Weak: Eugenics and America's Attempt to Create a Master Race* (Four Corners Press, 2003)

Brayer, Franklin T., M.D., editor, *World Population and U.S. Government Policy and Programs* (Georgetown University Press, 1968)

Callahan, Daniel, editor, *The American Population Debate* (Doubleday, 1971)

Callahan, Daniel, *At What Price Better Health: The Hazards of the Research Imperative* (University of California, 2003)

Callahan, Daniel, *False Hopes: Why America's Quest for Perfect Health Is a Recipe for Failure* (Simon & Schuster, 1998)

Callahan, Daniel, *What Kind of Life: The Limits of Medical Progress* (Georgetown University Press, 1990)

Caplan, Arthur L., *If I Were a Rich Man Could I Buy a Pancreas? and Other Essays on the Ethics of Health Care* (Indiana University Press, 1992)

Chase, Allan, *The Legacy of Malthus: The Social Costs of the New Scientific Racism* (Alfred A. Knopf, 1975)

Childress, James F., *Deliberations of the Human Fetal Tissue Transplantation Research Panel* (National Academies Press, 1991)

Crick, Francis, *The Astonishing Hypothesis: The Scientific Search for the Soul* (Scribner, 1994)

Crick, Francis, *Life Itself* (Simon & Schuster 1981)

Critchlow, Donald T., *Intended Consequences: Birth Control, Abortion, and the Federal Government in Modern America* (Oxford University Press, 1999)

Crombie, A.C., *The History of Science from Augustine to Galileo* (Dover, 1995)

Darwin, Charles, *Autobiography* (Henry Schuman, 1950)

Darwin, Charles, *The Origin of Species* (Gramercy, 1995 edition)

Dawkins, Richard, *The Blind Watchmaker: Why the Evidence of Evolution Reveals a Universe without Design* (W.W. Norton, 1986)

Dawkins, Richard, *The Selfish Gene* (Oxford University Press, 1989 edition)

Dembski, William, *The Design Revolution: Answering the Toughest Questions about Intelligent Design* (Intervarsity Press, 2004)

Dennett, Daniel C., *Darwin's Dangerous Idea* (Touchstone, 1995)

Denton, Michael, *Evolution: A Theory in Crisis* (Adler & Adler, 1986)

Desmond, Adrian, and James Moore, *Darwin: The Life of a Tormented Evolutionist* (W.W. Norton, 1992)

Ehrlich, Paul R., *The Population Bomb* (Buccaneer Books, 1968)

Faden, Ruth R., and Tom L. Beauchamp, *A History and Theory of Informed Consent* (Oxford University Press, 1986)

Fletcher, Joseph, *The Ethics of Genetic Control* (Anchor Press, 1974)

Fletcher, Joseph, *Humanhood: Essays in Biomedical Ethics* (Prometheus Books, 1979)

Gaylin, Willard, and Ruth Macklin, editors, *Who Speaks for the Child: The Problems of Proxy Consent* (Plenum Press, 1982)

Gish, Duane T., *Evolution: The Fossils Still Say No* (Institute for Creation Research, 1995)

Gould, Stephen Jay, *Ever Since Darwin: Reflections in Natural History* (W.W. Norton, 1977)

Gould, Stephen Jay, *The Mismeasure of Man* (W.W. Norton, 1996)

Gould, Stephen Jay, *Rocks of Ages: Religion and Science in the Fullness of Life* (Ballantine Books, 2002)

Greenberg, Daniel S., *The Politics of American Science* (Harmondsworth Penguin Books, 1969)

Greenberg, Daniel S., *Science, Money, and Politics: Political Triumph and Ethical Erosion* (University of Chicago Press, 2001)

Grogman, Arnold B., *The Changing Classroom: The Role of the Biological Curriculum Study* (Doubleday, 1969)

Hardin, Garrett, *The Ostrich Factor: Our Population Myopia* (Oxford University Press, 1999)

Hartmann, Betsy, *Reproductive Rights and Wrongs: The Global Politics of Population Control* (South End Press, 1995)

Haught, John F., *Responses to 101 Questions on God and Evolution* (Paulist Press, 2001)

Hawking, Stephen, *A Brief History of Time* (Bantam, 1996)

Henig, Robin Marantz, *Pandora's Baby* (Houghton-Mifflin, 2004)

Himmelfarb, Gertrude, *Darwin and the Darwinian Revolution* (Elephant Paperback Edition, 1996)

Horgan, John, *The End of Science* (Helix Books, 1996)

Huxley, Aldous, *Brave New World* (Harper & Brothers, 1932)

Jastrow, Robert, *God and the Astronomers* (Reader's Library, 1978)

Johnson, Phillip, *Darwin on Trial* (InterVarsity Press, 1993)

Johnson, Phillip, *The Wedge of Truth: Splitting the Foundations of Naturalism* (InterVarsity Press, 2002)

Jonas, Hans, *The Imperative of Responsibility: In Search of an Ethics for the Technological Age* (University of Chicago Press, 1985)

Jonsen, Albert R., *The Birth of Bioethics* (Oxford University Press, 1998)

Joshi, S.T., editor, *H.L. Mencken on Religion* (Prometheus Books, 2002)

Kass, Leon R., M.D., *Being Human: Core Readings in the Humanities* (W.W. Norton, 2004)

Kass, Leon R., M.D., *The Ethics of Human Cloning* (American Enterprise Institute, 1998)

Kass, Leon R., M.D., *Life, Liberty, and the Defense of Dignity: The Challenge for Bioethics* (Encounter, 2002)

Kass, Leon R., M.D., *The New Biology: What Price Relieving Mans Estate?* (American Association for the Advancement of Science, 1971)

Kass, Leon R., M.D., *Towards a More Natural Science* (Free Press, 1988)

Kevles, Daniel J., *In the Name of Eugenics* (Harvard University Press, 1995)

Kristol, William, and Eric Cohen, editors, *The Future Is Now: America Confronts the New Genetics* (School and Library Binding, 2002)

Kuhn, Thomas S., *The Structure of Scientific Revolutions*, second edition (University of Chicago Press, 1962, 1970)

LaFollette, Marcel C., *Making Science Our Own: Public Images of Science* (University of Chicago Press, 1990)

Langston, J. William M.D., and Jon Palfreman, *The Case of the Frozen Addicts* (Pantheon, 1995)

Larson, Edward J., *Summer for the Gods: The Scopes Trial and America's Continuing Debate over Science and Religion* (Harvard University Press, 1998)

Lawrence, Jerome, and Robert E. Lee, *Inherit the Wind* (1955), *Best American Plays, Fourth Series 1951-1957* (Crown Publishers, 1958, 1987)

Lifton, Robert Jay, *The Nazi Doctors* (Basic Books, 1986)

Mayer, Ernst, *What Evolution Is* (Basic Books, 2001)

Maynard-Moody, Steven, *The Dilemma of the Fetus* (St. Martin's Press, 1995)

Meilaender, Gilbert, *Bioethics: A Primer for Christians*, second edition (Wm. B. Eerdmans Publishing Company, 2004)

Moore, John A., *Science as a Way of Knowing: The Foundations of Modern Biology* (Harvard University Press, 1993)

Morris, Henry, *The Biblical Basis for Modern Science* (Baker Book House, 1984)

Morris, Henry, *Scientific Creationism* (Creation Life Publishers, 1974)

National Academy of Sciences, *Human Reproductive Cloning* (National Academy Press, 2002)

Nelkin, Dorothy, *The Creation Controversy: Science or Scripture in the Schools* (W.W. Norton, 1982, 2000)

Nelkin, Dorothy, *Selling Science: How the Press Covers Science and Technology* (W.H. Freeman, 1987)

Nolan, William A., *The Baby in the Bottle* (Coward, McCann & Geoghegan, 1978)

Pence, Gregory E., *Classic Cases in Medical Ethics*, third edition (McGraw Hill, 2000)

Pennock, Robert T., *The Tower of Babel: The Evidence against the New Creationism* (MIT Press, 2000)

President's Council on Bioethics, *Human Cloning and Human Dignity* (2004)

President's Council on Bioethics, *Monitoring Stem Cell Research* (2004)

President's Council on Bioethics, *Reproduction and Responsibility: The Regulation of the New Biotechnologies* (2004)

Ramsey, Paul, *The Ethics of Fetal Research* (Yale University Press, 1975)

Ramsey, Paul, *Fabricated Man: The Ethics of Genetic Control* (Yale University Press, 1970)

Ramsey, Paul, *The Patient as Person* (Yale University Press, 1970)

Rawls, John, *A Theory of Justice* (Harvard University Press, 1967)

Reeve, Dana, *Care Packages: Letters to Christopher Reeve from Strangers and Other Friends* (Random House, 1999)

Rifkin, Jeremy, *The Biotech Century* (Jeremy Tarcher/Putnam, 1998)

Rose, Hilary and Steven Rose, *Alas, Poor Darwin: Arguments against Evolutionary Psychology* (Random House, 2000)

Rosen, Christine, *Preaching Eugenics: Religious Leaders and the American Eugenics Movement* (Oxford University Press, 2004)

Ruse, Michael, *Mystery of Mysteries* (Harvard University Press, 2001)

Ruse, Michael, and Christopher A. Pynes, editors, *The Stem Cell Controversy: Debating the Issues* (Prometheus, 2003)

Sagan, Carl, *Cosmos* (Ballantine Books, 1985, reissue)

Sagan, Carl, *The Demon-Haunted World: Science as a Candle in the Dark* (Ballantine Books, 1996)

Sagan, Carl, *Intelligent Life in the Universe* (Pan Books, 1977)

Sanger, Margaret, *An Autobiography* (Dover Publications, 1938)

Sanger, Margaret, *Women and the New Race* (Brentanos, 1920)

Schroeder, Gerald L., *The Hidden Face of God: Science Reveals the Ultimate Truth* (Free Press, 2002)

Schroeder, Gerald L., *The Science of God* (Free Press, 1997)

Shreeve, James, *The Genome War: How Craig Venter Tried to Capture the Code of Life and Save the World* (Alfred Knopf, 2004)

Simon, Julian, *Hoodwinking the Nation* (Transaction Publishers, 1999)

Singer, Peter, *Animal Liberation* (Random House, 1990)

Singer, Peter, *Practical Ethics* (Cambridge University Press, 1993)

Singer, Peter, *Rethinking Life and Death: The Collapse of Our Traditional Ethics* (St. Martin's Griffin, 1996)

Singer, Peter, *Unsanctifying Human Life* (Blackwell Publishers, 2002)

Smith, Bruce L.R., *American Science Policy since World War II* (Brookings Institution Press, 1990)

Smith, Wesley J., *Consumer's Guide to the Brave New World* (Encounter, 2004)

Smith, Wesley J., *Culture of Death: The Assault on Medical Ethics in America* (Encounter, 2002)

Smith, Wesley J., *Forced Exit: The Slippery Slope from Assisted Suicide to Legalized Murder* (Crown, 1997)

Stevenson, Leslie, and Henry Byerly, *The Many Faces of Science* (Westview Press, 2000)

Tattersall, Ian, *The Monkey in the Mirror: Essays on the Science of What Makes Us Human* (Harcourt, 2002)

Taylor, Gordon Rattray, *The Great Evolution Mystery* (Harper & Row, 1983)

Teachout, Terry, *The Skeptic: A Life of H.L. Mencken* (HarperCollins, 2002)

Veatch, Robert M., *A Theory of Medical Ethics* (Basic Books, 1981)

Wickelgren, Ingrid, *The Gene Masters: How a New Breed of Scientific Entrepreneurs Raced for the Biggest Prize in Biology* (Times Books, 2002)

INDEX

Peoples Business Commission, 222, 312
Pfizer, 234
Pharmaceutical Manufacturers Association, 222
Pinker, Steven, 163–64
Pitt, Brad, 263, 269
Pius XII, 137
Planned Parenthood, 18, 45, 51, 61–63
polio, 27, 221
Pontifical Academy of Sciences, 224
Popper, Karl, 112
Powell, Lewis, 148–51
Press, Frank, 144
population, 13, 33–50, 55, 59–60, 62–67, 84–86, 111, 117, 123, 127–28, 164, 185, 214, 218, 301–3, 308, 319–21
The Population Bomb, 34, 41–42, 44, 47, 302
Population Council, 63
Prentice, David, 273–74, 316
President's Council on Bioethics, 26, 223, 252, 274, 293, 314, 316, 322
Proposition 71, 264, 266, 269–96

R
racism, 29, 41, 47–48, 55, 62, 65–66, 127, 182, 189
Ramsey, Paul, 25, 82, 85, 209, 301, 305, 312, 322
Randall, Tony, 105
Raulston, John T., 102
Reagan, Nancy, 263, 269, 281
Reagan, Ron, 276, 281
Reagan, Ronald, 144, 150, 156, 195, 204–5, 263, 276, 281
Redmond, Eugene Jr., 216–18
Reed, Donald, 257, 316
Reed, Fred, 169
Reed, John C., 281

Reed, Ralph, 179
Reed, Roman, 257–58, 276
Reeve–Irvine Research Center for Spinal Cord Injury, 258
Reeve, Christopher, 239–45, 255–57, 262–63, 271, 281, 287, 314–15, 322
Rehnquist, William, 150–51
Rifkin, Jeremy, 222, 227, 314
Robertson, Pat, 193
Rockefellers, 84–85
Rockefeller Foundation, 39
Rockefeller, John D. III, 39
Roe v. Wade, 1–2, 8, 13–15, 18, 47, 84, 89, 208, 226, 290
Roncallo, Angeloo D., 23
rubella (German measles), 27–28, 80
Rupe, Carol, 197
Ryan, Kenneth, 78, 207, 213

S
Sabin, Albert B., 27
Sagan, Carl, 155–61, 165, 168, 170, 172, 181, 310
Sacramento Bee, 266, 281–82, 317–18
Salk, Jonas, 221
San Diego Union Tribune, 261, 315–16
San Francisco Chronicle, 40, 270, 280, 316–17
San Jose Mercury News, 175, 311, 317
Sandoz Pharmaceutical Corporation, 226
Sanger, Margaret, 51, 59–61, 304
Sarewitz, 297, 317
Scalia, Antonin, 148, 150
Schechter, Alan, 233
Schmanske, Stephen, 269
Schwarzenegger, Arnold, 23, 263, 265
Science (magazine), 141
Scientific American, 168, 191, 213, 310–11

NELSON CURRENT

A Subsidiary of Thomas Nelson, Inc.

Nelson Current, the political imprint of Thomas Nelson Inc., publishes probing, engaging, thought-provoking titles that explore the political landscape with audacity and integrity. With a stable of news-making writers including both veteran journalists and rising stars, as well as *New York Times* best-selling authors, Nelson Current has quickly established itself as a clear leader in the ever-expanding genre of political publishing.

Check out other provocative, relevant, and timely books at *NelsonCurrent.com.*

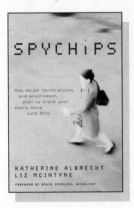

Spychips
How Major Corporations and Government Plan to Track Your Every Move with RFID
By Katherine Albrecht and Liz McIntyre
1-5955-5020-8

RFID, which stands for Radio Frequency IDentification, is a technology that uses computer chips smaller than a grain of sand to track items from a distance. And as this mind-blowing book explains, plans and efforts are being made now by global corporations and the U.S government to turn this advanced technology, these spychips, into a way to track our daily activities—and keep us all on Big Brother's short leash. Compiling massive amounts of research with firsthand knowledge, *Spychips* explains RFID technology and reveals the history and future of the master planners' strategies to imbed these trackers on everything—from postage stamps to shoes to people themselves—and spy on Americans without our knowledge or consent.

NELSON CURRENT

A Subsidiary of Thomas Nelson, Inc.

Hoodwinked
How Intellectual Hucksters Have Hijacked American Culture
By Jack Cashill
1-5955-5011-9

For the last century, many "progressive" intellectuals responsible for shaping the way we think about guns, corporations, the legal system, sex, and even our very history have been completely fabricating the facts. And yet they have been published, praised, promoted, and protected by the cultural establishment who have their own radical agendas advanced by their misinformation. This book tells the stories behind the fraud—targeting everyone from Michael Moore to Margaret Mead, Alfred Kinsey to Alex Haley—and proves how their corrosive lies have completely perverted our society, culture, and understanding of the world at large.

Big Fat Liars
How Politicians, Corporations, and the Media Use Science and Statistics to Manipulate the Public
By Morris E. Chafetz M.D.
1-5955-5008-9

Morris Chafetz, president of the Health Education Foundation, has spent decades carefully observing trends in science, government, the legal system, and the media, and now he reveals his unexpected findings in this sharp exposé of the many statistical lies—lies about everything from terrorism to the environment to alcohol and tobacco addiction—that manipulate Americans for the sinister motives of government, the media, corporations, and meretricious lawyers. Clear-sighted and far-reaching, this book will change how you look and listen to the scads of stats that are thrust on us every day.

NELSON CURRENT
A Subsidiary of Thomas Nelson, Inc.

Size Matters
How Big Government Puts the Squeeze on
America's Families, Finances, and Freedom
By Joel Miller
1-5955-5037-2

The federal government has seventeen million
employees, an annual budget of $2.5 trillion, and
heaps up thousands of pages worth of new regulations every year. This continually swelling government is squeezing entrepreneurs, workers, and
families in ways that reduce wealth, hurt finances, and
constrict our lives. Using studies about economic freedom and the near endless extent of government regulation, along with vivid anecdotes of individuals struggling to make it in an environment where the state hampers their
lifestyle and liberty, Joel Miller reveals the real daily drawbacks of Big
Government and the outlook for turning things around.

Something for Nothing
The All-Consuming Desire that Turns the
American Dream into a Social Nightmare
By Brian Tracy
1-5955-50038-0

America's greatness comes from people working
hard to fulfill their dreams. But today that greatness
is being undermined by people using the government
to steal other people's dreams (and money). *Something
for Nothing* reveals the social and personal threats
inherent in this emerging "grabbing match" culture,
juxtaposing free-market virtues against government vices, explaining how
the something-for-nothing mentality corrupts the political system,
undermines corporate success, and stifles the individual's ability
to prosper and contribute long-term to society.

NELSON CURRENT
A Subsidiary of Thomas Nelson, Inc.

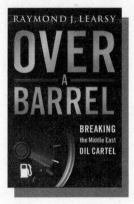

Over a Barrel
Breaking the Middle East Oil Cartel
By Raymond J. Learsy
1-5955-5036-4

Longtime commodities trader Raymond J. Learsy lifts the veil of the Mideast oil cartel, showing how OPEC manipulates the oil markets and destabilizes the world's economy by twisting bogus perceptions of oil scarcity to hike prices and gain political power; using Islamist terrorist connections that fuel anti-American hatreds with dollars from our own wallets; keeping Third-World nations in abject poverty despite their rich oil deposits; becoming the *de facto* master of Iraq's newly liberated oil fields. A sharp, sweeping survey of OPEC's methods of economic dominance, this book explains how to bust the Mideast oil cartel and chart our own course toward energy independence.

China: The Gathering Threat
By Constantine C. Menges, Ph.D.
Foreword by Bill Gertz
1-5955-5005-4

In a book that is as controversial as it is meticulously researched, a former special assistant to the president for National Security Affairs and senior official of the Central Intelligence Agency shows that the U.S. could be headed toward a nuclear face-off with communist China within four years. And it definitively reveals how China is steadily pursuing a stealthy, systematic strategy to attain geopolitical and economic dominance within the next twenty years. Using recently declassified documents and groundbreaking analysis and investigative work, Menges explains China's plan thoroughly, exposing their methods of economic control, their secret alliance with Russia and other anti-America nations, and their growing military and nuclear power.

NELSON CURRENT
A Subsidiary of Thomas Nelson, Inc.